Dear Health Plan Member,

We are delighted to give you this *Kaiser Permanente Healthwise® Handbook* as an additional benefit of membership. Members who use this book tell us that it is an extremely useful tool in helping them care for themselves and their families.

The *Kaiser Permanente Healthwise® Handbook* is designed to help you increase your confidence in managing your health in partnership with us. It is a comprehensive, easy-to-understand guide that has been reviewed and revised by hundreds of Kaiser Permanente physicians and other health professionals. The book provides information on over 180 health topics, including everything from headaches to ingrown toenails. For helpful hints on convenient home treatment or sound advice on when to call for professional help, check out the book. It also has the answers to many questions you might have about how to stay healthy, including how to start an exercise program, how to eat healthfully, and how to manage stress. So whether it's allergies or arthritis, backache or burns, rashes or relaxation, runny nose or ringing in the ears—you'll find a wealth of good information right at your fingertips in this home health guide.

Take a few minutes now to glance through it. We think you will find it of interest even when you are well. And, when you are sick, knowing what's in the book can help you quickly decide on the most appropriate care for yourself and your family. Keep the book handy—perhaps by your telephone along with your local Kaiser Permanente member guide to services.

Your Kaiser Permanente health care team will always be there when you need them. We value our role as your "partner in health" and look forward to helping you and your family stay healthy.

Francis J. Crosson, M.D.
Executive Director
The Permanente Federation

David M. Lawrence, M.D.
Chairman and Chief Executive Officer
Kaiser Foundation Health Plan and
Hospitals

KAISER PERMANENTE
HEALTHWISE®
H A N D B O O K

A Self-Care Guide For You And Your Family

- *Over 180 Health Care Problems*
- *Prevention*
- *Home Treatment*
- *When To Call Your Doctor*

DONALD W. KEMPER

THE HEALTHWISE STAFF

THE PHYSICIANS AND STAFF OF KAISER PERMANENTE

A Healthwise® Publication
Healthwise, Incorporated, Boise, Idaho
(A nonprofit organization)

Kaiser Permanente cover concept by Seventeenth Street Studios, current Kaiser Permanente cover design and illustrations by Kathy Locke of Locke Veach Communications Group

Illustrations by Jim Perkins of Nucleus Interactive

Healthwise Handbook, Thirteenth Edition, 1997

First Edition, 1976
Thirteenth Edition, 1997
Kaiser Permanente Edition (First Printing), 1994
Kaiser Permanente Revised Edition, 1999

13hwhb / Kaiser California / 2-99

ISBN: 1-877930-64-4

Printed in the United States of America.

Table of Contents

Part I: Self-Care Basics

Part II: Health Problems

Part V: Self-Care Resources

To Our Readers

No book can replace the need for doctors — and no doctor can replace the need for people to care for themselves. The purpose of this book is to help you and your health care professionals work together to manage your health problems.

The *Kaiser Permanente Healthwise® Handbook* includes basic guidelines on how to recognize and cope with over 180 of the most common health problems. These guidelines are based on sound medical information from leading medical and consumer publications, with review and input from doctors, nurses, pharmacists, physical therapists, and other health professionals. We have worked to present the information in a straightforward way that is free from medical jargon. We hope you find it easy to read and easy to use.

While this book does not eliminate the need for professional medical help, it does provide a better basis for you to work with your doctors to prevent and jointly care for health problems. If you receive professional advice in conflict with this book, look first to your health professional. Because your doctor is able to take your specific history and needs into consideration, his or her recommendations may prove to be the best. Likewise, if any self-care advice fails to provide positive results within a reasonable period, you should consult a health professional or advice nurse at Kaiser Permanente.

This book is as good as we can make it, but we cannot guarantee that it will work for you in every case. Nor will the authors, publishers, or Kaiser Permanente accept responsibility for any problems that may develop from following its guidelines. This book is only a guide; your common sense and good judgment are also needed.

We are continually adding to and improving this book. If you have a suggestion that will make this book better, or if you have a story about how the self-care guidelines in the *Kaiser Permanente Healthwise® Handbook* helped you, please write us at Healthwise Handbook Suggestions, c/o Healthwise, P.O. Box 1989, Boise, ID 83701, call us at 1-800-706-9646, or visit our Web site at www.healthwise.org.

We wish you the best of health!

About Healthwise

Healthwise is a nonprofit organization working to help people do a better job of staying healthy and taking care of their health problems. Since its founding in 1975, Healthwise has won awards of excellence and recognition from the Centers for Disease Control, the U.S. Department of Health and Human Services, the American Society on Aging, and the World Health Organization. Our clients range from volunteer organizations and church groups to Fortune 500 companies, major unions, state governments, hospitals, insurers, and health maintenance organizations.

Healthwise Program—This nationally replicated program gives consumers the resources and skills to improve the quality of care provided at home and helps them decide when to call a health professional. Program components include the *Healthwise® Handbook* (available in English and Spanish) and self-care workshop (live or video-based).

Healthwise for Life Program—This program meets the self-care and medical consumer needs of older adults, retirees, and Medicare participants. Program components include the award-winning *Healthwise for Life: Medical Self-Care for People Age 50 and Better* and Healthwise for Life workshop (live or video-based).

Partnership Program—This training and orientation program helps health professionals learn how they can better support their patients' self-care efforts (CME credit).

Healthwise Knowledgebase® Software—This computer-based source of consumer health information is used by managed care organizations, health clinics, nurse call centers, and as a part of online services. The Knowledgebase has comprehensive, useful, understandable, and medically accurate information on health problems, medical tests, treatments, medications, and support groups. See our Web site for a demo: www.healthwise.com.

International Programs—Healthwise programs have been implemented in South Africa, Canada, the United Kingdom, and Switzerland.

It's About Time: Better Health Care in a Minute (or two)—This 32-page booklet offers quick, easy-to-use action steps that promote good doctor-patient relationships.

For more information on our programs and publications, please contact Healthwise at P.O. Box 1989, Boise, ID 83701, 1-800-706-9646, or visit our Web site at www.healthwise.org.

Acknowledgements

This Kaiser Permanente version of the 13th edition of the *Healthwise® Handbook* has been produced as a partnership between two nonprofit organizations. Healthwise, Incorporated, founded in 1975, has been a pioneer in empowering medical care consumers through education. Kaiser Permanente has been dedicated to improving the health of its members by providing high quality group-practice prepaid medical care since 1945. Kaiser Permanente includes a rich collaboration between Kaiser Foundation Health Plan and Hospitals and the Permanente Medical Groups, as well as an affiliation with Group Health Cooperative, based in Seattle, Washington. Kaiser Permamente is now America's leading integrated health care organization with over 8.5 million members in 17 states and the District of Columbia, with its headquarters in Oakland, California.

Healthwise and Kaiser Permanente are both committed to helping patients become true partners with their team of health care professionals. The shared goals are to improve health, prevent disease, and promote the wise use of medical care. The *Kaiser Permanente Healthwise® Handbook* is an integral part of a larger effort to educate members, patients, and professionals through print, electronic media, and face-to-face interactions.

Healthwise, Incorporated

The first edition of the *Healthwise® Handbook*, published in 1976, was written and edited with major contributions from Kathleen McIntosh and Toni Roberts. Funding for the original development of the handbook was provided by the W. K. Kellogg Foundation of Battle Creek, Michigan. Since then, scores of people have helped to improve and update the book. The editors of the 13th edition are Terrance Smith and Jody Bower, with major contributions of writing and editing from Molly Mettler. Jane Woychick and Jo-Ann Kachigian provided proofreading and editing assistance, while layout and production were provided by Andrea Blum, Terrie Britton, and Elaine Wencl. Invaluable assistance was also provided by Cindy Hovland, Hollie Flint, and Mary Ellen Lemon. The principal medical reviewer for this edition was Steven Schneider, MD.

Kaiser Permanente

The first Kaiser Permanente edition of the *Healthwise® Handbook* was published in 1994, under the leadership of Steven M. Freedman, MD, who coordinated the book's medical review by more than 300 Kaiser Permanente physicians and other health professionals. The handbook is the cornerstone for the Kaiser Permanente Self-Care Program, with its goal to support member self-care and integration within all aspects of medical care delivery and patient education. Leadership for this effort was provided by Dr. Freedman, as well as by Pamela J. Larson, MPH; David S. Sobel, MD, MPH; and Joyce O. Arango, DrPH. Many other individuals provided valuable assistance as well, with cover customization, design of promotional materials, and with efforts to support dissemination in the medical centers and other Kaiser Permanente regions.

This edition of the *Kaiser Permanente Healthwise® Handbook* is the first national edition for Kaiser Permanente. The principal medical reviewers were David S. Sobel, MD, MPH, and Alan T. Elliot, MD. Coordination of the book revision process was provided by Joyce O. Arango, DrPH, with a great deal of support from Ann Banchoff, MSW, MPH; Frayne B. Rosenfield, MPH; Ron B. Nakamura, MPH; Joel D. Hyatt, MD; Jack Hudes; and Pamela J. Larson, MPH.

We would like to especially thank the Kaiser Permanente health care professionals across the country who contributed their time and expertise in the medical review of this edition, including:

Physicians

Travis Abbott, MD

Vernon Ansdell, MD

Mark Binstock MD, MPH

John Charde, MD

Mark Clark, MD

Nancy Cohen, MD

Jong Davis, MD

Catherine Dragstedt, MD

Alan T. Elliott, MD

Kenneth M. Ellner, MD

Kitty Evers, MD

Nathan Fujimoto, MD

Carole Gardner, MD

Scott Gee, MD

Howard Gould, MD

Bev Green, MD

Jeffrey Hoffman, MD

Tim McAfee, MD, MPH

Harry Miller, MD

Adrienne Mims, MD, MPH

Jeffrey Palmer, MD

David Preskill, MD

Willie Rainey, MD

Paul Reiss, MD

Jerry Salkowe, MD

Larry Scherzer, MD

Robert Schreiner, MD

David S. Sobel, MD, MPH

Ken Spiegelman, MD

David Starr, MD

Thomas Syltebo, MD

Robert van der Meer, MD

Winkler Weinberg, MD

Martha Wilber, MD

David Zelman, MD

Dentist

Don Prasnikar, DDS

Nurses

Betty Dennis, RN, BSN

Catherine Futch, RN, MN, CNAA

Lynda Garrett, MPH, RN

Judith Griffith, RN, MS

Leanne Johnston, RN, BSN

Jennifer Miller, RN, BSN

JoAnn Somers, RN, BSN

Crystal Stokes, RN, BSN

Health Education Staff for Kaiser Permanente

Ann Banchoff, MSW, MPH

Ron Blidar, CHES

Sally Butler, LCSW

Joyce Cusack, MHS

Joanne Ferguson, RN

Joy R. Gray, MPH

Patricia Greenfield, RN, DNSc

Lorinda Sheets Hartwell, DrPH

Mary Hobbs, MPH

Jamie Hunter-Mitchell

Susan Kayman, DrPH, RD

Jean Kumamoto, MPH

Kecia Leatherwood, MS

Kimmie Y. Lee, MPH, RD

Linda Madsen, MSW

Lisa A. Morgan, PT, MPH

Ron B. Nakamura, MPH

Frayne B. Rosenfield, MPH

Carol Shenise, MS, RN

Janet Tobacman, MPA

Dennis Tolsma, MPH

Deborah Zahn

Proofreader

Lisa Killen, MA

We also wish to thank the many health professionals and consumers whose review, suggestions, and input on previous editions were the foundation for the current book.

Most of all, we would like to thank the millions of Kaiser Permanente members who use the *Kaiser Permanente Healthwise® Handbook*. It is your actions that reward us the most and inspire us to constantly look for ways to improve this self-care guide and other patient education resources.

Introduction

The *Kaiser Permanente Healthwise® Handbook* can help you improve your health and lower your health care costs. We hope it is a book you will turn to time and again as health problems arise.

The book is divided into five sections:

Self-Care Basics. What you need to know to be a wise medical consumer and to deal with first aid and emergencies.

Health Problems. Prevention, treatment, and when to call a doctor for over 180 common illnesses and injuries.

Men's and Women's Health. Health conditions relevant to men or women.

Staying Healthy. Tips and techniques for fitness, nutrition, stress management, and mental wellness.

Self-Care Resources. How to manage medications and what you need to have on hand in your home to cope with health problems.

Most people will not read through the book from cover to cover in one sitting. It is more of a topic-by-topic book that you can use to look up what you need when a problem or interest develops. We encourage you to use the index to find the information you need, or just browse to become familiar with the valuable topics inside.

We do recommend that you read pages 1 and 2 and three special chapters right away:

Page 1, **The Healthwise Self-Care Checklist,** is a process to follow every time a health problem arises. Page 2, the **Ask-the-Doctor Checklist,** will help you get the most out of every doctor visit.

Chapter 1, **Partners in Health,** offers important information you can use to improve the quality and lower the cost of the health care you need.

Chapter 2, **Staying Healthy and Preventing Disease,** discusses the important things you can do to protect your health and prevent disease.

Chapter 20, **Your Home Health Center,** lists medications, supplies, equipment, and resources you may wish to keep on hand.

The rest of the information in the book is there when you need it. We have enjoyed writing this book and keeping it up to date. We hope it will help you succeed in better managing your health problems.

The Healthwise Self-Care Checklist

Step 1. Observe the problem.

- When did it start? What are the symptoms? _____
_____
_____
_____
_____

- Where is the pain? Dull ache or stabbing pain? _____
_____
_____

- Measure your vital signs:

  Temperature: _____   Blood pressure: _____ / _____

  Pulse: _____ / minute   Breaths: _____ / minute

- Think back:

  Have you had this problem before?   Yes _____   No _____

  What did you do for it? _____
_____

  Any changes in your life (stress, medications, food, exercise, etc.)?
_____
_____

  Does anyone else at home or work have these symptoms? _____

Step 2. Learn more about it.

- *Healthwise Handbook* (note page number): _____
- Other books or articles: _____
- Advice from others (lay or professional): _____

Step 3. Make an action plan.

- Your "tentative" diagnosis: _____
- Home care plan: _____
_____
- When to call your doctor: _____

Step 4. Evaluate your progress.

- Are your actions working? _____

Ask-the-Doctor Checklist

Before the visit:

- Complete the Healthwise Self-Care Checklist on page 1 and take it with you.
- Take a list of medications and record of last visit for similar problems.

During the visit:

- State your main problem first.
- Describe your symptoms (use page 1).
- Describe past experiences with the same problem.

Write down:

- Temperature: _____   Blood pressure: _____ / _____
- The diagnosis (what's wrong): _____
- The prognosis (what might happen next): _____
- Your self-care plan (what you can do at home): _____
  _____
  _____

For drugs, tests, and treatments, ask: (See page 10.)

- What's its name? _____
- Why is it needed? _____
- What are the costs and risks? _____
- Are there alternatives? _____
- What if I do nothing? _____
- (For drugs) How do I take this? _____
- (For tests) How do I prepare? _____

At the end of the visit, ask:

- Am I to return for another visit? _____
- Am I to phone in for test results? _____
- What danger signs should I look for? _____
- When do I need to report back? _____
- What else do I need to know? _____
  _____
  _____

You, the individual, can do more for your health and well-being than any doctor, any hospital, any drug, and any exotic medical device.
Joseph Califano

Partners in Health

Throughout your life you will have to make health decisions for yourself and your family. The decisions you make will not only influence your overall well-being, but also the quality and cost of the care you receive. You will feel better about your health choices, get better care, and save money if you approach health decisions with:

- A **desire** to take an active role in your health

- **Skills** to do self-care and shared decision-making

- **Information** that will help you understand your health options

These are the three components for making wise health decisions. This chapter will teach you how to partner with your doctor and other health care professionals to gain more control over the quality and cost of your health care.

Take an Active Role in Your Health

It's a fact: People who partner with their doctors to make health decisions are happier with the care they receive and the outcomes they achieve. If you're ready to take an active role in your health, then you can become a good health partner.

Skills for Becoming a Good Health Partner

Good partnerships are based on a common goal, shared effort, and good communication. You can hold up your end of the partnership bargain with your doctor by doing the following:

1. Take good care of yourself. Both you and your doctor would prefer that you don't get sick in the first place. But if you do get sick, both of you want you to get healthy again as soon as possible.

 For more information, see the inside front cover.

2. At the first sign of a health problem, observe and record your symptoms. Your record of symptoms will help both you and your doctor make an accurate diagnosis. If you do a good job recording your early symptoms, you and your doctor will have an easier time managing the problem later on. Use the Healthwise Self-Care Checklist on page 1 to organize your observations and plans.

3. Practice medical self-care. You can manage a lot of minor problems on your own. All it takes is for you to trust your common sense and monitor how well your efforts are working. Use this book, your own experience, and help from others to create a self-care plan.

• Learn all you can about the problem. Throughout this book, special icons mark topics where getting more information will be useful to you. The pieces of information that you gather—from the library, the Internet, or your doctor—are your tools for making wise health decisions.

• Use the Healthwise Self-Care Checklist on page 1 to keep notes on your self-care plan and what you do. Note whether home treatment seems to help. If you do end up calling your doctor or an advice nurse, they will want to know what you've tried to do for the problem and how well it worked.

• Set a time to call a health professional if the problem continues. If the problem seems to be getting more severe, don't wait too long before calling for help.

4. Prepare for office visits. Most medical appointments are scheduled to last only 10 to 15 minutes. The better organized you are, the more value you can get from the visit.

• Prepare an Ask-the-Doctor Checklist like the one on page 2.

• Update and bring your list of symptoms and your self-care plan.

• Write down your main concern and practice describing it. Your doctor will want to hear that first.

• Write down your hunches or fears about what is wrong. These are often helpful to your doctor.

• Write down the three questions that you most want to have answered. There may not be time to ask a long list of questions.

• Bring along a list of the medications (prescription and nonprescription) that you are taking.

5. Play an active role in your medical visits.

• State your main concern, describe your symptoms, and share your hunches and fears.

• Be honest and straightforward. Don't hold anything back because you are embarrassed. If you don't intend to take a prescribed medication, say so. If you are getting alternative treatment such as acupuncture or chiropractic treatments, let your doctor know. To be a good partner, your doctor has to know what's going on.

- If your doctor prescribes a drug, test, or treatment, get more information.

- Take notes. Write down the diagnosis, the treatment and follow-up plan, and what you can do at home. Then read it back to the doctor to be sure you have it right. If you think it will help, take a friend along to write down your doctor's findings and suggestions.

Skills for Finding a Doctor Who Will Be a Partner

A doctor (primary care physician) who knows and understands your needs can be your most valuable health partner. A host of specialists working on separate health problems may not see your whole health picture or get a good understanding of what's important to you. In choosing a doctor there are lots of questions to ask, but these three matter the most:

- Is this doctor well-trained and experienced?

- Is this doctor available when needed?

- Will this doctor work in partnership with me?

Calling for Medical Advice

Often a phone call to the advice nurse is all you need to manage a problem at home or determine if a visit is needed. Here's how to get the most from every call:

Prepare for your call.

Write down a one-sentence description of your problem and why you are calling (list two to three questions at most).

Have your symptom list handy.

Have your calendar and Health Plan card handy in case you need to schedule an appointment.

Give a clear description.

Tell your one-sentence description to the person who answers, and ask to talk with an advice nurse.

Describe your symptoms to the advice nurse, what you suspect the problem may be, and what you have done so far to treat the symptoms.

Listen carefully and ask questions as needed to make sure you understand.

Follow through.

Follow any instructions the nurse may give for home treatment, or for further monitoring of the symptoms.

Call back if the symptoms do not improve or if you have other concerns.

Training and Experience

For most people, a good choice for a primary care doctor is a board-certified family practice doctor or internist. For children and teens, a pediatrician or family practice doctor is a good choice. These doctors have broad knowledge about medical problems. See page 13 for a brief description of medical specialists.

Availability

Because health problems rarely develop when it's convenient, it helps to have a doctor and health care team who can help you when needed. A few questions to consider in selecting a new doctor are:

• What are the office hours?

• If I called right now for a routine visit, how soon could I be seen?

• Will the doctor discuss health problems over the phone?

• Does this doctor work with nurse practitioners or physician assistants? These primary care providers have special training for managing minor and routine medical problems. For many health problems, these professionals can often see you sooner, spend more time with you, and help you just as well as a doctor can.

The Advice Nurse

Advice nurses are registered nurses who have special training to help you decide what to do about symptoms, how to manage minor illnesses, and answer your questions about health problems.

A call to the advice nurse can often save you a doctor visit, or help you decide if you need an urgent or routine appointment.

Advice nurses can also help when your doctor diagnoses a health problem or recommends a test or treatment that you don't fully understand. Sometimes the advice nurse can answer your questions. Other times, he or she may help you come up with questions you can ask your doctor at your next visit.

Partner Potential

During your first visit, tell your doctor that you would like to share in making treatment decisions.

Pay attention to how you feel during the visit.

• Does the doctor listen well?

• Do you think you could build a good working partnership with this doctor?

If the answers are "no," look for another doctor.

But I Want a Take-Charge Doctor

Not everyone wants to be a partner with his or her doctor. Maybe you don't like to ask your doctor questions and you don't want to share in any decisions. Would you rather just let your doctor tell you what is best for you? If that's what you prefer, tell your doctor. Most doctors have a lot of patients who don't want to be a partner. Let the doctor know what you expect.

Is It Time for a Change?

If you are unhappy with how your doctor treats you, it may be time for a change. Before you start looking for a new doctor, tell your current doctor how you would like to be treated. Your doctor would probably be pleased to work with you as a partner if only you would tell him or her that's what you want. Otherwise, your doctor may think that you, like many people, want him or her to do all the work.

Share in Medical Decisions

Except in an emergency, you cannot be given a treatment or test without your "informed consent." You must be informed of the risks and agree to the treatment. In a partnership, however, informed consent may not be enough. The real goal is **shared decision-making**, where you actively participate in every health decision.

Medical Ping-Pong

Shared decision-making requires two-way communication, like playing a game of ping-pong.

Ping: You describe your symptoms, main concern, and hunches.

Pong: Your doctor makes a diagnosis and describes treatment options.

Ping: You tell your doctor your personal preferences or ask about other options.

Pong: Your doctor restates the options and how they relate to your preferences.

Ping: You accept one of the recommended options or learn more about what you should do.

With good two-way discussion, the chances are better that you will end up with the treatment plan that is best for you.

Why should you help make decisions with your doctor? Aren't you paying him or her to know what to do? Well, the choices aren't always black and white. With many health problems, there is more than one option. Consider these examples:

- You have moderately high blood pressure (160/95). Your doctor says that exercise and diet might bring it down, but most people don't succeed that way. Your doctor recommends that you start on medication to control it. You would rather try relaxation, exercise, and changing your diet. The best decision depends on your values.

- Your three-year-old has a headache and a fever. The doctor says it's probably nothing to worry about. Then you mention some other symptoms your child has shown, such as being hard to wake up and refusing to eat. The doctor suggests some additional testing.

- You have been suffering from carpal tunnel syndrome for several months. Your doctor is now recommending a wrist splint and a steroid injection. You would prefer trying just the splint with aspirin first. If that doesn't work, you will consider other medications. Your doctor agrees that is a good plan.

In each case, the treatment you choose will have an effect on your life. Therefore, the best approach to making health decisions is to combine the most reliable medical facts with your personal values. Among your personal values are your beliefs, fears, needs, lifestyle, and experiences. They all play a role in helping you make decisions about your health.

Skills for Making Wise Health Decisions

The following are some simple steps for you to follow when you have a health decision to make. Depending on the decision, the process may take a few minutes or hours, or as long as several weeks. Take as much time as you need to make the decision that is right for you.

1. What are you trying to decide? Tell your doctor that you want to share in making a decision. Ask your doctor to clearly state the decision that needs to be made and what your choices are.

2. Get the facts. Learn all about each option by using resources like the library, the Internet, and your doctor. Make sure the information you collect is based on sound medical research, not the results of a single study or facts published by a company that will profit by your using their product. In this book, a special icon marks some of the health problems for which more information will help you make better decisions about your care.

3. What do you think? Think about your own needs and values and what you hope for as the best possible outcome. Then sort out the information you've gathered into a list of the pros and cons as you see them for each option. You may want to share your list with your doctor to make sure you have all the information you need.

4. Try on a decision. Write down what you expect will happen if you choose a particular option. Ask your doctor if what you expect is reasonable. Ask again about possible side effects, pain, recovery time, or long-term outcomes of that option. Then see if you still feel it's the best choice for you.

5. Make an action plan. Now that you and your doctor have made a decision, find out what you can do to make sure that you will have the best possible outcome. Write down the steps that you need to take next. Think positively about your decision, and do your part to ensure success by following your doctor's advice. Remember, when you share in making a decision, you share the responsibility for the outcome.

Skills for Cutting Costs (but not quality)

Once you decide to become an active partner with your doctor, there is a lot you can do to reduce your health care costs. The goal is to get just the care you need, nothing more, and certainly nothing less.

Billions of dollars are spent each year on medications, tests, and treatments that people may not need. To better manage your health care costs, get the care you

---

Prepare for the Emergency Room

• Call your doctor, if possible. He or she may be able to work closely with the emergency room team and provide them with important information.

• If you think you may have to wait to be seen by an emergency room doctor, take this book and your medical records with you. While you are waiting you can:

° Use page 1, the Healthwise Self-Care Checklist, to help you think through the problem and report symptoms to the doctor.

° Use page 2, the Ask-the-Doctor Checklist, to organize questions for the doctor.

° Use your home medical records to discuss your medications, past test results, or treatments. Information about your allergies, medications, and conditions may be critical.

• As soon as you arrive, tell the admissions staff person why you think it is an emergency.

---

need when you need it, avoid unnecessary doctor visits, tests, and treatment, and use emergency services wisely. Here's how:

1. Stay healthy. Healthy lifestyles and regular preventive services are the best ways to keep costs down. Keep up to date with immunizations, and ask your doctor about screening tests. These tests help identify serious problems early, when they are easier and less expensive to treat.

2. Don't put off needed services. If your symptoms and the guidelines in this book suggest that you should see a doctor, don't put it off. Ignoring problems often leads to complications that are more expensive to treat.

3. Use self-care when you can. For some health problems, self-care is all that you need. By using the information in this book, and calling your doctor or nurse for help when necessary, you can often care for a problem at home.

4. Reduce your medical test costs. It is okay to ask questions about medical tests your doctor is ordering, especially if you do not understand how they will help you. Unneeded tests are sometimes done if your doctor thinks you won't be satisfied unless tests are ordered, or occasionally out of fear of malpractice suits. Make it clear that you only want a test done if it will help.

5. Reduce your medication costs. You may ask your doctor about any prescribed medication. Ask what would happen if you chose not to take a medication. Don't expect to get a prescription for every illness; sometimes self-care or nondrug remedies are all you need.

6. Avoid surgery when the risks for you outweigh the benefits. Ask your doctor why he thinks you need the surgery. Is this surgery the common treatment for your problem? What are your options? If you are not convinced that the benefits to you outweigh the risks, don't have the surgery.

7. Use emergency services wisely. In life-threatening situations, modern emergency services are vital. However, emergency rooms are not set up to care for routine illnesses, and they do not work on a first-come, first-served basis. During busy times, people with minor illnesses may wait for hours.

Use good judgment in deciding when to use emergency medical services. Whenever you feel you can apply home treatment safely and wait to see your regular doctor, do so. However, if you believe your situation is life-threatening, by all means call 911 or go to the emergency department.

8. Use hospitals only when you need them. More than half of this country's health care dollars are spent on hospitalizations. A stay in a modern hospital costs far more than a vacation at most luxury resorts. (And hospitals are a lot less fun.)

Wise Use of Ambulance Services

Call 911 or your local emergency department to dispatch an ambulance if:

Someone has symptoms that may mean a heart attack: severe chest pain, sweating, shortness of breath. See page 133.

There is severe bleeding or a large blood loss from the stomach, rectum, or vagina. See page 39.

Someone is unconscious or is having severe difficulty breathing.

A seizure lasts longer than five minutes.

There is an injury with immediate severe neck pain.

You feel that the situation is life-threatening.

If you are not sure whether an ambulance is needed, call your Kaiser Permanente facility.

Do not drive yourself to the hospital if you have dizziness, fainting, new weakness on one side of the body, chest pain with pressure or shortness of breath.

If you do need inpatient care, get in and out of the hospital as quickly as possible. This will reduce costs and your risk of hospital-acquired infections.

Don't check in to the hospital just for tests. Hospitalization is no longer needed for most medical tests. Ask if the tests can be done on an outpatient basis. If you agree to control your diet and activities, the doctor will usually support your request.

Try to avoid additional days in the hospital by bringing in extra help at home. Ask about home nursing services to help while you recover. With help available, many patients can shorten a hospital stay. Hospitals are not the only choice for people with a terminal illness. Many people choose to spend their remaining time at home with people they know and love. Special arrangements for the needed care can be made through Kaiser Permanente hospice care programs. Ask your doctor for a referral, or call your facility's hospice office to learn more.

9. Save specialists for special problems. Specialists are doctors with in-depth training and experience in a particular area of medicine. For example, a cardiologist has years of special training to deal

For more information, see the inside front cover.

> ## Skills to Use in the Hospital
>
> When you need to be in the hospital, there are things you can do to improve the quality of care you receive. However, if you are very sick, ask your spouse or a friend to help watch out for your best interests.
>
> - Ask "why?" Don't agree to anything unless you have a good reason. Agree only to those procedures that make sense for you.
>
> - Provide an extra level of quality control. Check medications, tests, injections, and other treatments to see if they are correct. Your diligence can improve the quality of care that you receive.
>
> - Be friendly with the nurses and aides, and they may pay more attention to your needs.
>
> - Know your rights. Most hospitals have adopted the "Patient's Bill of Rights" developed by the American Hospital Association. Ask your hospital for a copy.
>
> - If you get an itemized bill, check it, and ask about any charges you don't understand.

with heart problems. A visit to a specialist often costs more than a visit to your regular doctor, and the tests and treatments you receive may be more expensive. Of course, specialists often provide the information you need to decide what to do about a major health problem.

When your primary care doctor refers you to a specialist, a little preparation and good communication can help you get your money's worth. Before you go see a specialist:

- Know the diagnosis or expected diagnosis.

- Learn about your basic treatment options.

- Know what your primary care doctor would like the specialist to do (take over the case, confirm the diagnosis, conduct tests, etc.).

- Make sure that any test results or records on your case are sent to the specialist.

Ask your primary care doctor to remain involved in your care. Ask the specialist to send new test results or recommendations to both you and your regular doctor.

Medical Specialists

Cardiologist: heart

Dermatologist: skin

Endocrinologist: diabetes and hormonal problems

Family Practitioner: primary care

Gastroenterologist: digestive system

Geriatrician: older adults

Gynecologist: female reproductive system

Internist: primary care

Neurologist: brain and nervous system disorders

Obstetrician: pregnancy and childbirth

Oncologist: cancer

Ophthalmologist: eyes

Optometrist (OD): primary care for many eye problems*

Orthopedist: bones, joints, and muscles

Otolaryngologist or Head and Neck Surgeon: ears, nose, and throat

Pediatrician: infants, children, and teens

Physiatrist: physical medicine

Podiatrist (DPM): foot care

Psychiatrist: mental and emotional problems

Psychologist (MA* or PhD): mental and emotional problems

Pulmonologist: lungs

Rheumatologist: arthritis and other connective tissue disorders

Urologist: urinary and male reproductive systems

Unless otherwise noted, specialist may be an MD (Doctor of Medicine) or DO (Doctor of Osteopathy).

* Varies by state.

Health Fraud and Quackery: Don't Be Taken In

Millions of people are taken in each year by medical fraud and worthless health products.

Bogus "cures" are advertised for many chronic problems, especially arthritis, cancer, baldness, and impotence. The ads target people who are ready to try anything. Unfortunately, these cures rarely help and often (one out of ten) cause harmful side effects. It is wise to be suspicious of products that:

• Are advertised by testimonials

• Claim to have a secret ingredient

• Are not evaluated in prominent medical journals

• Claim benefits that seem too good to be true

• Are available only by mail

Be suspicious of any doctor who:

• Prescribes medicines or gives injections at every visit

• Promises a no-risk cure

• Suggests something that seems unethical or illegal

The best way to protect yourself from fraud is to be observant and ask questions. If you don't like what you see or hear, find another doctor.

Do Your Own Research

Information is your greatest tool for making wise health decisions.

If you have a complicated problem or want to know more about your health options:

• Start by asking your doctor if he or she has information about your problem that you could take home with you. Some doctors offer videotapes, printed brochures, or reprints from medical journals.

• Call the Kaiser Permanente advice line, and ask if they can help you get more information.

• Review the introduction to the Self-Care Resources beginning on page 324 and the books and other publications on the pages that follow.

 When you see this symbol in this book, it's there to tell you that you will be better able to make wise health decisions if you get more information about the topic.

The inside front cover of this book offers tips to help you get more information about health problems and your testing and treatment choices. Get your information from sources that present solid, evidence-based data. If you have questions or concerns about the information you gather, discuss them with your doctor.

Also, please refer to your Kaiser Permanente member guide to services for more information on Kaiser Permanente facilities available in your area and how best to use services.

Your Rights and Responsibilities as a Kaiser Permanente Member

You have the right to:

• Participate in your health care.

• Express your wishes about future care.

• Receive personal medical records and/or information so you can participate in your health care.

• Receive information about the people who provide your health care.

• Receive care with dignity and respect.

• Have impartial access to treatment.

• Be assured of privacy and confidentiality.

• Have a safe, secure, clean, and accessible health care environment.

• Participate in physician selection.

• Know and use Member satisfaction resources.

You are responsible for:

• Providing accurate and complete information.

• Following the treatment plan you and your health professional agree on.

• Keeping appointments.

• Recognizing the effect of your lifestyle on your health.

• Being considerate of others.

• Knowing the extent and limitations of your health care benefits.

• Fulfilling financial obligations.

*If I'd known I was going to live this long, I'd have
taken better care of myself.*
Eubie Blake

2

Staying Healthy and Preventing Disease

Prevention works! You and your family can save a lot of pain, worry, and money by avoiding health problems in the first place. If you can't prevent a problem altogether, the next best thing is to discover it early, when it is easy to treat. This chapter helps you do both.

Ten Ways to Stay Healthy

1. Immunize. Immunizations are the best bargain in health care. When you immunize, you prevent illness for your family and help prevent epidemics in your community. Schedule your child's immunizations according to the Kaiser Permanente guidelines.

2. Keep moving. Any way you define it, fitness is essential to good health. Even moderate exercise makes a huge difference both in how you feel and what illnesses you get. For a three-part fitness plan, see page 266.

3. Eat right. Eating a well-balanced, low-fat diet of wholesome foods will keep you energetic and free of many illnesses. See Chapter 18. Consider breast-feeding your baby to help keep him or her in the best health. See page 200.

4. Control stress. Even with a hectic and hurried lifestyle, you can prevent stress from undermining your health. See page 272 for relaxation skills.

5. Be smoke-free. Smokers who quit gain tremendous health benefits. So do people who avoid secondhand smoke. See page 150.

6. Avoid drugs and excess alcohol. When you say "no" to drugs and limit what you drink, you prevent accidents and illnesses and avoid a lot of problems for yourself and your family. For more on drug and alcohol problems, see page 291.

7. Put safety first. Safety at home, at work, and at play; safe driving; firearm safety; and safer sex will all help keep you healthy.

8. Pursue healthy pleasures. Take naps, relax during meals, play with kids, care for a pet—they all can add to your health. See Resource 74 on page 329.

9. Think well of yourself. A good self-image is the foundation of good health. See pages 304 to 306.

10. Promote peace. Peace on earth begins at home. Seek nonviolent ways of resolving conflicts at home, at school, at work, and in your community. See pages 303 and 304.

Immunizations

 Immunizations work by helping your immune system recognize and quickly attack diseases before they can cause problems. Some immunizations are given in a single shot while others require several shots over a period of time.

Childhood immunizations protect against pertussis (whooping cough), polio, measles, mumps, rubella, haemophilus influenza, chickenpox, and hepatitis B. Immunizations also protect against tetanus and diphtheria, although booster shots are needed every 10 years to maintain lifelong protection.

If your children are immunized, these serious illnesses will not be a problem. Schedule your child's immunizations according to the Kaiser Permanente preventive care guidelines for your area. There is no need to delay immunizations because of colds or other minor illnesses.

Be sure to keep good records. Children often need to show immunization records at school.

Diphtheria, Pertussis, and Tetanus (DPT/DTaP)

Infectious diseases like diphtheria and pertussis were major killers before the DPT vaccine was developed. This vaccine also protects against tetanus ("lockjaw"), a bacterial infection that can result when a wound is contaminated. The bacteria enter the body through cuts and thrive only in the absence of oxygen. So the deeper and narrower the wound, the greater the possibility of tetanus. With proper immunization, these diseases are rare.

Childhood immunizations for these diseases are given together, with a series of shots starting at age two months. DTaP is a newer version of this vaccine. It may cause a less severe reaction in the person receiving the vaccine. Follow the DPT/DTaP guidelines provided by Kaiser Permanente.

The first booster is given during the preteen or teen years. After that, get a Td (tetanus and diphtheria) booster every 10 years.

Keeping up to date with Td boosters is important because tetanus can be fatal. If it has been at least five years since your last shot, and you have a wound (especially a puncture wound) that is very dirty or that you suspect may be contaminated, get a Td booster.

Otherwise there is no need for more frequent vaccinations because this increases the risk of an uncomfortable local reaction.

Polio

Polio is a viral illness that leads to loss of mobility or paralysis. It is rare today because of the polio vaccine. A series of four doses by the age of six gives lifelong immunity.

The polio vaccine is available in two forms: an oral vaccine (OPV), taken by mouth, and an injected vaccine (IPV). IPV is sometimes used for the first two doses in infants and is recommended for anyone who has had an illness that impairs the immune system or who takes medications that impair the immune system. Nonimmunized adults need immunization only if they have a high risk of polio exposure.

Measles, Mumps, and Rubella (MMR)

MMR is an immunization for measles, mumps, and rubella (German measles). See page 217. Two shots are recommended. If both doses are given, no further MMR immunization is needed.

If there is a measles outbreak in your area, and your infant has not yet been immunized, call your doctor or health department to discuss having an early MMR shot. If given early, the dose should be repeated at age 15 months.

If you don't have records showing that you received two doses of MMR vaccine, and you did not have these illnesses as a child, discuss your need for immunization with your doctor.

Chickenpox (Varivax)

A chickenpox vaccine (Varivax) is available. The vaccine can be given to children at age 12 months and older, and to teens and adults who have not had the illness. Immunity lasts at least 10 years, but it is not yet clear if booster shots will be needed. Chickenpox is more serious in teens and adults, so if a child has not had chickenpox by age 11, vaccination may be more important. Teens and adults who are not sure that they have had chickenpox should discuss possible testing and immunization with their doctor. A two-shot series is needed for adults.

Hepatitis B Virus (HBV)

The hepatitis B virus causes serious and sometimes fatal liver disease. Vaccination against HBV prevents infection and its complications. See page 261.

Reactions to Childhood Immunizations

Temporary, mild reactions to immunizations are common. Babies often develop a fever after the DPT shot, and the location of the shot may be hard. A mild rash or fever may develop 10 to 14 days after the MMR vaccine is given. The rash will go away without treatment. The hepatitis B vaccines have caused nausea, low-grade fever, rash, and joint pain in some adults.

- Acetaminophen drops may soothe the discomfort and relieve fever. Also see page 213. Some doctors recommend giving acetaminophen before the shot.

- Keep written notes on any reactions you observe.

- Tell your health professional if you think the reactions are excessive.

It is recommended that all infants be vaccinated against HBV. Three shots provide long-term immunity. Immunization is also recommended for:

- Adolescents who were not previously vaccinated, especially if they are at high risk.

- Health care workers.

- People planning extended travel to China, Southeast Asia, and other areas where HBV infection rates are high.

Haemophilus influenzae Type b (Hib)

Haemophilus influenzae type b does not cause the flu. It is a serious bacterial illness that causes meningitis and may lead to brain damage and death. Most serious Hib disease affects children between six months and one year of age. Every child between two months and five years should be immunized against Hib. Children over five and adults need immunizations only if they have sickle cell anemia or spleen problems.

Other Immunizations

Annual **influenza vaccinations** are recommended for everyone age 65 and older and those who have a chronic illness. Health care workers who may be exposed to the disease may also wish to get the vaccine every year. The vaccine can be given to anyone over age 6 months. The vaccine is most effective when given in the autumn. If you are younger than 65 but live with someone who is elderly or has a chronic illness, you may also want to get an annual flu vaccination.

The **pneumococcal vaccine** is recommended for those 65 and older. Younger people with chronic diseases, especially respiratory illnesses (except asthma), should also consider getting the pneumococcal vaccine. If you received this shot before age 65 and it has been more than five years since you had the shot, ask your doctor if you need a booster shot.

Be Wise, Immunize

It's wise to immunize.

Immunizations:

- Prevent disease.
- Cost much less than treating the diseases they prevent.
- Are safe and effective.
- Reduce the risk of epidemics.
- Are the law. Children must be immunized (or the parents must sign a certificate of exemption) before they can begin public school.

If you are in close contact with people who have an infectious disease or you are planning travel to areas where illnesses such as malaria, typhoid, and yellow fever are common, talk with your local public health department to ask if other immunizations are needed.

Tuberculin Test

A tuberculin test is a skin test for tuberculosis (see page 152), not an immunization. A positive result does not necessarily mean that you have tuberculosis, but it does mean the bacteria have probably entered your body. Whether you should be tested depends on the prevalence of tuberculosis in your area and your risk of exposure. Once you have had a positive skin test, the test should not be repeated. Subsequent tests will always be positive and may cause more severe reactions.

Screening and Early Detection

Another way to protect your health is to detect an illness early, while it is still easy to treat. You can do this in two ways: by getting periodic medical exams from health professionals and by becoming a good observer of your own body and health.

Periodic Medical Exams

 Many doctors used to recommend a complete physical every year. Now, most doctors recommend specific medical exams based on age, sex, and risk factors. These exams are more effective than the annual physical in detecting treatable illness.

See the recommended schedule for preventive exams provided by your local Kaiser Permanente facility. The most appropriate schedule of preventive exams is one you and your doctor agree upon, based on your health conditions, values, and risk factors.

The recommendations apply to healthy people in each age category. You may be at higher risk for certain diseases. Family history (whether your relatives have or had the disease), other health problems, or behaviors such as smoking all increase your risk. Talk with your doctor about whether you need more frequent exams.

Periodic self-exams are also an important part of staying healthy. See the breast self-exam on page 228 and the testicular self-exam on page 250. If you have high blood pressure, see page 224.

For more information on cholesterol screening, see page 223.

Flexible Sigmoidoscopy

Flexible sigmoidoscopy is a screening test for precancerous polyps and cancers of the colon and rectum. The sigmoidoscope is a flexible viewing instrument that is inserted into the rectum to examine the lower bowel. The exam takes about 10 to 15 minutes, is only mildly uncomfortable, and is very safe.

Having flexible sigmoidoscopy exams reduces your risk of dying from colorectal cancer. Most experts recommend that you have a flexible sigmoidoscopy exam around age 50. In addition to screening, doctors sometimes wish to examine the colon to check for the cause of rectal bleeding, diarrhea, or constipation.

Other Recommended Tests and Exams

Infants

Discuss the frequency of well-baby visits with your health care professional, or see the recommended schedule provided in the preventive care guidelines for your local Kaiser Permanente facility.

Children Age 2 to 5

Discuss the frequency of visits with your health professional. A vision test is recommended at age three to four. Some childhood immunizations are also given at this age. See page 18.

Regular blood pressure checks are recommended after age three and may be done during visits for other reasons.

Children Age 6 to 18

Discuss the frequency of visits with your health professional. A tetanus booster is recommended during the teen years. Regular blood pressure checks are recommended and may be done during any visit.

Pap tests are recommended starting when a female becomes sexually active. See pages 231 and 232.

Pregnant Women

Discuss the frequency of visits and testing with your doctor. During the first prenatal visit, blood tests, urinalysis, blood pressure, and screening for hepatitis B are recommended. Additional tests are needed during the pregnancy.

Fahrenheit-Centigrade Conversion Chart

°F		°C
98.5	=	36.9
99.0	=	37.2
99.5	=	37.5
100.0	=	37.8
100.5	=	38.1
101.0	=	38.3
101.5	=	38.6
102.0	=	38.9
102.5	=	39.2
103.0	=	39.4
103.5	=	39.7

Vital Signs

With a few tools and an eye for observation, you can help detect and monitor health problems in your family. Everyone needs to know how to take a temperature and count pulse and respiration rates. It is also good to learn how to take your own blood pressure. You may even want to learn to do simple ear exams. The tools you need are inexpensive and usually come with instructions.

Temperature

A normal temperature ranges from 97.6° to 99.6°F and for most people is 98.6°. Temperature varies with time of day and other factors, so don't worry about minor changes.

Whenever a person feels hot or cold to your touch, it is a good idea to take and record his or her temperature. If you have to call your doctor during an illness, knowing the exact temperature will be very helpful.

There are four ways to take a temperature:

- Orally (in the mouth)
- Rectally (in the anus)
- Axillary (under the armpit)
- Using an electronic oral or ear thermometer or temperature strip

Unless otherwise specified, **all temperatures in this book are oral Fahrenheit readings.** If you take a rectal or axillary temperature, adjust it accordingly. Rectal temperatures are the most accurate.

Oral temperatures are recommended for adults and children age six years and older.

- Clean the thermometer with soapy water or rubbing alcohol.

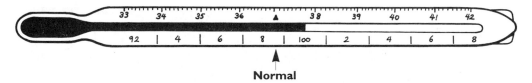

Normal

Shake the thermometer so that the mercury is below 95°F (35°C) before taking a temperature. This thermometer reads 100°F (37.8°C).

- Hold it firmly at the end opposite the bulb and shake the mercury down to 95° or lower.

- Do not drink hot or cold liquids beforehand.

- Place the bulb under the tongue and close the lips around it. Do not bite it. Breathe through the nose and do not talk.

- Wait three to five minutes.

Rectal temperatures are recommended for children younger than six years or anyone who cannot hold an oral thermometer in the mouth. Use only a rectal thermometer. Rectal temperature is 0.5° to 1° higher than oral temperature.

- Clean the thermometer and shake it down (see above).

- Put Vaseline or another lubricant on the bulb.

- Hold the child bottom-up across your lap.

- Hold the thermometer one inch from the bulb and gently insert it into the rectum no more than one inch. Do not let go. Hold it right at the anus so that it cannot slip in farther.

- Wait for three minutes.

Axillary temperatures are less accurate and about 1° lower than oral. They are safer for small children who will not hold still while you use a rectal thermometer.

- Use either an oral or rectal thermometer. Shake it down below 95°.

- Place the thermometer in the armpit and have the child cross her arm across the chest and hold her opposite upper arm.

- Wait five minutes.

How to Read a Thermometer

- Roll the thermometer between your fingers until you can see the thin ribbon of mercury. Note that the thermometer is marked from 92° to 108°.

- Each large mark indicates one degree of temperature. Each small mark indicates 0.2°.

Normal Resting Pulse		Normal Resting Respiration	
Infant–1 year	100–160 beats/minute	Infant–1 year	40–60 breaths/minute
1–6 years	65–140 beats/minute	1–6 years	18–26 breaths/minute
7–10 years	60–110 beats/minute	7–adult	12–24 breaths/minute
11–adult	50–100 beats/minute		

Electronic thermometers are convenient and easy to use. They are quite accurate, but some are expensive. Temperature strips should only be used to measure axillary (armpit) temperature. They are inaccurate when used on the forehead.

Taking a Pulse

The pulse is the rate at which your heart is beating. As the heart forces blood through your body, you can feel a throbbing in the arteries wherever they come close to the skin surface. The pulse can be taken at the wrist, neck, or upper arm.

Certain illnesses can cause the pulse to increase, so it is helpful to know what your resting pulse rate is when you are well. The pulse rate rises about 10 beats per minute for every degree of fever.

- Count the pulse after the person has been sitting or resting quietly for 5 to 10 minutes.

- Place two fingers gently against the wrist as shown (don't use your thumb).

- If it is hard to feel the pulse in the wrist, locate the carotid artery in the neck, just to either side of the windpipe. Press gently.

- Count the beats for 30 seconds, then double the result for beats per minute.

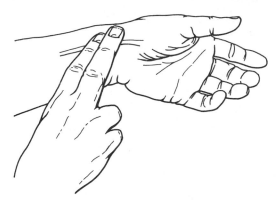

To check your pulse, place two fingers on your forearm below the base of the thumb.

Counting Respiration Rates

Your respiration rate is how many breaths you take in a minute. It increases with fever and some illnesses. The best time to count respiration is when a person is resting, perhaps after taking the pulse while your fingers are still on his or her wrist. The person's breathing is likely to change if the person knows you are counting it.

- Count the number of times the chest rises in one full minute.

- Notice whether there is any sucking in beneath the ribs or any apparent wheezing or difficulty breathing.

Measuring Blood Pressure

Blood pressure is the force of the blood pulsing against the walls of your arteries. The pressure when the heart beats is called the systolic pressure (the first number in blood pressure readings). The pressure between beats, when the heart is at rest, is called the diastolic pressure. A blood pressure reading below 140/90 is considered normal for an adult over 18. See page 224 for information about high blood pressure.

Most people with good hearing can learn to measure blood pressure using a stethoscope and a blood pressure cuff (sphygmomanometer). Electronic blood pressure cuffs are also available, which do not require a stethoscope or good hearing.

- Ask your pharmacist to recommend a blood pressure kit and show you how to use it.

- Regular in-home blood pressure monitoring may be useful for anyone who has heart disease or high blood pressure.

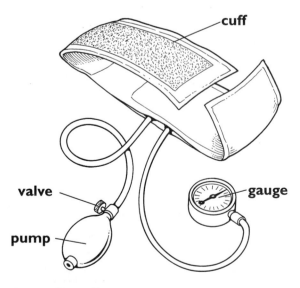

Blood pressure can be measured at home with a blood pressure cuff.

Warning Signs

Some symptoms act as warning signs that a serious disease may be developing. If you know these warning signs and heed them, you may detect the disease before it becomes life-threatening. Some diseases, like cancer, are often curable if they are detected early. Other diseases, like diabetes, cannot be cured, but early detection and treatment may reduce the injury they cause the body.

Here are the warning signs for four diseases that, if detected early, can often be stopped or controlled.

Cancer

The American Cancer Society lists the following seven warning signs for cancer. Let your doctor know immediately if you experience any of these signs.

- Change in bowel or bladder habits. Most people occasionally have a brief period of constipation, diarrhea, or a change in the frequency of bowel movements or urination. These do not necessarily indicate cancer but can be due to flu, changes in your diet, stress, etc. Tell your doctor about any changes in bowel or bladder habits that last more than two weeks.

- A sore that does not heal. See Skin Cancer, page 195.

- Unusual bleeding or discharge. Coughing up blood, blood in vomit, blood in the urine, or significant amounts of blood in the stool should be called to your doctor's attention. Small amounts of blood in the stool can be due to hemorrhoids. Tell your doctor about even small amounts of blood in the stool if it does not go away in a few days.

• Thickening or lump in breast or elsewhere. Most lumps, even in the breast, are not cancer. However, they should not be ignored. See Breast Health, page 228, and Testicular Self-Exam, page 250.

• Difficulty swallowing or indigestion that lasts more than a month and causes more than occasional minor discomfort.

• Change in the appearance or size of a wart or mole. See Skin Cancer, page 195.

• Nagging cough or hoarseness. Cough and hoarseness are commonly associated with a cold. However, if either lasts more than a few weeks, tell your doctor.

Diabetes

The warning signs of diabetes are often vague and might not cause you to think you need to see a doctor. However, if you have any of the following symptoms and there is no other obvious cause (fatigue from working hard, or frequent urination because of drinking lots of fluids, for example), discuss the symptoms with your doctor. For more information on diabetes, see page 219.

• Increased thirst

• Frequent urination (especially at night)

• Increased appetite

• Unexplained weight loss

• Fatigue

• Frequent unexplained skin infections

• Slow-healing wounds

• Frequent vaginal infections

• Difficulty with erections

• Persistent blurred vision

• Persistent tingling or numbness in hands or feet

Heart Attack

Call 911 or other emergency services immediately if you or someone you are with has warning signs of a heart attack. Early treatment can save your life.

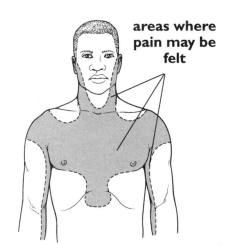

areas where pain may be felt

Chest pain caused by a heart attack can spread up the neck, down one or both arms, into the upper abdomen, or to the upper back.

• Chest pain that is crushing, squeezing, increases in intensity, or occurs with other symptoms of a heart attack is the key warning sign of a heart attack.

Other symptoms of a heart attack include:

• Sweating

• Shortness of breath

• Chest pain radiating to the arm, neck, or jaw

• Nausea or vomiting

• Dizziness

• Rapid and/or irregular pulse

Stroke

The National Stroke Association lists five warning signs of stroke. Certain stroke treatments can only be effective if given within three hours of the start of symptoms. If you or someone you are with experiences any of these symptoms, **call 911 or other emergency services immediately**.

• Weakness, numbness, or paralysis of the face, arm, or leg, especially on only one side of the body, that does not go away in a few minutes

• Blurred or decreased vision in one or both eyes that does not clear with blinking

• Newly developed difficulty speaking or understanding simple statements

• Sudden unexplainable and intense headache

• Severe dizziness, loss of balance, or loss of coordination, especially if another warning sign is present at the same time

If the symptom was definitely there and then goes away in a few minutes, call your doctor immediately. Symptoms that go away in a few minutes may be caused by a transient ischemic attack (TIA). TIAs are a strong sign that a major stroke may soon occur.

*It is by presence of mind in untried emergencies
that the native metal of a man (or woman) is tested.*
James Russell Lowell

3

First Aid and Emergencies

This chapter covers both serious medical emergencies and minor first aid situations. Review this chapter before you need it. Then, when you are faced with an emergency or injury, you will know where to turn. Your confidence in dealing with both major and minor emergencies will be reassuring to an injured person. Also see Resource 34 on page 327.

Medical emergencies covered in this chapter include:

- Bleeding, page 39.

- Head Injuries, page 44.

- Poisoning, page 54.

- Rescue Breathing and CPR, page 56.

- Shock, page 61.

- Unconsciousness, page 65.

Dealing With Emergencies

Take a deep breath. Count to 10. Tell yourself you can handle this situation.

Assess the danger. Protect yourself and the injured person from fire, explosions, or other hazards. If you suspect a spinal injury, do not move the person unless the danger is great.

If the person is unconscious or unresponsive, check the ABCs: Airway, Breathing, Circulation. If the person is not breathing, see Rescue Breathing and CPR on page 56.

Identify and prioritize the injuries. Treat the most life-threatening problems (bleeding, shock) first. Check for broken bones and other injuries. If you need emergency assistance, call 911 or emergency services.

Legal Protection

If you are needed in an emergency, give what help you can. Most states have a Good Samaritan law to protect people who help in an emergency. You cannot be sued for giving first aid unless it can be shown that you are guilty of gross negligence.

When to Call the Dentist

- If a permanent tooth is knocked out.

- If a baby tooth is knocked out, schedule an appointment within two weeks to determine if a spacer is needed until permanent teeth come in.

Accidental Tooth Loss

If a permanent tooth is knocked out, a dentist may be able to reimplant it in the mouth. Baby teeth need to come out anyway, so they are not usually reimplanted.

Home Treatment

- Call your dentist immediately for an emergency visit. Teeth reimplanted within 30 minutes have the best chance of success. After two hours, it is unlikely the procedure will be successful.

- Clean the tooth and replace it in the socket, or between the gum and cheek (use care not to swallow the tooth), or in a small container of milk. Do not transport the tooth in tap water.

Animal and Human Bites

When bitten by an animal, most people want to know if they need a rabies shot. The main wild animal carriers of rabies are raccoons, skunks, foxes, and bats. Pet dogs and cats that have been vaccinated rarely have rabies. However, many stray animals have not been vaccinated. Rabies is quite rare, but it is fatal if not treated. The treatment is no more painful than a typical injection. Report all wild animal bites to your doctor or health department.

Bites that break the skin can cause bacterial infections. Cat and human bites are particularly prone to infection. Tetanus can occur if shots are not up to date. See page 18.

Prevention

- Vaccinate all pets against rabies. Do not keep wild animals as pets.

- Do not disturb animals while they are eating, even your family pet.

- Teach children not to approach or play with stray dogs or cats.

- Do not touch wild animals or provoke them to attack. Do not handle sick or injured animals.

Home Treatment

- Scrub the bite immediately with soap and water. Treat it as a puncture wound. See page 55.

- If you are bitten by a pet dog or cat, find out whether it has been vaccinated for rabies.

- A healthy pet that has bitten someone should be confined and observed for 10 days to see if it develops symptoms of rabies. If the owner cannot be located or relied on to confine and watch the animal, contact the local health department.

- If you are bitten by a wild animal, contact the health department. They can tell you whether that animal is a rabies carrier in your area, and whether treatment is needed.

When to Call Kaiser Permanente

- If the bite is from a wild animal.

- If the bite is from a dog or cat that is acting strangely, foaming at the mouth, or if it attacked for no apparent reason.

- If the bite is from a pet whose owner cannot confirm that it has been vaccinated for rabies.

- If the bite is severe and may need stitches or if it is on the face, hand,

or foot. If stitches are needed they usually should be done within 8 hours.

- If signs of infection develop:

  ° Increased pain, swelling, redness, or tenderness

  ° Heat or red streaks extending from the bite

  ° Discharge of pus

  ° Fever of 100° or higher with no other cause

Blood Under a Nail

Fingernails and toenails often get crunched, bashed, or smashed. These injuries usually aren't too serious, but if there is bleeding under the nail, the pressure can be very painful.

The only way to relieve the throbbing and pain is by making a hole in the nail to drain the blood. You may feel squeamish about trying this at home, but it is the same thing a health professional would do.

Draining is helpful only if there is severe, throbbing pain (you can feel the pulse beating under the nail) that is bad enough to keep you from sleeping.

Home Treatment

- Apply ice and elevate the injured area as soon as possible after the injury to minimize swelling and relieve pain. Acetaminophen will also ease discomfort.

First Aid and Emergencies

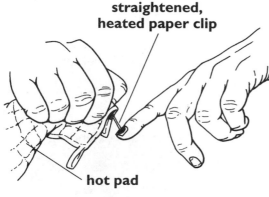

straightened, heated paper clip

hot pad

Use a red-hot paper clip to relieve the pain caused by blood under a fingernail or toenail.

First Aid and Emergencies

- To make a hole in the nail and relieve throbbing, follow these steps:

  ° Straighten a paper clip and heat the tip in a flame until it is red hot.

  ° Place the tip of the paper clip on the nail and let it melt through. You do not need to push. This will not be painful, because the nail has no nerves. A thick nail may take several tries.

  ° As soon as the hole is complete, blood will escape and the pain will be relieved.

- Soak the finger three times a day in a half-and-half mixture of hydrogen peroxide and warm water.

- If the pressure builds up again in a few days, repeat the procedure, using the same hole.

When to Call Kaiser Permanente

- If the person is uncooperative and won't let you try the procedure.

- If signs of infection appear:

  ° Increased pain, swelling, redness, or tenderness

  ° Heat or red streaks extending away from the area

  ° Discharge of pus

  ° Fever of 100° or higher with no other cause

- If there are signs of a more serious injury, see page 117.

Blunt Abdominal Wounds

Blunt abdominal wounds caused by a blow to the stomach can cause severe bruising of the abdominal wall and bleeding from the internal organs. Such injuries are often caused by automobile, bicycle, tobogganing, or skiing accidents, where the victim is thrown into something or to the ground.

The symptoms of abdominal injury are similar to those of shock: rapid pulse, low blood pressure, and cold, clammy skin. The abdomen may become rigid or tender. The injured person may become confused and unable to remember or describe the injury.

Home Treatment

- Monitor the injured person's pulse, blood pressure, and breathing. A rapid, weak pulse, falling blood pressure, or very rapid or very slow breathing may indicate internal bleeding. If these signs develop, call 911 or take the person to the emergency room.

- Have the injured person lie down with the feet elevated above the heart. Loosen the person's clothing and cover the person with a blanket to keep him or her warm. Do not give the person anything to eat or drink, even though he or she may be thirsty.

- Watch for signs of shock: faintness, weakness, drowsiness, or confusion; sweating; and cool, clammy skin.

When to Call Kaiser Permanente

- If signs of shock or internal bleeding (see above) develop up to 48 hours after an abdominal injury. See page 61.

- If there is bleeding from the rectum, urethra, or unexpected vaginal bleeding following a blow to the abdomen.

- If the injury causes nausea, vomiting, heartburn, or loss of appetite.

- If the abdomen is swollen and hard, or if pressing on the abdomen causes severe pain.

- If you have any concerns about the symptoms you observe.

Bruises

Bruises (contusions) are caused by ruptured small blood vessels under the skin, which are usually caused by a bump or fall. Blood seeps into the surrounding tissues, causing the black and blue color of a bruise.

People who take aspirin or blood thinners (anticoagulants) may bruise easily. A bruise may also develop after blood is drawn.

A black eye is a type of bruise. Apply home treatment for a bruise and inspect the eye.

Home Treatment

- Apply ice or cold packs for 15 minutes every 1 to 2 hours during the first 48 hours to help vessels constrict and to reduce swelling. The sooner you apply ice, the less bleeding will result.

- If possible, elevate the bruised area. Blood will leave the area and there will be less swelling.

- Rest the injured limb so you don't injure it further.

- If the area is still painful after 48 hours, apply heat with warm towels, a hot water bottle, or a heating pad.

When to Call Kaiser Permanente

- If signs of infection develop:

  ° Increased pain, swelling, redness, or tenderness (after the initial bruise)

First Aid and Emergencies

° Heat or red streaks extending away from the area

° Discharge of pus

° Fever of 100° or higher with no other cause

• If a blow to the eye causes:

° Blood in the colored part of the eye or blood in the white part of the eye (see page 156)

° Impaired or double vision

° Inability to move the eye normally in all directions

° Severe pain in the eyeball rather than in the eye socket

• If you suddenly begin to bruise easily, or if you have unexplained recurrent or multiple bruises.

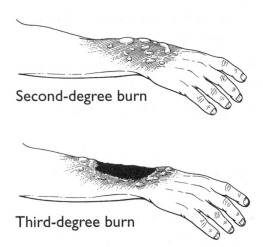

Second-degree burn

Third-degree burn

or damaged, so there may be little pain except on the edge, where there may be a second-degree burn.

Prevention

• Install smoke detectors on each story of your home. Check and replace batteries regularly.

• Keep a fire extinguisher near the kitchen. Have it inspected yearly.

• Set your water heater at 120° or lower to avoid burns.

• Don't smoke in bed.

If your clothing catches fire:

• Do not run, because running will fan the flames. Stop, drop, and roll on the ground to smother the flames.

• Smother the flames with a blanket, rug, or coat.

• Use water to douse the fire and cool the skin.

To avoid kitchen burns:

• Use caution when handling hot foods.

Burns

Burns are classified as first, second, or third degree depending on their depth, not on the amount of pain or the extent of the burn. A first-degree burn involves only the outer layer of skin. The skin is dry, painful, and sensitive to touch. A mild sunburn is an example.

A second-degree burn involves several layers of skin. The skin becomes swollen, puffy, weepy, or blistered.

A third-degree burn involves all layers of skin and may include any underlying tissue or organs. The skin is dry, pale white or charred black, swollen, and sometimes breaks open. Nerves are destroyed

First Aid and Emergencies

- Turn pot handles toward the back of the stove.

- Smother burning food or grease with a lid or pot.

- Supervise children closely.

Home Treatment

- For home treatment of sunburn, see page 63.

- Run cold tap water over the burn for 10 to 15 minutes. Cold water is the best immediate treatment for minor burns. The cold lowers the skin temperature and lessens the severity of the burn. Do not use ice, because it may further damage the injured skin.

- Remove rings, bracelets, watches, or shoes from the burned limb. Swelling may make them difficult to remove later.

For first-degree burns and second-degree burns with intact blisters:

- Leave the burn alone for 24 hours. Don't cover the burn unless clothing rubs on it. If it rubs, cover it with a gauze pad taped well away from the burn. Do not encircle a hand, arm, or leg with tape. Change the bandage after 24 hours, and then every two days.

- Do not put salve, butter, grease, oil, or ointment on a burn. They increase the risk of infection and don't help heal the burn.

- After two to three days of healing, the juice from an aloe leaf can soothe minor burns.

- For second-degree burns: Do not break blisters. If the blisters break, clean the area by running tap water over it. Apply an antibiotic ointment, such as Polysporin or Bacitracin, and cover the burn with a sterile dressing. Don't touch the wound with your hands or any unsterile objects. Remove the dressing every day, clean the wound, and cover it again.

- Aspirin or ibuprofen can help relieve pain from minor burns.

Third-degree burns require immediate medical treatment. Call a health professional and apply home treatment:

- Make sure the source of the burn has been extinguished.

- Have the person lie down to prevent shock.

- Cover the burned area with a clean sheet soaked in cool water.

- Do not apply any salve or medication to the burn.

When to Call Kaiser Permanente

- For all third-degree burns.

- If in doubt about the extent of a burn, or in doubt if it is a second- or third-degree burn.

- If a second-degree burn involves the face, hands, feet, genitals, or a joint and is more than one inch in diameter.

- If the burn encircles an arm or leg, or covers more than one-quarter of the body part involved.

First Aid and Emergencies

First Aid and Emergencies

• If it is an electrical burn. Electrical burns are often more extensive than they appear.

• If the pain lasts longer than 48 hours.

• If signs of infection develop:

  ° Increased pain, swelling, redness, or tenderness

  ° Heat or red streaks extending from the area

  ° Discharge of pus

  ° Fever of 100° or higher with no other cause

• If an infant, older adult, or person with diabetes is burned.

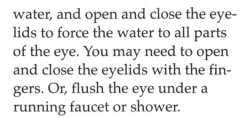

Chemical Burns

Chemical burns occur when something caustic, such as a cleaning product, gasoline, or turpentine, is splashed into the eye or onto the skin. The vapors or fumes of strong chemicals can also burn or irritate the eyes.

The eye becomes red, watery, and may be sensitive to light. If the damage is severe, the eye appears whitish. The skin may become red, blistered, or blackened, depending on how strong the caustic material is.

Home Treatment

• Immediately flush the eye or skin with water. If the eyes are involved, fill a sink or dishpan with water, immerse the face in the water, and open and close the eyelids to force the water to all parts of the eye. You may need to open and close the eyelids with the fingers. Or, flush the eye under a running faucet or shower.

• Continue flushing for 15 to 20 minutes, or until the pain stops, whichever takes longer.

• After flushing, cover the eye or skin with a clean bandage or cloth.

When to Call Kaiser Permanente

• Call 911 or seek emergency services if a strong chemical such as acid or lye is splashed into the eye.

• If there is major skin exposure (more than $\frac{1}{4}$ of any part of the body or on the face) to a strong acid, such as battery acid, or to a caustic substance, such as lye or Drano.

• If the eye still hurts after 20 minutes of home treatment.

• If the eye appears to be damaged. Symptoms include:

  ° Persistent redness

  ° Discharge or watering

  ° Any visual impairment, such as double vision, blurring, or sensitivity to light

  ° Colored part of the eye (iris) appears white

• If the skin shows signs of a burn, see page 34.

Choking

Choking is usually caused by food or an object stuck in the windpipe. A person who is choking cannot cough, talk, or breathe, and may turn blue or dusky. The **Heimlich maneuver**, described at right, can help dislodge the food or object.

Prevention

- Don't drink too much alcohol before eating. It may dull your senses and you might not chew food properly or might try to swallow too large a portion of food.

- Take small bites. Cut meat into small pieces. Chew your food thoroughly.

- Do not give popcorn, peanuts, or hard candy to children under age three, and supervise older children when they eat these foods.

- Do not allow children under age three to play with toys that have very small parts (smaller than a 50-cent piece) that could be swallowed.

- Keep balloons away from any child who may put them in his or her mouth.

When to Call Kaiser Permanente

- Call 911 or seek emergency services if you are unable to dislodge the object or the person loses consciousness. Attempt rescue breathing while waiting for help to arrive. See page 56.

- Call even if the food has been dislodged. The throat could be damaged by the object or there could be abdominal damage from the maneuver.

Choking Rescue Procedure (Heimlich Maneuver)

WARNING: Do not begin the choking rescue procedure unless the person cannot breathe or is turning blue and cannot speak, and you are certain that the person is choking.

Adults and Children Over One Year

If the victim is standing or sitting:

- Stand behind the victim and wrap your arms around his or her waist. Place one foot between the victim's legs so you can support the victim's body if he or she loses consciousness.

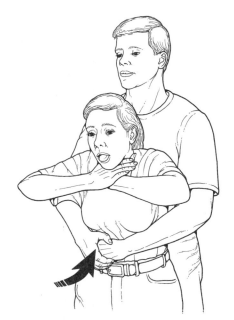

A. Give quick upward thrusts to dislodge the object.

First Aid and Emergencies

First Aid and Emergencies

• Make a fist with one hand. Place the thumb side of your fist against the victim's abdomen, just above the navel but well below the breastbone. See Illustration A (page 37).

• Grasp your fist with the other hand. Give a quick upward thrust into the victim's abdomen. This may cause the object to pop out. Use less force for young children.

• Repeat until the object is dislodged or the victim loses consciousness.

• If you choke while alone, do abdominal thrusts on yourself, or lean hard over the back of a chair to pop out the food.

If the victim loses consciousness, gently lower the victim to the ground. Call 911 or emergency services.

• Straddle the victim on your knees.

• Place the heel of one hand against the victim's abdomen, just above the navel but well below the breastbone. Place your other hand directly over the first. See Illustration B.

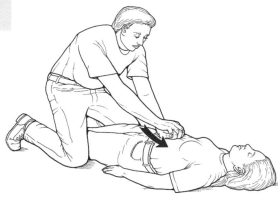

B. Proper positioning for performing choking rescue on an unconscious victim.

• Give five quick, upward thrusts into the victim's abdomen. Use less force for children.

• If you have been trained to do the mouth sweep and to give rescue breaths, continue with the choking rescue procedure by doing mouth sweeps, rescue breathing, and abdominal thrusts until the object is dislodged and you can breathe into the victim, or until an ambulance arrives.

C. To help a baby who is choking, put him face down on your forearm so his head is lower than his chest. Support the baby's head in your palm against your thigh (don't cover the baby's mouth or twist his neck). Use the heel of the other hand to give back blows between the baby's shoulders.

Infant Under One Year

• Hold infant as in Illustration C.

• Use the heel of one hand to jar the child between the shoulder blades in an attempt to dislodge the object. Repeat four times.

• If the airway remains blocked, support the infant's head and turn the infant face up on your thigh with his or her head down.

Stopping Severe Bleeding

- Have the person lie down and elevate the site that is bleeding.

- Remove any visible objects. Do not attempt to clean out the wound.

- Press firmly on the wound with a clean cloth or the cleanest material available. If the edges of the wound gape, hold them together. If there is an object in the wound, apply pressure around the cut, not directly over it.

- Apply steady continuous pressure for 15 minutes. If blood soaks through the cloth, apply another one without lifting the first.

- If direct pressure does not slow or stop bleeding after 15 minutes, press firmly on a pressure point between the wound and the heart (see illustration). Continuous pressure on these points can stop the bleeding with less risk than a tourniquet. Tourniquets should be used only as a last resort.

- Watch for shock. See page 61.

- Call 911 or go to the emergency room if severe bleeding has not been controlled after 15 minutes.

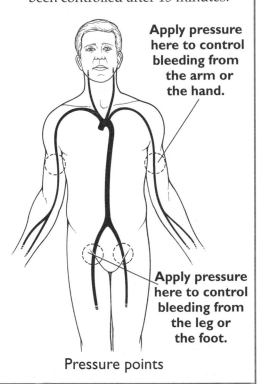

Apply pressure here to control bleeding from the arm or the hand.

Apply pressure here to control bleeding from the leg or the foot.

Pressure points

- Place two or three fingers just below a line between the nipples, and give up to four upward thrusts until the object pops out.

Cuts

When you see a cut (laceration), the first steps are to stop the bleeding and determine whether or not stitches are needed.

If the cut is bleeding heavily or spurting blood, see "Stopping Severe Bleeding," above.

Bleeding from minor cuts will usually stop on its own or with a little direct pressure. To decide whether stitches are needed, see "Are Sutures Necessary?" on page 40. If stitches are needed, apply home treatment and seek medical care as soon as possible, certainly within eight hours.

If stitches are not needed, you can clean and bandage the cut at home.

First Aid and Emergencies

Home Treatment

- Wash the cut well with soap and water. Treat an animal bite like a puncture wound. See page 55.

- Stop any bleeding by applying direct continuous pressure over the wound for 10 to 15 minutes.

- Leave small cuts unbandaged, unless they will become irritated. They heal best when exposed to the air.

- If a cut needs bandaging, but not stitches, apply antibiotic ointment (Polysporin or Bacitracin). The ointment will keep the cut from sticking to the bandage. Do not use rubbing alcohol, hydrogen peroxide, iodine, or mercurochrome, which can harm tissue and slow healing.

- Use an adhesive bandage (Band-Aid) to continue the pressure. Always put an adhesive strip across a cut rather than lengthwise. A butterfly bandage (made at home or purchased) can help hold cut skin edges together:

  ° Cut a strip from a roll of one-inch adhesive tape and fold it sticky side out. Cut notches into the tape as shown in the illustration on page 41.

  ° Unfold the tape, then fold the notched pieces together sticky side in. The center of the tape will be non-sticky. Keep the part that will be over the cut clean.

Are Sutures Necessary?

For best results, cuts that need stitches should be sutured within eight hours. Wash the cut well and stop the bleeding, then pinch the sides of the cut together. If it looks better, you may want to consider stitches. If stitches are needed, avoid using an antibiotic ointment until after a health professional has examined the cut.

Sutures may be needed for:

- Deep cuts (more than $\frac{1}{4}$ inch deep) that have jagged edges or gape open.

- Deep cuts on a joint: elbow, knuckle, knee.

- Deep cuts on the palm side of the hand or fingers.

- Cuts on the face, eyelids, or lips.

- Cuts in an area where you are worried about scarring, especially the face.

- Cuts that go down to the muscle or bone.

- Cuts that continue to bleed after 15 minutes of direct pressure.

Cuts like these that are sutured usually heal with less scarring than those that are not.

Sutures may not be needed for:

- Cuts with smooth edges that tend to stay together during normal movement of the affected body part.

- Shallow cuts less than $\frac{1}{4}$ inch deep that are less than one inch long.

First Aid and Emergencies

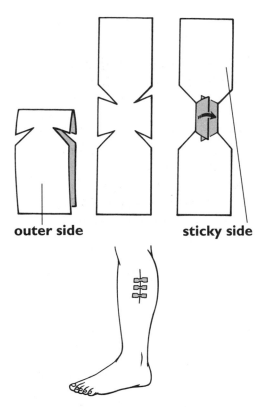

outer side   **sticky side**

Butterfly bandages are best for closing a long cut.

- ° Place one end of the tape on the skin, then pull the other end to close the wound tightly.

- ° If the cut is long, use more than one bandage.

- • Apply a clean bandage at least once a day, or when it gets wet. Leave the bandage off whenever possible.

When to Call Kaiser Permanente

- • If the person goes into shock, even if bleeding has stopped. See Shock on page 61.

- • If a cut continues to bleed through bandages after 15 minutes of direct pressure.

- • If blood or clear fluid drains from the ears or nose following a blow to the head (not due to a cut or direct blow to the nose).

- • If there is blue, white, or cold skin, numbness, tingling, or loss of feeling, or if the person is unable to move a limb below the wound.

- • If the cut contains, or might contain, foreign objects such as wood or gravel.

- • If the cut needs stitches. They usually need to be done within eight hours.

- • If your tetanus shots are not up to date. See page 18. If you need a tetanus booster, you should have it within 2 days of being injured.

- • If signs of infection develop:

  - ° Increased pain, swelling, or tenderness

  - ° Heat and redness or red streaks extending away from the cut

  - ° Discharge of pus

  - ° Fever of 100° or higher with no other cause

Fishhook Removal

In the excitement of fishing, sometimes fingers are hooked instead of fish. It is useful to know how to remove a fishhook, especially if you are far from medical help.

Home Treatment

Remove the hook as follows:

- Use ice, cold water, or hard pressure to provide temporary numbing.

- Tie a piece of fishing line to the hook near the skin surface.

- Grasp the eye of the hook with one hand and press down about $\frac{1}{8}$ inch to disengage the barb.

- While still pressing the hook down (barb disengaged), jerk the line parallel to the skin surface so that the hook shaft leads the barb out of the skin.

- If the fishhook is deeply embedded, another option is to push the hook the rest of the way through the skin, snip off the barb, and remove the hook.

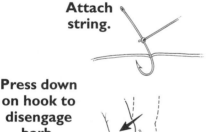

Attach string.

Press down on hook to disengage barb.

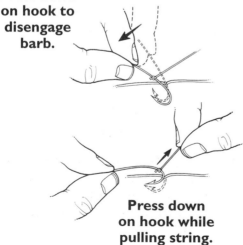

Press down on hook while pulling string.

- Wash the wound thoroughly with soap if possible. Treat as you would a puncture wound. See page 55.

- Do not try to remove a fishhook from the eyeball. Seek medical care immediately.

When to Call Kaiser Permanente

- If the hook is in the eyeball.

- If you cannot remove the hook.

- If your tetanus shots are not up to date. See page 18. If you need a tetanus booster, you should have it within two days of being injured.

- If signs of infection develop:

  ° Increased pain, swelling, redness, or tenderness

  ° Heat or red streaks extending from the area

  ° Discharge of pus

  ° Fever of 100° or higher with no other cause

Freeing Trapped Limbs

Fingers, arms, or legs sometimes get caught in objects such as bottles, jars, or pipes. Stay calm; panic will only make the situation worse.

Home Treatment

- Don't force the limb, because doing so will make it swell and become more difficult to remove.

- Try to relax the limb. Relaxation alone will sometimes enable you to free the limb.

- If possible, elevate the limb.

- Apply ice around the exposed part of the limb. This may reduce any swelling and allow the limb to be released.

- If ice doesn't work, dribble soapy water or cooking oil on the limb. Turn the limb or the object so you "unscrew" it rather than pulling it out directly.

When to Call Kaiser Permanente

Call if you are unable to free the trapped limb.

Frostbite

Frostbite is freezing of the skin or underlying tissues that occurs as a result of prolonged exposure to cold.

Frostbitten skin is pale or blue, stiff or rubbery to touch, and feels cold and numb. The severity is divided into three degrees:

First degree: Frostnip. Numbness and whitening of the skin with little likelihood of blistering if rewarmed promptly.

Second degree: Superficial frostbite. Outer skin feels hard and frozen but tissue underneath has normal resilience. Blistering is likely.

Third degree: Deep frostbite. Skin is white or blotchy and blue. Skin and tissue underneath are hard and very cold.

Prevention

Stay dry and out of the wind in extreme cold, and cover areas of exposed skin. Keep the body's core temperature up:

- Wear layers of clothing. Wool and polypropylene are good insulators. Wear wind- and waterproof outer layers. Wear wool socks and well-fitting, waterproof boots.

- Wear a hat to prevent heat loss from your head. Wear mittens rather than gloves.

- Keep protective clothing and blankets in your car in case of a breakdown in an isolated area.

- Don't drink alcohol or smoke when out in extreme cold.

Home Treatment

- Get inside or take shelter from the wind.

- Check for signs of hypothermia (see page 47) and treat it before treating frostbite.

- Protect the frozen body part from further exposure. Don't rewarm the area if refreezing is possible. Wait until you reach shelter.

- Warm small areas (ears, face, nose, fingers, toes) with warm breath or by tucking hands or feet inside warm clothing next to bare skin.

First Aid and Emergencies

First Aid and Emergencies

- Don't rub or massage the frozen area, because doing so will further damage tissues. Avoid walking on frostbitten feet if possible.

- Keep the frostbitten part warm and elevated. Wrap with blankets or soft material to prevent bruising. If possible, immerse it in warm water (104° to 108°) for 15 to 30 minutes.

- Blisters may appear as the skin warms. Do not break them. The skin may turn red, burn, tingle, or be very painful. Aspirin or acetaminophen may help.

When to Call Kaiser Permanente

- If skin is white or blue, hard, and cold (third-degree frostbite). Careful rewarming and antibiotic treatment are needed to prevent infection and permanent tissue damage.

- If blisters develop during rewarming (second- or third-degree frostbite). Do not break blisters. The risk of infection is very high.

- If signs of infection develop:

  ° Increased pain, swelling, redness, or tenderness

  ° Heat or red streaks extending from the area

  ° Discharge of pus

  ° Fever of 100° or higher with no other cause

Automobile Seat Restraints

Wearing seat belts saves lives and prevents injuries. No one is strong enough to brace against a sudden impact, even at very low speeds. Seat belts reduce the risk of serious injury and death.

- Wear your seat belt every time you are in a vehicle. Keep the belt snug and close to your body. Always use both the lap and shoulder belts.

- Seat belts are necessary even if your car is equipped with air bags. Air bags inflate from the steering wheel or dashboard of your car in the event of sudden impact. They are very effective in protecting front-seat riders, but they must be used with seat belts.

- Children younger than 12 years of age should sit in the back seat. Use child car seats for infants, children under four, and those weighing under 40 pounds. See page 200.

Head Injuries

Most bumps on the head are minor and heal as easily as bumps anywhere else. Head injuries that cause cuts often bleed heavily because the blood vessels of the scalp are close to the surface. This bleeding is alarming, but it does not always mean the injury is severe.

However, head injuries that do not cause visible external bleeding may have caused life-threatening bleeding and swelling inside the skull. Anyone who has experienced a head injury should be watched carefully for 24 hours for signs of a severe head injury.

Prevention

- Wear your seat belt when in a motor vehicle. Use child car seats.

- Wear a helmet while biking, motorcycling, and skating.

- Don't dive into shallow or unfamiliar water.

Home Treatment

- If the victim is unconscious, make sure there is no spinal injury before moving him or her (see page 62). Check for other injuries.

- If there is bleeding, apply firm pressure directly over the wound with a clean cloth or bandage for 15 minutes. If the blood soaks through, apply additional cloths over the first one. See page 39.

- Apply ice or cold packs to reduce the swelling. A "goose egg" may appear anyway, but ice will help ease the pain.

- Watch for the following signs of a severe head injury immediately afterwards and then every two hours for the next 24 hours:

  ° Confusion. Ask the person his or her name, address, age, the date, etc.

  ° Inability to move arms and legs on one side of the body, or slower movement on one side than the other.

  ° Lethargy, abnormally deep sleep, or difficulty waking up.

  ° Vomiting that continues after the first two hours.

  ° Seizures or convulsions.

- Continue observing the person every two hours during the night. Wake the person up and check for any unusual symptoms. Call 911 or go to an emergency room immediately if you cannot wake the person or if he or she has any of the above symptoms.

- Check for injuries to other parts of the body, especially if the person has fallen. The alarm from seeing a head injury may cause you to overlook other injuries that need attention.

When to Call Kaiser Permanente

- If the person loses consciousness anytime after the injury.

- If double vision or speech difficulty occurs after the first minute.

- If weakness or numbness occurs on one side.

- If blood or clear fluid drains from the ears or nose following a blow to the head (not due to a cut or direct blow to the nose).

- If the person is confused or has any loss of memory after the first few minutes.

First Aid and Emergencies

First Aid and Emergencies

- If a severe headache develops: "The worst headache I've ever had."

- If vomiting occurs after the first two hours or violent vomiting persists after the first 15 minutes. Mild nausea or vomiting at first is usually not serious.

- If there are seizures or convulsions.

- If bleeding cannot be stopped (see page 39) or the wound needs stitches (see page 40).

Heat Exhaustion and Heat Stroke

Heat exhaustion occurs when your body cannot sweat enough to cool you off. It generally happens when you are working or exercising in hot weather. Symptoms include:

- Fatigue, weakness, dizziness, or nausea

- Cool, clammy, pale, red, or flushed skin

Heat exhaustion can sometimes lead to **heat stroke**, which requires emergency treatment. Heat stroke happens when your body stops sweating but the body temperature continues to rise, often to 105° or higher.

Symptoms of heat stroke include:

- Confusion, delirium, or unconsciousness

- Hot, dry, red or flushed skin, even under the armpits

Prevention

- Avoid strenuous outdoor physical activity during the hottest part of the day.

- Wear light-colored, loose-fitting clothing to reflect the sun.

- Avoid sudden changes of temperature. Air out a hot car before getting into it.

- If you take diuretics, ask your doctor about taking a lower dose during hot weather.

- Drink 8 to 10 glasses of water per day. Drink even more if you are working or exercising in hot weather.

- If you exercise strenuously in hot weather, drink more liquid than your thirst seems to require. For example, runners should drink about one cup of water 10 to 15 minutes before running and another cup of water every two miles or so.

Home Treatment

- Get out of the sun to a cool spot and drink lots of cool water, a little at a time. If you are nauseated or dizzy, lie down.

- Sponge the body with cool water.

- If the body temperature reaches 105°, immediate cooling is essential. Use cold, wet cloths all over the body or a cool water bath.

- If the temperature is lowered to 102°, use care to avoid overcooling.

When to Call Kaiser Permanente

Call 911 or seek emergency care if signs of heat stroke develop. Work fast to lower the temperature and seek immediate help if:

- The skin is dry, even under the armpits, and bright red or flushed.

- The body temperature reaches 104° and keeps rising.

- The person is delirious, disoriented, or unconscious.

Hyperventilation

When you breathe very fast and deep (hyperventilate), the carbon dioxide (CO_2) level in your blood can drop too low. Symptoms that may occur with hyperventilation include:

- Numbness or tingling in the hands, feet, or around the mouth

- Pounding, racing heartbeat and anxiety

- Feeling you can't get enough air

- Lightheadedness

- Chest pain

In a severe case, you may lose consciousness.

Prevention

If you have hyperventilated before:

- Ask people to mention it if you start to breathe too fast.

- As soon as you notice fast breathing or other symptoms, slow your breathing to one breath every five seconds, or slow enough that symptoms subside.

Home Treatment

- Sit down and concentrate on slowing your breathing.

- Practice a relaxation technique. See page 272.

- Breathe in and out of a paper bag held over the nose and mouth. This will help bring the amount of CO_2 in the blood back to normal. Continue this treatment intermittently for 5 to 15 minutes.

When to Call Kaiser Permanente

- If hyperventilation occurs in a person who doesn't appear tense or anxious. See page 294 to help determine if a person is anxious.

- If anxiety and hyperventilation are frequent and interfere with your daily activities.

Hypothermia

Hypothermia occurs when the body temperature drops below normal. It occurs when the body loses heat faster than heat can be produced by muscle contractions and shivering.

Early symptoms include:

- Shivering

- Cold, pale skin

- Apathy

- Impaired judgment

Later symptoms include:

- Cold abdomen
- Slow pulse and breathing
- Weakness or drowsiness
- Confusion

Shivering may stop if body temperature drops below 96°.

Hypothermia is an emergency. It can quickly lead to unconsciousness and death if the heat loss continues. Hypothermia can happen at temperatures of 45° or even higher in wet and windy weather. Frail and inactive people can develop hypothermia indoors if they are not dressed warmly.

Early recognition is very important in the treatment of hypothermia. Often a hiker or skier will lose heat to a critical degree before others notice anything is wrong. If someone begins to shiver violently, stumble, or respond incoherently to questions, suspect hypothermia and warm the person quickly.

Prevention

Whenever you plan to be outdoors for several hours in cold weather, take the following precautions:

- Dress warmly and wear wind- and waterproof clothing. Wear fabric that remains warm even when wet, such as wool or polypropylene.
- Wear a warm hat. An unprotected head loses a great deal of the body's total heat production.

- Head for shelter if you get wet or cold.
- Eat well before going out and carry extra food.
- Don't drink alcohol while in the cold. It makes the body lose heat faster.
- Older or less active people can prevent indoor hypothermia by dressing warmly and keeping temperatures above 65°.

Home Treatment

The goal of home or "in-the-field" treatment is to stop additional heat loss and slowly rewarm the person. Warming one degree per hour is best.

- For mild cases, get the person out of the cold and wind. Give the person dry or wool clothing, and warm liquids to drink.
- For moderate cases, remove cold, wet clothes first, then warm the person with your own body heat by wrapping a blanket or sleeping bag around both of you.
- Give warm liquids to drink and high-energy foods, such as candy. Do not give food or drink if the person is disoriented or unconscious. Do not give alcoholic beverages.
- Rewarming the person in warm water can cause shock or heart attack. However, in emergency situations when help is not available and other home treatments are not working, you can use a warm water bath (100° to 105°) as a last resort.

First Aid and Emergencies

When to Call Kaiser Permanente

- Call 911 or seek emergency care if the person loses consciousness and remains unconscious or seems confused.

- If the victim is a child or older adult. It's a good idea to call regardless of the severity of the symptoms.

- If the body temperature does not return to normal after four hours of warming.

Insect and Spider Bites and Stings

Insect and spider bites and bee, yellow jacket, and wasp stings usually cause a localized reaction with swelling, redness, and itching. In some people, especially children, the redness and swelling may be worse, and the local reaction may last up to a few days. In most cases, bites and stings do not cause reactions all over the body. (In a few areas, mosquitoes may spread illnesses, including encephalitis and malaria.)

Some people have severe skin reactions to insect or spider bites or stings, and a few have allergic (anaphylactic) reactions that affect the whole body. Symptoms may include hives all over the body, shortness of breath and tightness in the chest, dizziness, wheezing, or swelling of the tongue and face. If

these symptoms develop, immediate medical attention is needed.

Few spiders cause serious bites, although any bite may be serious if the person has an allergic reaction.

Black widow spiders can be up to two inches across (although they are generally much smaller) and are shiny black with a red hourglass mark on their undersides. Their bites may cause chills, fever, nausea, and abdominal muscle pain. A severe reaction may cause breathing problems. People with high blood pressure, elderly people, and children are at the greatest risk for a severe reaction.

Brown recluse (fiddler) spiders are smaller than black widows and have long legs. They are brown with a white, violin-shaped mark on their back. Their bites result in intense pain (although the bite itself may be painless) and may result in a blister that turns into a larger open sore. Their bites also may cause nausea, vomiting, headaches, and chills.

Also see Tick Bites on page 64.

Prevention

- To avoid bee stings, wear white or light-colored solid fabrics. Bees are attracted to dark colors and flowered prints.

- Avoid wearing perfumes and colognes when you are outside.

- Apply an insect repellent containing DEET every few hours when in insect- and spider-infested areas. Use a lower-concentration DEET product for small children and pregnant women. Wash DEET

First Aid and Emergencies

off when you come inside. Alpha-Keri and Skin-So-Soft bath oils also seem to repel insects.

- Wear gloves and tuck pants into socks when working in woodpiles, sheds, and basements where spiders are found.

Home Treatment

- Remove a bee stinger by scraping or flicking it out (if the stinger isn't visible, assume there isn't one). Don't squeeze the stinger; you may release more venom into the skin.

- If the bite is from a black widow or brown recluse spider, apply ice to the bite and call your doctor.

- Apply a cold pack or ice cube to the bite or sting. Some people also find that a paste of baking soda, meat tenderizer, or activated charcoal mixed with a little water helps relieve pain and decrease the reaction.

- An oral antihistamine (Benadryl, Chlor-Trimeton) may help relieve pain and swelling and relieve itching if there are many bites. Calamine lotion or hydrocortisone cream may also help.

- Anyone who has had a severe systemic allergic reaction to insect venom should carry an emergency kit containing a syringe and adrenaline (epinephrine). Ask your doctor or pharmacist how to use the kit.

- Trim fingernails to prevent scratching, which can lead to infection.

When to Call Kaiser Permanente

- Call 911 or seek emergency services if signs of a severe allergic reaction develop soon after being stung by an insect:

  ° Wheezing, difficulty breathing

  ° Swelling around the lips, tongue, or face, or significant swelling around the site of the insect sting (e.g., entire arm or leg is swollen)

  ° Spreading skin rash, itching, feeling of warmth, or hives

- If a bite by the same type of spider or insect previously caused a serious reaction.

- If a blister appears at the site of a spider bite, or if the surrounding skin becomes discolored.

- If symptoms are not improving in 2 to 3 days or there are signs of infection.

- To talk with your doctor about adrenaline kits or allergy shots (immunotherapy) for insect venom if you have had a serious allergic reaction.

Jellyfish Stings

Jellyfish stings cause pain and hive-like swellings. If the stings are numerous and a large amount of poison is released into the skin, there may be shortness of breath, nausea, and stomach cramps. In severe cases there can be muscle cramps, fainting, vomiting, and difficulty breathing.

First Aid and Emergencies

Home Treatment

- Rinse the area immediately with sea water. Do not use fresh water and do not rub; doing so will release more poison.

- Splash vinegar, rubbing alcohol, or meat tenderizer dissolved in saltwater on the area to neutralize the poison.

- Remove any attached tentacles carefully. Protect your hand with a towel and apply a paste of sand or baking soda and saltwater to the area. Scrape the tentacles off with the towel or the edge of a credit card.

- Apply calamine lotion to relieve pain and itching.

- If you are stung by a Portuguese man-of-war jellyfish, scrape the stinging tentacles off with sand and seek medical care immediately.

When to Call Kaiser Permanente

- Call 911 or seek emergency care if signs of a severe allergic reaction develop soon after being stung by a jellyfish:

  ° Wheezing, difficulty breathing

  ° Swelling around the lips, tongue, or face or significant swelling around the sting (e.g., entire arm or leg is swollen)

- If there is some swelling around the site of the jellyfish sting.

- If the skin around the sting becomes discolored.

- If over-the-counter pain medications are not able to control the pain.

- Call your doctor to talk about adrenaline kits or allergy shots (immunotherapy) for jellyfish venom if you have had a serious allergic reaction.

Nosebleeds

Nosebleeds are inconvenient and messy, but they can usually be stopped with home treatment. Some common causes of nosebleeds are low humidity, colds and allergies, blows to the nose, medications (especially aspirin), high altitudes, and blowing or picking the nose.

Prevention

- Low humidity is a common cause of nosebleeds. Humidify your home, especially the bedrooms, and keep the heat low (60° to 64°) in sleeping areas.

- If your nose becomes very dry, breathe moist air for a while (e.g., from a shower) and then put a little petroleum jelly on the inside of your nose to help prevent bleeding. A saline nasal spray may also help.

- Limit your use of aspirin, which can contribute to nosebleeds.

Home Treatment

- Sit up straight and tip your head slightly forward. Tilting the head back may cause blood to run down the throat.

First Aid and Emergencies

First Aid and Emergencies

- Blow all the clots out of the nose. Pinch the nostrils shut between your thumb and forefinger or apply firm pressure against the bleeding nostril for 10 full minutes. Resist the urge to peek after a few minutes to see if the nose has stopped bleeding.

- After 10 minutes, check to see if the nose is still bleeding. If it is, hold it for 10 more minutes. Most nosebleeds will stop after 10 to 30 minutes of direct pressure.

- Stay quiet for a few hours and do not blow the nose for at least 12 hours after the bleeding has stopped.

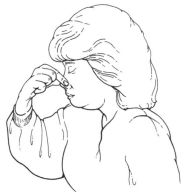

To stop a nosebleed, tilt your head forward and pinch your nostrils together below the bridge of your nose. Hold for at least 10 minutes.

When to Call Kaiser Permanente

- If the bleeding hasn't stopped after 30 minutes of direct pressure.

- If blood runs down the back of your throat even when the nose is pinched.

- If the nose is deformed after an injury and may be broken.

- If nosebleeds recur often.

Objects in the Ear

Children sometimes put small objects in their ears, or an insect may crawl into the ear. It may be hard to know if an insect is in the ear. Your child may say, "My ear is bumping around."

Home Treatment

- Don't try to kill an insect in the ear. Pull the ear up and back and point it toward the sun or a bright light. Insects are attracted to light, so the insect may crawl out.

- If the insect doesn't crawl out, fill the ear canal with mineral, olive, or baby oil. The insect may float out.

- To remove other objects in the ear, tilt the head to the side and shake it. Gently pulling the ear up and back may straighten the ear canal and help dislodge the object.

- If the object is soft and can be easily seen, try carefully to remove it with tweezers. Do not try this if the person will not hold very still or if the object is in the ear so far that you can't see the tips of the tweezers. Use care not to push the object farther in.

When to Call Kaiser Permanente

Call if you cannot remove the insect or object.

Objects in the Eye

A speck of dirt or small object in the eye will often wash out with your tears. If the object is not removed, it may scratch the covering of the eye (cornea). Most corneal scratches are minor and heal on their own in a day or two.

If an object is thrown forcefully into the eye (e.g., from a machine), seek emergency care, especially if the eye is punctured.

Home Treatment

• Don't rub the eye, because doing so could scratch the cornea. You may have to restrain small children from rubbing.

• Do not try to remove an object that is on the pupil or that is stuck in the white of the eye. Cover both eyes and call a health professional.

• Wash your hands before touching the eye.

• If the object is at the side of the eye or on the lower lid, moisten a cotton swab or the tip of a twisted piece of tissue and touch the end to the speck. The object should cling to the swab or tissue. Some minor irritation is common after you have removed the object.

• Gently wash the eye with cool water. An eyedropper helps.

• Never use tweezers, toothpicks, or other hard items to remove any object. Eye damage may result.

When to Call Kaiser Permanente

• Call 911 or seek emergency care if the eyeball is punctured.

• If the object is on the pupil or is embedded in the eye. Do not pull out an object that is stuck in the eye.

• If you cannot remove the object.

• If pain is severe or persists, if it feels like there is still something in the eye, or if vision is blurred after the object is removed. The cornea may be scratched. Keep the eye closed.

Objects in the Nose

Children sometimes put small objects, like beads or popcorn, up their noses. If the child doesn't tell you about it, your first clue may be a foul-smelling green or yellow discharge from just one nostril. The nose may also be tender and swollen.

Home Treatment

• Spray a nasal decongestant (see page 313) in the affected nostril to reduce the swelling.

• Have the child pinch the other nostril closed and try to blow the object out.

First Aid and Emergencies

• If you can see the object, try to remove it with blunt-nosed tweezers. Hold the child's head still and use care not to push the object in farther. If the child resists, do not try tweezers. Some minor bleeding from the nostril is not serious.

When to Call Kaiser Permanente

Call if you are unable to remove the object after several tries.

Poisoning

FOR ANY POISONING: Call 911 or your local poison control number immediately.

Children will swallow just about anything, including poisons. When in doubt, assume the worst. Always believe a child who indicates that some poison has been swallowed, no matter how unappetizing the substance is. Even if it turns out that a child has not swallowed poison, following the steps below will not hurt.

If you suspect food poisoning, see page 81.

Prevention

About 80 percent of poisonings occur in children age one to four. Develop poison prevention habits before your child is born and certainly before he or she is crawling. Infants grow so fast that sometimes they are crawling and walking before you have time to protect them.

Lead Poisoning

Infants and young children exposed to lead are at risk of developing learning disabilities and growth problems.

Your child is at risk for lead poisoning if he or she:

• Lives in or regularly visits a house built before 1960 and is exposed to peeling or chipping paint or home renovations.

• Has a sibling or parent who uses lead paints in hobbies.

• Is in contact with someone who has been treated for lead poisoning.

• Eats dirt or clay on purpose.

If your child is at risk, have his or her blood level tested at one year of age.

To reduce the risk of lead poisoning:

• Get rid of peeling or chipping paint.

• Prevent contact with hobby paints and home remodeling supplies.

• If your home has lead or lead-soldered water pipes, let the water run for a few minutes before using.

• Never leave a poisonous product unattended, even for a moment.

• Lock all drugs and vitamins away from children. Aspirin is the most common source of childhood

First Aid and Emergencies

poisoning, especially flavored baby aspirin. Lock up drugs between doses.

• Do not keep poisons such as drain opener, dishwasher detergent, oven cleaner, or plant food under your kitchen sink. Keep them completely out of reach of children. Dishwasher detergent is especially dangerous.

• Keep products in their original containers. Never store poisonous products in food containers.

• Use childproof latches on your cupboards.

• Use "Mr. Yuk" stickers and teach your children to recognize them.

• Purchase syrup of ipecac (see page 318) and keep the poison control center number near your phone.

Home Treatment

• Call a poison control center, hospital, or health professional immediately. Have the poison container with you so you can tell them what the poison is. They will tell you whether it is safe to make the person vomit.

• Do not have the person vomit if he or she:

° Is having convulsions.

° Is unconscious.

° Has a burning sensation in the mouth or throat.

° Has swallowed a corrosive agent or petroleum product (dishwasher detergent, lye, bleach, disinfectant, drain opener, floor wax, kerosene, grease remover).

• If suggested by poison control, induce vomiting by:

° Giving syrup of ipecac, if available. See page 318.

° Placing a spoon or finger at the back of the throat.

• When vomiting begins, place the head lower than the chest to prevent vomited material from entering the lungs.

Puncture Wounds

Puncture wounds are caused by sharp, pointed objects that penetrate the skin. Nails, tacks, ice picks, knives, needles, and animal bites can all cause puncture wounds. Puncture wounds are easily infected because they are difficult to clean and provide a warm, moist place for bacteria to grow.

Home Treatment

• Make sure that nothing is left in the wound, such as the tip of a needle. Check to see if the object is intact.

• Allow the wound to bleed freely to clean itself out unless there has been a large loss of blood or the blood is squirting out. If bleeding is heavy, see page 39.

• Clean the wound thoroughly with soap and water.

• For the next four to five days, soak the wound in warm water several times a day. This will clean the

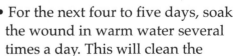

wound from the inside out. If the wound is closed, an infection under the skin may not be detected for several days.

When to Call Kaiser Permanente

- If the wound is in the head, neck, chest, or abdomen, unless it is minor.

- If there is blue, white, or cold skin, numbness, tingling, loss of feeling, or the person is unable to move a limb below the wound.

- If an animal bite is severe and may need stitches, or if it is on the hand or face. Stitches usually need to be done in eight hours.

- If you are unable to remove an object from the wound.

- If your tetanus shots are not up to date (see page 18), especially if the object that caused the puncture wound was dirty, such as a rusty nail or a farm implement.

- If a deep wound to the foot occurred through a shoe.

- If signs of infection develop:

  ° Increased pain, swelling, redness, or tenderness

  ° Heat or red streaks extending from the wound

  ° Discharge of pus

  ° Fever of 100° with no other cause

First Aid and Emergencies

Rescue Breathing and CPR

Warning: **Improper CPR or CPR performed on a person whose heart is still beating can cause serious injury. Never perform CPR unless:**

1. Breathing has stopped.

2. There is no heartbeat.

3. No one with more training in CPR is present.

Be prepared: Take a CPR course from the American Red Cross or the American Heart Association.

For basic life support, think **ABC: A**irway, **B**reathing, and **C**irculation, in that order. You must establish an open airway to start breathing, and you must give rescue breathing before you can begin the chest compressions needed if the victim's heart has stopped.

Step 1: Check for consciousness.

Tap or gently shake the victim and shout, "Are you okay?" If the victim does not respond, roll the victim

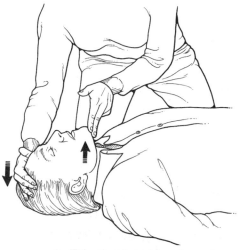

A. Tilt the head back and lift the chin.

onto his or her back, unless there is a possible spinal injury. If the victim may have suffered a spinal injury, gently roll the head, neck, and shoulders together as a unit until the victim is on his or her back.

When a victim does not respond:

• **Adults and children age 9 and older:** Call 911 or emergency services immediately. Then give rescue breathing (and CPR if there is no pulse).

• **Children age 8 and younger:** Give one full minute of rescue breathing (and CPR if there is no pulse); then call 911 or emergency services.

Step 2: Open the airway.

• Kneel next to the victim. Clear any foreign material from the mouth with your fingers.

• Place one hand on the victim's forehead and tilt the head back gently.

• Place the fingers of your other hand under the chin and lift to

pull it forward. See Illustration A (page 56). **For an infant:** Use care not to tilt the head back too far.

• Look to see if the victim's chest is rising and falling. Listen and feel for air moving out of the mouth.

• Sometimes, just opening the airway will allow the victim to breathe. If the victim does not start breathing, begin rescue breathing immediately.

Step 3: Begin rescue breathing.

• Pinch the victim's nostrils shut with your thumb and forefinger (of the hand on the forehead). With your other hand, continue tilting the chin forward to keep the airway open.

• Take a deep breath and place your mouth over the victim's, making a tight seal. See Illustration B.

For an infant: Place your mouth over the baby's mouth and nose.

• Slowly blow air in until the victim's chest rises. Take $1\frac{1}{2}$ to 2 seconds to give each breath. Remove your mouth from the victim's and take a deep breath between rescue breaths. Allow the victim's chest to fall and feel the air escape.

• Give two full breaths; then check for circulation.

Step 4: Check for circulation.

Locate the carotid artery in the neck:

• Find the voice box or Adam's apple. Slide the tips of your index and middle fingers into the groove beside it.

B. Blow air in slowly; look to see if chest rises.

First Aid and Emergencies

- Feel for a pulse for 5 to 10 seconds.

If there is no pulse: Begin chest compressions. See Step 5.

If there is a pulse: Continue rescue breathing until help arrives or the victim starts to breathe on his or her own. If the victim begins breathing again, he or she still needs to be seen by a health professional.

Give rescue breaths:

- Adult (age 9 and older): 1 breath every 5 seconds

- Children age 1 to 8: 1 breath every 3 seconds

- Infant under 1 year: 1 breath every 3 seconds

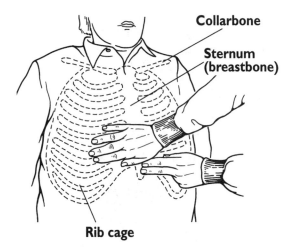

Collarbone

Sternum (breastbone)

Rib cage

C. Put your hand two fingers' width above the bottom of the sternum.

CPR Ready Reference

	Adults	Children	Infants
If the victim has a pulse, give one rescue breath every:	5 seconds	3 seconds	3 seconds
If the victim has no pulse, locate the chest compression landmark:	Trace ribs into notch; place 2 fingers on sternum	Same as adult	1 finger-width below nipple line
Do chest compressions with:	2 hands stacked; heel of 1 hand on sternum	Heel of 1 hand on sternum	2 or 3 fingers on sternum
Rate of compressions per minute:	80 to 100	100	100
Compression depth:	$1\frac{1}{2}$ to 2"	1 to $1\frac{1}{2}$"	$\frac{1}{2}$ to 1"
Ratio of compressions to breaths:			
1 rescuer	15:2	5:1	5:1
2 rescuers	5:1	5:1	N/A

Guidelines from the American Heart Association

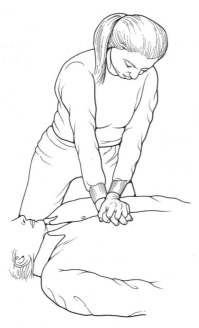

D. Keep your shoulders directly over your hands with your elbows straight as you give chest compressions.

Step 5: Begin chest compressions.

Infants and children: See right.

- **For adults:** Kneel next to the victim. Use your fingers to locate the end of the breastbone (sternum), where the ribs come together. Place two fingers at the tip of the breastbone. Place the heel of one hand directly above your fingers. See Illustration C (page 58).

- Place your other hand on top of the one that is in position. Do not allow your fingers to touch the chest, because that may damage the ribs.

- Straighten your arms, lock your elbows, and center your shoulders directly over your hands. See Illustration D.

- Press down in a steady rhythm, using your body weight and keeping your elbows locked. The force from each thrust should go straight down onto the sternum, compressing it $1\frac{1}{2}$ to 2 inches. It may help to count "one and two and three and four...," up to 15 compressions. Give one downward thrust each time you say a number. Lift your weight, but not your hands, from the victim's chest each time you say "and."

- After 15 compressions, open the airway with the head tilt/chin lift, and give 2 full, slow breaths, taking one breath in between.

- Repeat the 15 compressions-2 breaths cycle 4 times. Check the pulse again. If there is still no pulse, continue the rescue breathing and chest compressions until help arrives or the victim's pulse and breathing return.

- **For an infant:** Place 2 fingers on the sternum, about one finger-width below an imaginary line connecting the nipples. Press with gentle force, compressing the sternum about $\frac{1}{2}$ inch.

- **For a child:** Using the heel of one hand, press with less force, compressing the sternum 1 to $1\frac{1}{2}$ inches.

- **For infants and children:** Give 5 chest compressions, then 1 breath. Repeat 20 times (one minute) and

First Aid and Emergencies

check the pulse again. If there is still no pulse, continue rescue breathing and chest compressions until help arrives or until the pulse and breathing are restored.

Scrapes

Scrapes or abrasions happen so often that they seem unimportant. Good home treatment will reduce scarring and prevent infection.

Home Treatment

• Scrapes are usually very dirty. Remove large pieces of debris with tweezers, then scrub vigorously with soap and water and a wash-cloth. The injured person will probably complain loudly, but cleaning is necessary to prevent infection and scarring. If you have a water sprayer in your kitchen sink, try using that on the scrape with additional scrubbing.

• Apply steady pressure with a clean bandage or cloth to stop bleeding.

• Ice may help reduce swelling and bruising.

• If the scrape is large or in an area rubbed by clothing, apply an anti-biotic ointment and cover it with a non-stick (Telfa) bandage. This type of bandage won't stick and is held in place by adhesive around the edges. Putting the ointment on the bandage first will be less painful.

Removing Splinters

If you can grasp the end of the splinter with tweezers, gently pull it out. If the splinter is embedded in the skin, clean a needle with alcohol and make a small hole in the skin over the end of the splinter. Then lift the splinter with the tip of the needle until it can be grasped with the tweezers and pulled out.

After the splinter has been removed, wash the area with soap and water. Apply a ban-dage if needed to keep the wound clean; otherwise, leave it open to the air. Watch for signs of infection (see below).

Call a health professional if the splinter is very large or deeply embedded and cannot be easily removed, or if the splinter is in the eye.

When to Call Kaiser Permanente

• If your tetanus shots are not up to date. See page 18.

• If the scrape is very large and dirty.

• If you cannot remove dirt and debris embedded under the skin. They may cause tattooing or infec-tion if not removed.

• If signs of infection develop:

° Increased pain, swelling, redness, or tenderness

First Aid and Emergencies

° Heat or red streaks extending from the scrape

° Discharge of pus

° Fever of 100° or higher with no other cause

Shock

Shock may occur due to sudden illness or injury. When the circulatory system is unable to get enough blood to the vital organs, the body goes into shock. Sometimes even a mild injury will lead to shock.

The signs of shock include:

- Cool, pale, clammy skin
- Weak, rapid pulse
- Shallow, rapid breathing
- Low blood pressure
- Thirst, nausea, or vomiting
- Confusion or anxiety
- Faintness, weakness, dizziness, or loss of consciousness

Shock is a life-threatening condition. Prompt home treatment can save lives.

Home Treatment

- Have the person lie down and elevate his or her legs 12 inches or more. If the injury is to the head, neck, or chest, keep the legs flat. If the person vomits, roll him or her to one side to let fluids drain from the mouth. Use care if there could be a spinal injury (see page 62).

- Control any bleeding (see page 39) and splint any fractures (see page 118).

- Keep the person warm, but not hot. Place a blanket underneath the person and cover him or her with a sheet or blanket, depending on the weather. If the person is in a hot place, try to keep him or her cool.

- Take and record the person's pulse every five minutes.

- Comfort and reassure the person to relieve anxiety.

When to Call Kaiser Permanente

Call 911 or seek emergency services if signs of shock develop.

Snake Bites

While thousands of people are bitten by snakes every year in the United States, only about 10 people die as a result. Most poisonous snake bites are from rattlesnakes. Other poisonous snakes in North America are copperheads, cottonmouths (also called water moccasins), and coral snakes. Even if a poisonous snake bites you, it may not inject poison. However, if your skin is broken by the bite, assume that poison has been injected.

If you are bitten and it is safe for someone with you to kill the snake, have the person do so and take the dead snake with you when you get medical care. Be very careful in handling the dead snake. The biting

First Aid and Emergencies

reflex remains even after the snake has been dead up to 60 minutes. By knowing what kind of snake has bitten you, a health professional can quickly select the correct treatment.

Get medical care as quickly as possible. Antivenin treatment is best started within four hours and is of little use if more than 12 hours have passed.

Prevention

- Be aware if the area you are in is inhabited by poisonous snakes.

- Wear high leather boots and long pants when in areas that snakes inhabit.

- Do not reach into areas where snakes may be resting if you cannot see it is safe. Do not step over logs or rocks if you cannot see the other side.

- Avoid walking at night in snake-infested areas.

- Do not handle snakes, even if they are dead, unless you know how to identify snakes and know their habits.

Home Treatment

If you may have been bitten by a poisonous snake:

- Keep calm. Frantic activity will cause the poison to spread faster.

- If possible, lie down and keep the area of the bite lower than the heart.

- Tie a band or strip of cloth around the limb between the bite and the heart. This band should be tight

enough to indent the skin like a rubber band (it is not intended to stop blood flow).

- Do not allow the person to eat or drink, especially alcoholic beverages.

- Get medical attention as soon as possible.

- Snake bite kits are of minimal benefit. Use them only if you have been instructed by an expert.

When to Call Kaiser Permanente

- Call 911 or seek emergency services if you or someone you are with is bitten by a poisonous snake or if you feel odd (more than just scared) or have any unusual symptoms after being bitten by a snake.

- If you are not certain whether the snake is poisonous or not, even if you are feeling well.

Spinal Injuries

Any accident involving the neck or back must be considered a possible spinal injury. Permanent paralysis may be avoided if the injured person is immobilized and transported correctly.

Signs of a spinal injury include:

- Severe pain in neck or back

- Bruises on head, neck, shoulders, or back

- Weakness, tingling, or numbness in the arms or legs

- Loss of bowel or bladder control

First Aid and Emergencies

- Bleeding or clear fluid discharge from ears or nose (not directly due to the injury)

- Unconsciousness

Home Treatment

- If you suspect a spinal injury, do not move the person unless there is an immediate threat to life, such as fire. Don't drag victims from automobile accidents.

- If the person is in immediate danger, keep the head and neck supported and aligned while you move him or her to safety.

- If it was a diving accident, don't pull the injured person from the water, because you may cause permanent damage. Float the person face up in the water until help arrives. The water will act as a splint and keep the spine immobile.

When to Call Kaiser Permanente

Call 911 or seek emergency services to transport the injured person if you suspect a spinal injury.

Sunburn

A sunburn is usually a first-degree burn that involves just the outer surface of the skin. Sunburns are uncomfortable but are usually not dangerous unless they are extensive. Severe sunburns can be serious in infants and small children.

Repeated sun exposure and sunburns increase the risk of skin cancer.

Prevention

If you are going to be in the sun for more than 15 minutes, take the following precautions:

- Use a sunscreen with a sun protection factor (SPF) of at least 15.

- Apply the sunscreen 15 minutes before exposure. Reapply every two hours or as directed.

- If you are allergic to PABA, the active ingredient in many sunscreens, ask your pharmacist about non-PABA alternatives.

- Wear light-colored, loose-fitting, long-sleeved clothes and a broad-brimmed hat to shade your face.

- Drink lots of water. Sweating helps cool the skin.

- Avoid the sun between 10 a.m. and 2 p.m., when the burning rays are strongest.

- Don't forget the kids. Sun exposure may be very hard on their tender skin. Teach your young children safe sun habits—hats and sunscreen—early, and set a good example by following these rules yourself.

Home Treatment

- Watch sunburned infants or children for signs of dehydration. See page 72. Also watch for signs of heat exhaustion. See page 46. Drink lots of water.

First Aid and Emergencies

• Cool baths or compresses can be very soothing. Take acetaminophen or aspirin for pain. Don't give aspirin to children under 20 years of age.

• A mild fever and headache can accompany a sunburn. Lie down in a cool, quiet room to relieve headache.

• There is nothing you can do to prevent peeling; it is part of the healing process. Lotion can help relieve itching.

When to Call Kaiser Permanente

• If signs of heat stroke develop (dry, flushed skin, confusion). See page 46.

• If there is severe blistering (over half of the affected body part) with fever or if you feel very ill.

• If there is fever of 102° or higher.

• If dizziness or vision problems persist after you have cooled off.

Tick Bites

 Ticks are parasites that fasten themselves to the skin and feed on blood. A tick should be removed as soon as you discover it.

Lyme disease is a bacterial infection spread by deer ticks. This can occur in the Northeast, upper Midwest, and the West Coast, especially northern California. In other areas it is very rare. Deer ticks are tiny, about the size of the period at the end of this sentence. Therefore, if the tick is large enough to be seen easily, it is probably not a deer tick.

Early symptoms of Lyme disease usually include a red "bull's-eye" rash with a white center around the bite. The rash develops four days to three weeks after the bite. Flu-like symptoms such as fever, fatigue, headache, muscle aches, and joint pain may also occur. Lyme disease can be treated with antibiotics to prevent later symptoms, such as arthritis and heart problems.

Prevention

• Wear light-colored clothing and tuck pant legs into socks.

• Apply an insect repellent containing DEET to exposed areas of skin or to clothing when in tick-infested areas. Apply carefully around eyes and mouth.

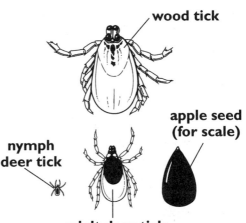

Lyme disease is usually spread by nymph deer ticks, which are too small to see. Adult deer ticks are about the size of an apple seed. All ticks grow larger as they fill up with blood.

° Use a lower-concentration product on children and pregnant women.

° Don't put repellent on small children's hands, because they often put their hands in their mouths.

° After returning indoors, wash the repellent off with soap and water.

Home Treatment

• Check regularly for ticks when you are out in the woods and thoroughly examine your skin and scalp when you return home. Check your pets too. The sooner ticks are removed, the less likely they are to spread bacteria.

• Remove a tick by gently pulling with tweezers, as close to the skin as possible. Pull straight out and try not to crush the body. Save the tick in a jar for tests if symptoms of Lyme disease develop.

• Wash the area and apply an antiseptic.

When to Call Kaiser Permanente

• If you are unable to remove the entire tick.

• In areas where Lyme disease is common, see a doctor if a tick has been attached for more than 24 hours.

• If a red "bull's-eye" rash, fever, fatigue, or flu-like symptoms develop up to three weeks after a possible tick bite.

Unconsciousness

An **unconscious** person is completely unaware of what is going on and is unable to make purposeful movements. Fainting is a brief form of unconsciousness; a coma is a deep, prolonged state of unconsciousness.

Causes of unconsciousness include stroke, epilepsy, heat stroke, diabetic coma, insulin shock, head or spinal injury, suffocation, alcohol or drug overdose, shock, bleeding, and heart attack.

Fainting is usually a short loss of consciousness most often due to a momentary drop in blood flow to the brain. When you fall or lie down, blood flow is improved and you regain consciousness. This lightheadedness is a mild form of shock and is usually not serious. If it happens often, there may be a more serious problem. Dizziness and fainting can also be brought on by sudden emotional stress or injury. See page 158.

Home Treatment

• Make sure the unconscious person can breathe. Check for breathing and, if necessary, open the airway and begin rescue breathing. See page 56.

• Check the pulse. If there is none, call for help and start cardiopulmonary resuscitation (CPR). See page 56.

• Keep the person lying down.

First Aid and Emergencies

- Look for a medical identification bracelet, necklace, or card that identifies a medical problem such as epilepsy, diabetes, or drug allergy.

- Treat any injuries.

- Do not give the person anything to eat or drink.

When to Call Kaiser Permanente

- Call 911 or seek emergency services if a person remains unconscious.

- If someone has completely lost consciousness even if the person is now awake.

- If unconsciousness follows a head injury and the victim is now awake. A head injury victim needs to be carefully observed. See page 44.

- Whenever a person with diabetes loses consciousness, even if he or she is now awake. He or she may have **insulin shock** (low blood sugar) or be in a **diabetic coma** (too much sugar in the blood).

First Aid and Emergencies

*A great step towards independence
is a good-humored stomach.*
Seneca

4

Abdominal Problems

The cause of abdominal problems can be hard to pin down. Stomach cramps due to gas pain, which is not often serious, can be much more painful than the early stages of appendicitis, a much more serious problem. Fortunately, most abdominal problems are minor and require only home treatment.

When you have stomach pain, note the location and severity of the pain, and any other symptoms, such as fever. Review page 68 and note your observations to help you or your doctor figure out the cause.

Remember that even for a doctor, abdominal pain is difficult to evaluate. In addition to the information in the When to Call Kaiser Permanente sections of this chapter, call your doctor whenever stomach pain:

• Is severe or persistent.

• Increases over several hours.

• Moves (localizes) to one area of the abdomen (e.g., upper right, lower left). See page 69.

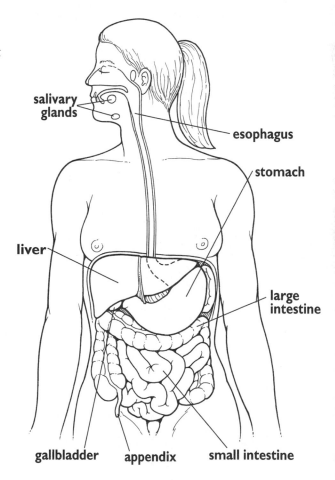

Organs of the digestive tract

For more information, see the inside front cover. 67

Abdominal Problems

Symptoms	Possible Causes
Nausea or vomiting	See Nausea and Vomiting, p. 80; watch for dehydration, p. 72. Medication reaction. Call your doctor or pharmacist. See "Adverse Drug Reactions," p. 321.

Bowel Movements

Symptoms	Possible Causes
Frequent, watery stools	See Diarrhea, p. 73; Stomach Flu and Food Poisoning, p. 81. Watch for dehydration, p. 72. See Antibiotics, p. 319.
Stools are dry and difficult to pass	See Constipation, p. 70.
Bloody or black, tarry stools	See Ulcers, p. 83; Diarrhea, p. 73.
Pain during bowel movements; bright red blood on surface of stool or on toilet paper	See Hemorrhoids, p. 76.

Abdominal Pain

Symptoms	Possible Causes
Pain and tenderness in the lower right abdomen with nausea, vomiting, and fever	See Appendicitis, p. 69; Urinary Tract Infections, p. 243.
Bloating with diarrhea, constipation, or both	See Irritable Bowel Syndrome, p. 78.
Burning or discomfort just below the breastbone	See Heartburn, p. 74; Ulcers, p. 83; Chest Pain, p. 133.
Pain in lower abdomen and lower back just before menstrual period	See Menstrual Cramps, p. 239.

Urination

Symptoms	Possible Causes
Pain or burning on urination	See Urinary Tract Infections, p. 243; Prostate Problems, p. 252; Sexually Transmitted Diseases, p. 260.
Difficulty urinating or weak urine stream (men)	See Prostate Problems, p. 252.
Blood in the urine	See p. 244.

Abdominal Lumps or Swelling

Symptoms	Possible Causes
Painless lump or swelling in groin that comes and goes	See Hernia, p. 77.
Blow to the stomach; very rigid or distended abdomen	See Blunt Abdominal Wounds, p. 32. Watch for shock, p. 61.

Appendicitis

The appendix is a small sac extending from the large intestine. It is normally self-cleaning and does not cause problems. However, if its opening becomes blocked (usually by bowel material), bacteria can build up and the appendix may become inflamed and infected. This condition is known as appendicitis.

Appendicitis is most common in people age 10 to 30, although it does occur in younger children and older adults. It is rare before age two. Since small children often cannot describe pain well, their cases may become quite serious before they are diagnosed.

Once appendicitis begins, it usually worsens until the appendix ruptures, which spreads the infection to the other abdominal organs.

However, the appendix rarely ruptures within the first 24 hours. Observing the symptoms for 8 to 12 hours is usually safe and is often necessary to confirm the diagnosis. In most cases, appendicitis requires surgery.

Symptoms of appendicitis may include:

- Pain that begins around the navel or upper stomach and moves (localizes) to the lower right abdomen over the course of 2 to 12 hours.

- Nausea, vomiting, loss of appetite, and constipation. Diarrhea is sometimes present but usually indicates the pain is due to some other cause.

- Low-grade fever (100° to 101°).

Home Treatment

- Check the vital signs. See page 23.

- Keep a careful record of the following symptoms:
  - Abdominal pain and tenderness
  - Nausea, vomiting, constipation, or diarrhea
  - Fever

- Keep the person quiet and in a comfortable position.

- Try to identify or rule out other causes of abdominal pain, such as stomach flu (see page 81) or overeating.

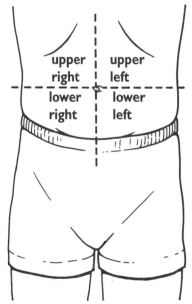

If you have abdominal pain, it helps to tell your doctor exactly where the pain is.

• Do not give laxatives. They can stimulate the intestine and cause the appendix to rupture sooner.

• Do not give strong pain medication. The location and severity of pain are diagnostic clues and strong pain relievers may mask them.

When to Call Kaiser Permanente

• If you suspect appendicitis. Review your observations of the symptoms with your doctor.

• If there is severe, increasing, and continuous pain in the lower right abdomen for more than four hours.

• If any stomach pain localizes to a specific point in the abdomen.

Constipation

 Constipation occurs when bowel movements are difficult to pass. Some people are overly concerned with frequency because they have been taught that a healthy person has a bowel movement every day. This is a misconception. Most people pass stools anywhere from three times a day to three times a week. If your stools are soft and pass easily, you are not constipated.

Constipation may be accompanied by cramping and pain in the rectum from the strain of trying to pass hard, dry stools. There may be some bloating and nausea. There may also be small amounts of bright red blood on the stool caused by slight tearing as the stool is pushed through the anus. This should stop when the constipation is controlled.

Rarely, a stool may become lodged in the rectum (impacted). If this happens, mucus and fluid may leak out around the stool, or there may be uncontrollable leakage of stool (fecal incontinence).

Lack of fiber and inadequate water in the diet are common causes of constipation. Other causes include travel, lack of exercise, delaying bowel movements, medications, pain due to hemorrhoids, and laxative overuse. Irritable bowel syndrome (see page 78) may also cause constipation.

Stress related to toilet training may contribute to constipation in young children. Children who are involved in play or other activities and ignore the urge to pass stools may become constipated. Children and adults may get constipated because they are reluctant to use toilets away from home.

Prevention

• Eat plenty of high-fiber foods such as fruits, vegetables, and whole grains. Other ways to add fiber include (also see page 278):

 ° A bowl of bran cereal with 10 grams of bran per serving.

 ° Two tablespoons of bran added to cereal or soup.

 ° Two tablespoons of psyllium (found in Metamucil and other bulk-forming agents). Start with one tablespoon or less and increase slowly to avoid bloating.

• Avoid foods that are high in fat and sugar.

• Drink $1\frac{1}{2}$ to 2 quarts of water and other liquids every day. (However, some people find milk constipating.)

• Exercise more. A walking program would be a good start. See page 266.

• Go when you feel the urge. Your bowels send signals when a stool needs to pass. If you ignore the signal, the urge will go away and the stool will eventually become dry and difficult to pass.

Home Treatment

• Set aside relaxed times for having bowel movements. Urges usually occur sometime after meals. Establishing a daily routine, after breakfast, for example, may help.

• Drink two to four extra glasses of water per day, especially in the morning.

• Add fruits, vegetables, and high-fiber foods, such as bran cereal, beans, or prunes, to your diet.

• If necessary, use a stool softener or very mild laxative, such as milk of magnesia. Do not use mineral oil or any other laxative for more than two weeks without consulting your doctor. See page 316.

For babies and children up to age two:

• Make sure you are adding the correct amount of water to the baby's formula.

• Give one to two ounces of water before feeding.

• After age six months, give $\frac{1}{2}$ teaspoon to 2 ounces (increase amount slowly over time) of prune juice. At age nine months, add $1\frac{1}{2}$ to 3 tablespoons of strained prunes per day.

When to Call Kaiser Permanente

• If acute constipation persists after the above treatment has been followed for one week for adults or three days for infants.

• If bleeding is heavy (more than a few bright red streaks), if the blood is dark red or brown, or if blood is mixed in the stool.

• If bleeding persists longer than two to three days after constipation has improved, or if bleeding occurs more than once.

• If sharp or severe pain occurs in the abdomen.

• If constipation and major changes in bowel movement patterns persist longer than two weeks without clear reason.

• If you have uncontrollable leakage of fecal material (fecal incontinence).

• If you are unable to have bowel movements without using laxatives.

Dehydration

Dehydration occurs when your body loses too much water. When you stop drinking water or lose large amounts of fluids through diarrhea, vomiting, or sweating, the body cells reabsorb liquid from the blood and other body fluids. When too much water is lost, the blood vessels may collapse. Without medical attention, death may result.

Dehydration is very dangerous for infants, small children, and older adults. Watch closely for its early signs anytime there is an illness that causes high fever, vomiting, or diarrhea. The early symptoms are:

- Dry mouth and sticky saliva

- Reduced urine output with dark yellow urine

Prevention

- Prompt home treatment for illnesses that cause diarrhea, vomiting, or fever will help prevent dehydration.

  ° Diarrhea, page 73

  ° Vomiting, page 80

  ° Diarrhea and vomiting in children, page 210

  ° Fever, page 139

  ° Fever in children, page 212

- To prevent dehydration during hot weather or exercise, drink 8 to 10 glasses of liquids (water and/or rehydration drinks) each day. Drink extra water before exercise and every half hour during activity.

Rehydration Drinks

When you have diarrhea or are vomiting, your body can lose large amounts of water and essential minerals called electrolytes. If you are unable to eat for a few days, you are also losing nutrients. This happens faster and is more serious in infants, young children, and older adults.

A rehydration drink (Pedialyte, Lytren, Rehydralyte) replaces fluids and electrolytes in amounts that are best used by your body. Sports drinks (Gatorade, PowerAde, All Sport) and other sugared drinks will replace fluid, but most contain too much sugar (which can make the diarrhea worse) and not enough of the other essential ingredients. Plain water won't provide any necessary nutrients or electrolytes.

Rehydration drinks won't make the diarrhea or vomiting go away faster, but they will prevent serious dehydration from developing.

You can make an inexpensive homemade rehydration drink. However, do not give this homemade drink to children under age 12.

Measure all ingredients precisely. Small variations can make the drink less effective or even harmful.

- 1 quart water

- $\frac{1}{2}$ teaspoon baking soda

- $\frac{1}{2}$ teaspoon table salt

- 3 to 4 tablespoons sugar

- Add $\frac{1}{4}$ teaspoon salt substitute ("lite" salt), if available

Home Treatment

Treatment of mild dehydration involves stopping the fluid loss and gradually replacing lost fluids.

- To stop vomiting, do not eat for several hours or until you are feeling better. Take frequent, small sips of water or a rehydration drink.

- To prevent dehydration, start taking small sips of water or rehydration fluid even if you are still having diarrhea or vomiting.

- If vomiting or diarrhea lasts longer than 24 hours, use only a rehydration drink to restore lost electrolytes. See page 72 for a drink you can make at home. Do not give the homemade drink to children under 12.

- Watch for signs of more severe dehydration (see below).

For infants and children under four:

- Give small sips of a rehydration drink (Pedialyte, Lytren) as soon as vomiting or diarrhea starts. See page 210 for home treatment of vomiting or diarrhea in children.

When to Call Kaiser Permanente

- If someone cannot hold down even small sips of liquid after 12 hours of no food or drink.

- If the following signs of severe dehydration develop:

  ° Sunken eyes, no tears, dry mouth and tongue

  ° Sunken soft spot on an infant's head

  ° Little or no urine for eight hours

  ° Skin that is doughy or doesn't bounce back when pinched

  ° Rapid breathing and heartbeat

  ° Sleepy, difficult to wake up, listless, and extremely irritable

- If vomiting lasts longer than 24 hours in an adult.

- If severe diarrhea (large loose stools every one to two hours) lasts longer than two days in an adult.

Diarrhea

Diarrhea is an increase in the frequency of bowel movements and the discharge of watery, loose stools. A person with diarrhea may also have abdominal cramps and nausea.

Diarrhea occurs when the intestines push stools through before the water in them can be reabsorbed by the body. It is your body's way of quickly clearing out any viruses or bacteria.

Most diarrhea is caused by viral stomach flu (gastroenteritis). Some medications, especially antibiotics, may also cause diarrhea. For some people, emotional stress, anxiety, or food intolerance may bring on the condition. Irritable bowel syndrome (see page 78) may also cause diarrhea.

Drinking untreated water that contains the *Giardia lamblia* parasite can also cause diarrhea that develops one to four weeks later.

Since most cases of diarrhea are viral, they will clear up in a few days with good home treatment.

Home Treatment

The following home treatment applies to adults and children over age four. For home treatment for diarrhea in infants and children under age four, see page 210.

- Eat small amounts of bland food several times a day. Take frequent, small sips of water or a rehydration drink.

- Since diarrhea may sometimes speed recovery of the underlying problem, avoid antidiarrheal drugs for the first six hours. After that, use them only if there are no other signs of illness, such as fever, and if cramping or discomfort continues. See antidiarrheal preparations on page 312.

- Begin eating mild foods, such as rice, dry toast or crackers, bananas, and applesauce, the next day or sooner, depending on how you feel. Avoid spicy foods, fruit, alcohol, and coffee until 48 hours after all symptoms have disappeared. Avoid dairy products for three days.

- Take care to avoid dehydration. See page 72.

When to Call Kaiser Permanente

- If the stools are black or bloody. However, Pepto-Bismol or other medications containing bismuth can cause stools to look black.

- If abdominal pain or severe discomfort accompanies diarrhea and is not relieved by passing stools or gas.

- If diarrhea is accompanied by fever of 101° or higher, chills, vomiting, or fainting.

- If signs of severe dehydration appear. See page 73.

- If severe diarrhea (large loose stools every one to two hours) lasts longer than two days in an adult.

- If mild diarrhea continues for one to two weeks without obvious cause.

- If diarrhea occurs after drinking untreated water.

Heartburn

Heartburn (indigestion) is caused by stomach acids backing up into the lower esophagus, the tube that leads from the mouth to the stomach. The medical term for heartburn is gastroesophageal reflux disease (GERD). The acids produce a burning sensation and discomfort between the ribs just below the breastbone. Another symptom is sour or bitter fluid backing up into the throat or mouth. Heartburn can occur after overeating and sometimes in reaction to medications.

Don't be concerned if you experience heartburn now and then; nearly everyone does (25 percent of pregnant women have it every day). However, months of constant heartburn can injure the esophageal lining.

Most cases of heartburn can be prevented by following the home treatment tips below.

Home Treatment

- Eat smaller meals, and avoid late-night snacks.

- Avoid foods that bring on heartburn. Chocolate, orange and tomato juices, peppermint- and spearmint-flavored foods, caffeine-containing foods, fatty or fried foods, and carbonated drinks may make heartburn worse.

- Avoid alcohol, which irritates your stomach and esophagus and may make your symptoms worse.

- Stop smoking. This is especially important because smoking promotes heartburn. Quitting will often relieve heartburn completely.

- If you are overweight, lose weight, even a few pounds. Being overweight can worsen heartburn.

- Avoid tight-fitting clothes, such as tight belts and waistbands.

- Raise the head of your bed six inches by placing a foam wedge or thick telephone books under the mattress or legs of the bed frame.

- Don't lie down too soon after eating. Try to stay upright for at least two to three hours after each meal. Avoid large meals and snacks before bedtime.

- Try acetaminophen rather than aspirin, ibuprofen, naproxen, or other anti-inflammatory drugs, which may cause heartburn.

- Take an over-the-counter product for heartburn. Antacids, such as Maalox, Mylanta, Tums, and Gelusil, neutralize stomach acid.

  Acid blockers, such as Pepcid AC, Tagamet HB, etc., reduce the production of stomach acid. Ask your pharmacist for advice in choosing one of these medications, and follow the package instructions and your doctor's advice for their use.

When to Call Kaiser Permanente

- If pain occurs with shortness of breath or other symptoms that suggest heart problems. See Chest Pain on page 133.

- If stools are deep red, black, or tarry. If there are small amounts of bright red blood on stool or toilet paper, see Hemorrhoids on page 76.

- If you suspect that a prescribed medication is causing heartburn. Antihistamines, Valium, birth control pills, and anti-inflammatory drugs including aspirin, ibuprofen, and naproxen can sometimes cause heartburn.

- If you have difficulty swallowing, especially bread and meat.

• If heartburn persists for one to two weeks despite home treatment. Call sooner if symptoms are severe or are not relieved at all by antacids or acid blockers. See Ulcers on page 83.

Hemorrhoids

 Hemorrhoids and piles are two terms used to describe inflammation and swelling in the veins around the anus. Hemorrhoids may develop either inside (internal) or outside (external) the anus. Straining to pass hard, compacted stools sometimes causes these veins to become enlarged and inflamed.

The symptoms of hemorrhoids are tenderness, pain, itching, and sometimes bleeding. There may be a small lump at the opening to the anus. Hemorrhoids generally last several days and often come back (recur).

Anal itching is usually caused by other conditions. Skin may become irritated by leakage of stool or by irritating foods in the diet, such as spicy food or coffee. If the anus is not kept clean, itching may result. However, trying to keep the area too clean by rubbing with dry toilet paper or using excess soap will injure the skin and is usually a more common problem. It is important to be gentle with the skin in the anal area.

Prevention

• Keep your stools soft. Include plenty of water, fresh fruits and vegetables, and whole grains in your diet. Include up to two tablespoons of bran or Metamucil in your diet each day. Also see Constipation on page 70.

• Try not to strain during bowel movements. Take your time and never hold your breath.

• Avoid sitting too much, which restricts blood flow around your anus.

• Keep the anal area clean, but even more importantly, be gentle when cleaning it.

Home Treatment

• For hemorrhoids warm baths are soothing and cleansing, especially after a bowel movement. Sitz baths (hot baths with just enough water to cover the anal area) are also helpful for hemorrhoids but may worsen anal itching. Try using premoistened tissues (baby wipes) instead of toilet paper.

• Wear cotton underwear and loose clothing.

• Relieve itching by using cold compresses on the anus for 10 minutes four times a day.

• Ease itching and irritation with zinc oxide, petroleum jelly, hydrocortisone (0.5%), or an over-the-counter medicated cream or suppository (Anusol, Tucks, Preparation H, etc.). Avoid products with a local anesthetic, which can cause an allergic reaction. These products will have the suffix "-caine" in the name or ingredients.

When to Call Kaiser Permanente

- If a lump on the anus is increasing in size or becoming more painful.

- If pain is severe or lasts longer than one week.

- If bleeding occurs for no apparent reason and is not associated with straining to pass stools.

- If bleeding is heavy (more than a few bright red streaks), if the blood is dark red or brown, or if blood is mixed in the stool.

- If any bleeding continues for longer than one week or occurs more than once despite home treatment.

Hernia

A hernia occurs when tissue from inside the abdomen bulges out through a weak spot in the abdominal wall. Hernias are more common in men than in women. They commonly occur in the groin and, in men, may bulge into the scrotum.

Hernias are often caused by increased abdominal pressure resulting from lifting heavy weights, coughing, or straining during a bowel movement. Sometimes a weak spot in the abdominal wall is present at birth.

The symptoms of a hernia may come on gradually or suddenly. There may be a feeling that something has given way and varying degrees of pain.

Symptoms may include:

- Feeling of weakness, pressure, burning, or pain in the groin or scrotum.

- A bulge or lump in the groin or scrotum. These bulges may be easier to see when the person coughs and may disappear when the person lies down.

- Pain in the groin when straining, lifting, or coughing.

A hernia is called reducible if it can be pushed back into place in the abdomen; irreducible if it cannot.

A hernia becomes incarcerated when the tissue becomes trapped outside the abdominal wall. If the blood supply is cut off, the hernia is said to be strangulated. When this occurs, the tissue swells and dies. The dead tissue quickly becomes infected, requiring immediate medical attention. Rapidly increasing pain in the groin or scrotum is a sign that the hernia has become strangulated.

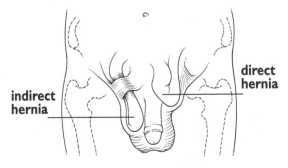

indirect hernia

direct hernia

A hernia can cause a bulge or lump in the groin or scrotum.

 For more information, see the inside front cover.

Prevention

- Use proper lifting techniques (see page 91), and avoid lifting weights that are too heavy for you.

- Avoid constipation and do not strain during bowel movements and urination.

- Stop smoking, especially if you have a chronic cough.

When to Call Kaiser Permanente

- If you suspect a hernia, to confirm the diagnosis and discuss treatment options.

- If mild groin pain or an unexplained groin bump or swelling continues for more than one week.

If you have been diagnosed with a hernia, call a health professional:

- If you experience sudden, severe, pain in the area of the hernia, scrotum, or groin.

- If the hernia cannot be pushed back into place with gentle pressure when you are lying down.

Irritable Bowel Syndrome

Irritable bowel syndrome (IBS) is one of the most common disorders of the digestive tract. Symptoms of IBS often increase with stress or after eating, and include:

- Abdominal bloating, pain, and gas

- Mucus in the stool

- Feeling that a bowel movement hasn't been completed

- Irregular bowel habits, with constipation, diarrhea, or both

IBS is a functional bowel disorder, which means that function of the digestive tract is impaired. There are no physical signs of this disorder and no tests that diagnose it.

IBS can persist for many years. An episode may be milder or more severe than the one before it, but the disorder itself does not worsen over time. It does not lead to more serious diseases such as cancer.

Prevention

There is no way to prevent IBS. However, because symptoms often worsen or improve due to diet, stress, medications, exercise, or for unknown reasons, identifying those things that trigger your symptoms may help you avoid or minimize attacks.

Home Treatment

If constipation is the main symptom:

- Try an over-the-counter fiber supplement or bulk-forming agent that contains crushed psyllium seeds or methylcellulose. Examples include Metamucil, Fiberall, and Citrucel.

- Add fiber-rich foods to your diet slowly so they do not worsen gas or cramps. See page 278.

- Use laxatives (e.g., Feen-a-Mint, Correctol) only on a doctor's recommendation.

If diarrhea is the main symptom:

- Using the fiber suggestions for constipation can sometimes help diarrhea by absorbing liquid in the large intestine.

- Avoid foods that make diarrhea worse. Try eliminating one at a time, then add it back gradually. If a food doesn't seem to be related to symptoms, there is no need to avoid it. Many people find that the following foods or drinks worsen their symptoms:

  ° Alcohol, caffeine, nicotine

  ° Beans, broccoli, apples

  ° Spicy foods

  ° Foods high in acid, such as citrus fruit

  ° Fatty foods, including bacon, sausage, butter, oils, and anything deep-fried

- Avoid dairy products that contain lactose (milk sugar) if they seem to worsen symptoms. However, get enough calcium in your diet from other sources. Yogurt may be a good choice, because some of the lactose has already been digested by the yogurt culture.

- Avoid sorbitol, an artificial sweetener found in some sugarless candies and gum.

- Add more starchy food (bread, rice, potatoes, pasta) to your diet.

- If diarrhea persists, an over-the-counter medication such as loperamide (Imodium) may help. Check with your doctor if you are using it twice a month or more.

To reduce stress:

- Keep a record of the life events that occur with your symptoms. This may help you see any connection between your symptoms and stressful occasions.

- Get regular, vigorous exercise such as swimming, jogging, or brisk walking to help reduce tension.

- See page 272 for more tips on managing stress. Also see Resource 43 on page 327.

When to Call Kaiser Permanente

- If you have continuous moderate to severe pain located in any part of the abdomen, especially if it is accompanied by a fever of 100.5° or higher.

- If pain is so severe that treatment is needed, or if symptoms gradually or suddenly become worse.

- If there is blood in the stool that is not obviously related to hemorrhoids which have already been diagnosed by a doctor.

- If you have been diagnosed with IBS and your symptoms change significantly from their usual pattern.

If none of these more serious symptoms are present, try to rule out other causes of stomach problems (e.g., eating a new food, nervousness, stomach flu). Try home treatment for a week or two. If there is no improvement, or if your symptoms worsen, call for an appointment.

Nausea and Vomiting

Nausea is a very unpleasant feeling in the pit of the stomach. Someone who is nauseated may feel weak and sweaty and produce lots of saliva. Intense nausea often leads to vomiting, which forces stomach contents up the esophagus and out the mouth. Home treatment will help ease the discomfort. Nausea and vomiting may be caused by:

- Viral stomach flu or food poisoning (see page 81)
- Stress or nervousness
- Medications, especially antibiotics and anti-inflammatories (e.g., aspirin, ibuprofen, naproxen, etc.)
- Pregnancy (see page 234)
- Diabetes
- Migraine (see page 168)
- Head injury (see page 44)

Nausea and vomiting can also be signs of other serious illnesses.

Home Treatment

The following home treatment applies to adults and children over age four. For home treatment of vomiting in children under age four, see page 210.

- If vomiting is severe and persistent, stop all food for several hours or until you are feeling better. Take frequent small sips of water or a rehydration drink (see page 72).

- Drink only clear noncarbonated liquids such as water, weak tea, diluted juice, or broth for the next 12 to 24 hours. Start with a few sips at a time and increase gradually.

- If vomiting lasts longer than 24 hours, sip a rehydration drink to restore lost fluids and nutrients. See page 72.

- Rest in bed until you are feeling better.

- Watch for and treat early signs of dehydration (see page 72). Infants, children, and older adults can quickly become dehydrated from vomiting.

- When you are feeling better, begin eating clear soups, mild foods, and liquids until all symptoms are gone for 12 to 48 hours, depending on how you feel. Flavored gelatin, dry toast, crackers, and cooked cereal are good choices.

When to Call Kaiser Permanente

- If vomiting is severe or violent (shoots out in large quantities).

- If there is blood in the vomit. It may look like red or black coffee grounds.

- If vomiting occurs with fever and increasing pain in the lower right abdomen. See Appendicitis on page 69.

- If pain is located in one area of the abdomen rather than generalized cramping.

- If vomiting occurs with severe headache, sleepiness, lethargy, or stiff neck.

- If vomiting lasts longer than 24 hours in an adult.

- If signs of severe dehydration develop. See page 73.

- If nausea and vomiting persist longer than two hours after a head injury, or if violent vomiting lasts longer than 15 minutes. Limited nausea or vomiting at first is usually not serious. See Head Injuries on page 44.

- If you suspect that medication is causing the problem. Antibiotics and anti-inflammatory medications (aspirin, ibuprofen, naproxen, etc.) may cause nausea or vomiting. Learn which of your medications can cause these symptoms.

Stomach Flu and Food Poisoning

 Stomach flu and food poisoning are different ailments with different causes. However, many people confuse the two because the symptoms are so similar. Most people who get food poisoning attribute their symptoms of nausea, vomiting, diarrhea, and stomach pain to a sudden case of stomach flu, and vice versa.

Stomach flu is usually caused by a viral infection in the digestive system, hence the medical name, viral gastroenteritis. To prevent stomach flu, you must avoid contact with the virus, which is not always easy to do.

Food poisoning is usually caused by a poison (toxin) from bacteria that grow in food which is not handled or stored properly. Bacteria can grow rapidly when certain foods, especially meats, dairy products, and sauces, are not handled properly during preparation or are kept at temperatures between 40° and 140°. The bacteria produce a poison (toxin) that causes an acute inflammation of the intestines.

Suspect food poisoning when symptoms are shared by others who ate the same food, or after eating unrefrigerated foods. Symptoms of food poisoning may begin as soon as 1 or 2 hours or as long as 48 hours after eating. Nausea, vomiting, and diarrhea may last from 12 to 48 hours for common food poisoning.

Botulism is a rare but often fatal type of food poisoning. It is generally caused by improper home canning methods for low-acid foods like beans and corn. Bacteria that survive the canning process may grow and produce toxin in the jar. Symptoms include blurred or double vision, muscle weakness, and headache.

 For more information, see the inside front cover.

Prevention

To prevent food poisoning:

• Follow the 2-40-140 rule. Don't eat meats, dressing, salads, or other foods that have been kept for more than two hours between 40° and 140°.

• Be especially careful with large cooked meats like your holiday turkey, which require a long time to cool. Thick parts of the meat may stay over 40° long enough to allow bacteria to grow.

• Use a thermometer to check your refrigerator. It should be between 34° and 40°.

• Defrost meats in the refrigerator or by microwaving, not on the kitchen counter.

• Wash your hands, cutting boards, and counter tops frequently. After handling raw meats, especially chicken, wash your hands and utensils before preparing other foods.

• The USDA recommends you reheat meats to 165° to destroy any bacteria. Even then, the toxin may not be destroyed.

• Cook hamburger well done. Cook chicken until the juices run clear.

• Cover meats and poultry during microwave cooking to heat the surface of the meat.

• Do not eat raw eggs or uncooked sauces made with eggs.

• Keep party foods on ice.

• When you eat out, avoid rare and uncooked meats. Eat salad bar and deli items before they get warm.

• Discard any cans or jars with bulging lids or leaks.

• Follow home canning and freezing instructions carefully. Contact your County Agricultural Extension office for advice.

Home Treatment

• Viral stomach flu will usually go away within 24 to 48 hours. Good home care can speed recovery. For adults and children age four and older, see Nausea and Vomiting on page 80 and Diarrhea on page 73. For children younger than four years, see page 210.

• Watch for and treat early signs of dehydration (see page 72). Infants, children, and older adults can quickly become dehydrated from diarrhea and vomiting.

When to Call Kaiser Permanente

• If vomiting lasts longer than one day in an adult.

• If severe diarrhea (large loose stools every one to two hours) lasts longer than two days in an adult.

• If signs of severe dehydration develop. See page 73.

• If you suspect food poisoning from a canned food or have symptoms of botulism (blurred or double vision, difficulty swallowing or breathing). If you still have it, take a food sample with you for testing.

Ulcers

An ulcer (peptic ulcer) is a sore or crater in the lining of the gastrointestinal tract. Most ulcers develop in the stomach (gastric ulcers) or in the upper part of the small intestine (duodenal ulcers). Ulcers develop when something damages the protective lining of the gastrointestinal tract. This allows stomach acid and enzymes to eat away at the wall of the stomach or upper small intestine. Factors that increase the risk of ulcers include:

- Regular use of aspirin, ibuprofen, and other nonsteroidal anti-inflammatory drugs (NSAIDs), such as indomethacin, naproxen, clinoril, etc.

- Smoking

- Infection with bacteria called *Helicobacter pylori*

Symptoms of an ulcer may include a burning or sharp pain in the abdomen between the navel and the end of the breastbone. The pain often occurs between meals and may wake you during the night. The pain can usually be relieved by eating something or taking an antacid. Ulcers may also cause heartburn, nausea or vomiting, and a bloated or full feeling during or after meals.

Ulcers can cause bleeding in the stomach, which may produce dark red, black, or tarry bowel movements. Without treatment, ulcers may occasionally cause obstruction or break through (perforate) the stomach wall. Bleeding and perforation are serious situations that require immediate treatment.

Home Treatment

- Avoid foods, especially alcohol, caffeine, and spicy foods, that seem to bring on symptoms. It isn't necessary to eliminate any particular food from your diet if it doesn't cause you problems. Milk and milk products are not a problem unless they interfere with medication absorption or if you are lactose intolerant (see page 283).

- Try eating smaller, more frequent meals. If it doesn't help, return to a regular diet.

- Stop smoking. People who smoke are twice as likely to develop ulcers as nonsmokers are. Smoking also slows healing of ulcers.

- Do not take aspirin, ibuprofen, or naproxen. Try acetaminophen instead.

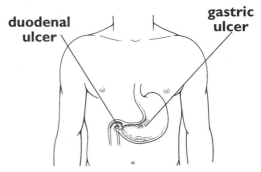

duodenal ulcer **gastric ulcer**

Most ulcers occur in the stomach (gastric ulcers) or in the opening to the small intestine (duodenal ulcers).

• Antacids are usually needed to neutralize stomach acid and allow the ulcer to heal. Talk with your doctor about the best dose. You may need frequent large doses. Nonabsorbable antacids like Maalox, Mylanta, and Gelusil are often best. If you are on a low-salt diet, talk with your doctor or pharmacist before choosing an antacid. Some antacids have a high sodium content.

• Too much stress may slow ulcer healing. Practice the relaxation techniques on page 272.

When to Call Kaiser Permanente

• If pain occurs with shortness of breath or other symptoms that suggest heart problems. See Chest Pain on page 133.

• If pain localizes to one area of the abdomen.

• If increasing pain in the lower right abdomen occurs with vomiting and fever.

• If stools are deep red, black, or tarry, which usually means there is blood in the stool. Ulcers are one of many possible causes of this condition, which needs to be evaluated.

• If you have an ulcer and develop sudden, severe abdominal pain that is not relieved by your usual home treatment.

• If you suspect an ulcer and your symptoms have not improved after two weeks of home treatment. Your doctor can evaluate your symptoms and prescribe a treatment plan that may include antacids or other medications.

• To discuss your use of prescription anti-inflammatory drugs.

Urinary Incontinence

If you suffer from loss of bladder control (urinary incontinence), you are not alone. Many people are coping with this problem.

Many cases of incontinence can be controlled, if not cured outright. Temporary incontinence can be caused by water pills (diuretics) and many other common medications. Constipation, urinary infections, stones in the urinary tract, or extended bed rest are other causes. If the underlying problem is corrected, the incontinence can be cured.

There are three types of bladder control problems:

Stress incontinence occurs when small amounts of urine leak out during exercise or when you cough, laugh, or sneeze. This is common in women, and men may experience it after prostate surgery. This type of incontinence is often helped by Kegel exercises.

Urge incontinence happens when the need to urinate comes on so quickly that there is not enough time to get to the toilet.

Overflow incontinence occurs when the bladder cannot empty itself completely.

Home Treatment

• Don't let incontinence embarrass you. Take charge and work with your doctor to treat any underlying conditions that may be causing the problem.

• Don't let incontinence keep you from doing the things you like to do. Absorbent pads or briefs, such as Attends and Depend, are available in pharmacies and supermarkets.

• Avoid coffee and other drinks that contain caffeine, which over-stimulates the bladder. Do not cut down on liquids overall; you need about two quarts a day to keep the rest of your body healthy.

• Practice "double-voiding." Empty your bladder as much as possible, relax for a minute, and then try to empty it again.

• Urinate on a schedule, perhaps every three to four hours during the day, whether the urge is there or not. This may help you to restore control.

Kegel Exercises

Kegel exercises can help cure or improve stress incontinence by strengthening the muscles that control the flow of urine.

• Locate the muscles by repeatedly stopping your urine in midstream and starting again. The muscles that you feel squeezing around your urethra and anus are the ones to focus on.

• Practice squeezing these muscles while you are not urinating. If your stomach or buttocks move, you are not using the right muscles.

• Hold the squeeze for three seconds, then relax for three seconds.

• Repeat the exercise 10 to 15 times per session. Do at least three Kegel exercise sessions per day.

Kegel exercises are simple and effective and can be done anywhere and anytime. No one will know you are doing them except you.

- Keep skin in the genital area dry to prevent rashes. Vaseline or Desitin ointment will help.

- Pay special attention to any medications you are taking, including over-the-counter drugs, since some affect bladder control.

- Incontinence is sometimes caused by a urinary tract infection. If you feel pain or burning when you urinate, see page 243.

When to Call Kaiser Permanente

- If you experience more than one episode of unexpected urinary incontinence, even in small amounts.

- If you feel that you cannot completely empty your bladder.

- If urinary incontinence continues for more than a few months or is interfering with your life.

Stand up straight!
Mom

5

Back and Neck Problems

Although back and neck problems are usually preventable, most of us will suffer from one or both at some time in our lives. Fortunately, 9 out of 10 acute back problems will heal on their own within 4 to 6 weeks.

By following the prevention and home treatment guidelines in this chapter, you can recover from most back and neck problems and prevent them from recurring.

Quick Reference Guide

- First aid for back problems, page 88.

- Back problems due to arthritis, page 89.

- Neck problems, page 98.

Back Problems

 Your back includes the bones of the spine (vertebrae that support body weight), their joints (facets that guide the direction of the movement of the spine), the discs that separate the vertebrae and absorb shock as you move, and the muscles and ligaments that hold it all together. One or more of these structures can be injured.

- You can strain or sprain the ligaments or muscles by a sudden or improper movement or by overuse.

- You can damage your discs the same way so that they bulge or tear. If the tear is large enough, the disc may press against a nerve. The nerve may also become irritated due to swelling or inflammation of the other parts of the back.

First Aid for Back Problems

When you first feel a catch or strain in your back, try these steps to avoid or reduce expected problems. These are the most important home treatments for the first few days of a back problem. Also see Home Treatment on page 95.

First Aid #1: Activity

Stick to your usual routine as much as you can. Take a short walk for a few minutes every hour or two on a flat surface. Try to work up to 20-minute walks. If you have pain down your leg, start with shorter walks less often. Walk only distances you can manage without making your back or leg worse. Swimming is also a good activity for a back problem.

Walk

First Aid #2: Ice and/or Heat

If your problem is in your neck, upper back, or shoulders, place the ice or moist heat on the back and sides of your neck. Otherwise, put it in the middle of your low back. Go for a walk afterward, when you feel more comfortable.

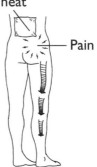

Ice pack or moist heat

Pain

An ice pack or moist heat in middle of low back

First Aid #3: Medicine

Medication can relieve pain and help you move around more easily. See page 96 for specific suggestions.

First Aid #4: Good Posture

Keep the small curves in your spine all the time. See pages 90, 91, 98, 99, and 100. Avoid sitting for very long.

Foot on ledge for prolonged standing activities

Any of these injuries can result in two or three days of acute pain and swelling in the injured tissue, followed by slow healing and a gradual reduction in pain. The problem may be felt in the low back, in the buttock, or down the leg. The goals of self-care are to relieve the inflammation, promote healing, and avoid reinjury.

Back problems can also be caused by conditions that affect the bones and joints of the spine. Arthritis pain may be a steady ache, unlike the sharp, acute pain of strains, sprains, or disc injuries. If you think your back problem may be caused by arthritis, combine the self-care guidelines for back problems with those for arthritis on page 104.

Osteoporosis weakens the bones of the spine, which can cause the bones to compress and lead to varying degrees of pain. See page 114.

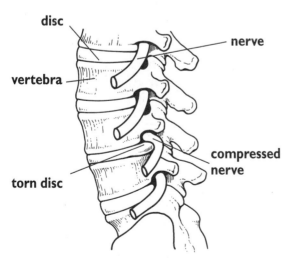

A torn (ruptured or herniated) disc in the spine can put pressure on a nerve, causing pain.

Sciatica

Sciatica is an irritation of the sciatic nerve, which runs from the low back down through the buttocks and to the feet. It can occur when an injured disc presses against the nerve. Its main symptom is radiating pain, numbness, tingling, or weakness that is usually worse in the leg than in the back. In addition to the Home Treatment for back problems on page 95, the following may help:

- Avoid sitting if possible, unless it is more comfortable than standing.

- Alternate standing or lying down with short walks. Increase the distance as you are able to tolerate without increasing your pain.

- Ice or moist heat will probably do the most good placed in the middle of your low back. See page 120.

The Upper Back

Tension, tightness, or aches in the upper back usually connect to a neck problem.

Prevention

The frequency of back problems has increased dramatically in all developed countries. The more time we spend sitting at desks, in cars, or in front of the TV, the more we must do to prevent back problems. Good posture and body mechanics will reduce the stress on your back.

For both men and women, extra weight in the abdomen area can make it harder to keep the natural curves in your back. For this reason, it is especially important to watch your posture and, if necessary, to reduce your weight. Also, smokers tend to have more back problems and take longer to recover from them.

Exercise (stretching, strengthening, and aerobic exercise) will help maintain your flexibility, strengthen the muscles that support your spine, and maintain your overall fitness.

Back Posture

Improper posture puts too much stress on your back and can lead to discomfort and damage. The key to good back posture is to keep the right amount of curve in your low back. Too much curve ("swayback") or too little curve ("flat back") can result in problems.

Standing and Walking

When you stand and walk with good posture, your ear, shoulder, hip, and ankle should be in a line. Do not lock your knees. Keep the small curve in your low back.

Sitting

When you sit, keep your shoulders back and down, chin back, abdomen in, and your low back supported in its natural curve. Slouching can stress the ligaments and muscles in your low back.

- Avoid sitting in one position for more than one hour at a time. Get up or change positions often.

- If you must sit a lot, the exercises on page 93 are particularly important.

- If your chair doesn't give enough support, use a small pillow or rolled towel to support your low back.

- See the illustration of proper sitting posture on page 99.

- To rise from a chair, keep the curves in your back and scoot forward to the edge of the chair. Use your leg muscles to stand up without leaning forward at the waist.

- For driving, pull your seat forward so that the pedals and steering wheel are within comfortable reach. Stop often to stretch and walk around. Consider using a small pillow for your lower back.

Sleeping

A firm bed is better than a soft mattress or waterbed. Sleep so that your back keeps its natural curves.

- If you sleep on your back, you may want to use a towel roll to support your lower back or a pillow under your knees.

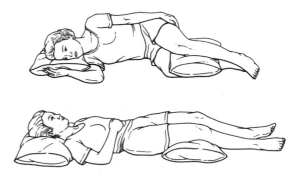

Use pillows while sleeping to prevent back or neck problems.

- If you sleep on your side, try placing a pillow between your knees.

- To rise from bed, lie on your side, bend both knees, and drop your feet over the side of the bed as you push with both arms to sit up. Scoot to the edge of the bed and position your feet under your buttocks. Stand up, keeping a small curve in your low back.

Body Mechanics

Good body mechanics means practicing good posture during daily activities. Use good body mechanics all the time, not just when you have a back problem.

- Keep the small curve in your low back.

- When you must stay in one position for long periods, take regular breaks to walk and stretch.

- When standing for long periods, stand with one foot on a small stool, ledge, or box.

Lifting

- Bend your knees and let your arms and legs do the work. Tighten your buttocks and abdomen to further support your back.

- Keep your upper back straight and keep the curve in your low back. Do not bend forward from the waist to lift.

- Keep the load as close to your body as possible, even if it is light.

- While holding a heavy object, turn your feet, not your back. Do not turn or twist your body.

- Never lift a heavy object above shoulder level.

- Get close to objects you need to reach. Use a stool or ladder for items that are above your head, and place it close to what you are doing.

- Use a hand truck or ask someone to help with heavy or awkward objects.

Exercises to Prevent Back Problems

Strengthening your entire body prevents future back problems and also improves your general health. Many exercises and sports strengthen your arms and legs. Doing special exercises to strengthen your abdominal muscles is also encouraged. See curl-ups and pelvic tilts on page 92.

Keeping your body flexible helps you to use proper body mechanics that protect your back.

Avoid back strain when lifting heavy objects by keeping your upper back straight, bending your knees, and keeping the load close to your body.

These exercises are *not recommended* for use during an acute back problem or spasm. Instead, see First Aid for Back Problems on page 88.

- If any exercise causes increased or continuing back pain, stop the exercise and try something else. Stop any exercise that causes the pain to radiate away from your spine into your buttocks or legs, either during or after the exercises.

- You do not need to do every exercise. Stick with the ones that help you most.

- Start with five repetitions three to four times a day, and gradually increase to 10 repetitions. Do all exercises slowly.

The basic types of exercises that can help your back include: flexion, extension, and stretching and strengthening.

Flexion Exercises

Flexion exercises stretch the low back muscles and strengthen the stomach muscles.

1. Pelvic Tilts

This exercise gently moves the spine and stretches the low back.

- Lie on your back with knees bent and feet flat on the floor.

- Slowly tighten your stomach muscles and press your low back against the floor. Hold for 10 seconds (do not hold your breath). Slowly relax.

2. Curl-Ups

Curl-ups strengthen your abdominal muscles, which work with your back muscles to support your spine.

- Lie on your back with knees bent (60° angle) and feet flat on the floor, arms crossed on your chest. Do not hook your feet under anything.

- Slowly curl your head and shoulders a few inches up until your shoulder blades barely rise from the floor. Keep your low back pressed to the floor. To avoid neck problems, remember to lift your shoulders and do not force your head up or forward. Hold for 5 to 10 seconds (do not hold your breath), then curl down very slowly. Do not do full sit-ups.

1. Pelvic tilt

2. Curl-ups: keep neck straight and chin tucked in

Extension Exercises

3. Press-Ups

- Lie face down with arms bent, hands at shoulders with palms flat on floor.

- Lift yourself up on your elbows, keeping lower half of body relaxed. If it's comfortable, press your chest forward.

- Keep hips pressed to the floor. Feel the stretch in your low back.

- Lower upper body to the floor. Repeat slowly 3 to 10 times.

4. Backward Bend

Practice the backward bend at least once a day and do it frequently when you work in a bent-forward position.

- Stand upright with your feet slightly apart. Back up to a counter top for greater support and stability.

- Place your hands in the small of your back and gently bend backward. Keep your knees straight (not locked) and bend only at the waist. See illustration.

- Hold the backward stretch for one to two seconds.

3. Press-ups

4. Backward bend
(keep neck straight
and chin down)

Additional Strengthening and Stretching Exercises

5. Prone Buttocks Squeeze

This exercise strengthens the buttocks muscles, which support the back and help you lift with your legs.

- Lie flat on your stomach with your arms at your sides.

- Slowly tighten your buttocks muscles and hold for 5 to 10 seconds (do not hold your breath). Relax slowly.

- You may need to place a small pillow under your stomach for comfort.

6. Hamstring Stretch

This exercise stretches the muscles in the back of your thigh, which will allow you to bend your legs while keeping your back in the neutral position.

- Lie on your back in a doorway with one leg through the doorway on the floor. Put the leg you want to stretch straight up with the heel resting on the wall next to the doorway.

- Keep the leg straight and slowly move your heel up the wall until you feel a gentle pull in the back of your thigh. Do not overstretch.

- Relax in this position for 30 seconds, then bend the knee to relieve the stretch. Repeat with the other leg.

7. Hip Flexor Stretch

This exercise stretches the muscles in the front of your hip, to avoid "swayback" caused by tight hip muscles.

- Kneel on one knee with your other leg bent and foot in front of you. Keep a natural curve in your back.

- Slowly shift your weight onto your front foot, maintaining a natural curve in your back. Hold for 10 seconds. You should feel a stretch in the groin of the leg you are kneeling on. Repeat with the other leg.

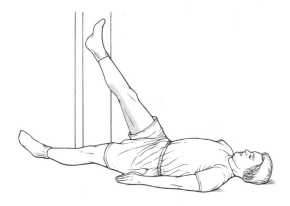

6. Hamstring stretch

7. Hip flexor stretch

Which Exercises for You?

- If you have no back problem now, try some of the prevention exercises on pages 91 to 94. *Do not* do the prevention exercises if you have just injured your back.

- If you have injured your back within the last two weeks, or you have more pain in your leg than in your back or buttocks, see Home Treatment and When to Call Kaiser Permanente on pages 95 to 97.

- Discontinue any exercise that increases pain.

- Gradually increase any exercise that helps you feel better.

Exercises to Avoid

Many common exercises actually increase the risk of low back problems. Avoid the following:

- Straight-leg sit-ups

- Leg lifts (lifting both legs while lying on your back)

- Lifting heavy weights above the waist (military press, biceps curls while standing)

- Any stretching done while sitting with the legs in a V

- Toe touches while standing

Home Treatment

It is important to stay as active as you can. The following tips may help you in your recovery:

- Use cold or moist heat on the injured area. See the icing guidelines on page 120. Ice your back until you feel numb, no more than 15 to 20 minutes every two hours. Always wrap the pack in a damp cloth to avoid harming your skin. Cold decreases inflammation, swelling, and pain.

- Moist heat often works well. Try taking warm showers, or use a warm, damp towel to apply heat. If you like, you can heat the towel in a microwave oven.

- If heat feels better, try a warm shower or use a warm towel. (Do not sit in the bathtub; this puts your back in the wrong position.) Use heat for no more than 20 minutes every two hours. Be careful not to irritate your skin. Be especially careful if you use electric heating pads, because people sometimes burn themselves by falling asleep on them.

- Avoid positions or activities that worsen your symptoms, such as sitting for long periods of time. Follow the posture and body mechanics guidelines discussed earlier.

- Keep a positive attitude. Most back injuries are temporary and heal. Healing improves when you keep active. Focus on what you *can* do rather than what you *can't* do.

- Keep moving, improving, and listening to your body. It hurts sometimes to move around, but hurt does not equal harm. Even for the first two to three days when it usually hurts the worst, it is important to stay as active as you can and gradually return to your usual activities. Soon you will be back to all your usual activities.

• The first few days you may need to take short breaks from your daily activities. If you lie down during your breaks, make sure you are on a firm surface.

• Medication can relieve pain and help you move around more easily. We recommend acetaminophen (Tylenol) because it has the fewest side effects. If Tylenol does not work for you, try coated aspirin (Ecotrin), ibuprofen (Advil, Motrin, Nuprin), naproxen (Aleve), or ketoprofen (Orudis KT). No matter which drug you use, it is important to follow the directions on the label.

• Take short walks for a few minutes every hour or two, and work up to 20-minute walks.

• Relax your muscles frequently. See page 273 for progressive muscle relaxation.

• See Resources 18 and 19 recommended on page 326.

After two to three days of home treatment:

• Because returning to work helps most people recover quickly, your goal is to get back to work or your usual activities as soon as possible. You may be able to go right back to your regular schedule. You may need to talk with your employer about how to modify your duties for the first few days or weeks.

• Continue frequent walks (increase as you can) and the exercises above.

• Try swimming, which is good for your back. It may be painful immediately after a back injury, but lap swimming, walking in water, or kicking with swim fins is often helpful to prevent back problems from recurring. Using a snorkel and mask also helps, since you do not need to raise your head to breathe.

• When your back has improved, begin easy exercises that do not increase your back problem. One or two of the exercises in the Prevention section (pages 91 to 94) may be helpful. Start with five repetitions twice a day and increase to 10 repetitions as you are able.

When to Call Kaiser Permanente

• If you have loss of bowel or bladder control. Although constipation and frequent or urgent urination are common in people with low back pain, any new problems with bowel or bladder control should be discussed with your doctor.

Back Surgery

Very few people benefit from surgery for back problems. If you have serious weakness or loss of bladder or bowel control, then surgery may be needed, and you may need to see a surgical specialist.

- If you have new numbness in the genital or rectal area.

- If you have leg weakness that is not solely due to pain. Many people with low back pain say their legs feel weak. However, significant leg weakness should be evaluated, especially if you are unable to bend your foot upward, get up out of a chair, or climb stairs.

- If you have new or increased back pain with unexplained fever, painful urination, or other signs of urinary tract infection. See page 243.

- If you have a dramatic increase in your chronic back pain, especially if it is unrelated to a new or changed physical activity.

- If you have a history of cancer or HIV infection and develop new or increased back pain.

- If you have new back pain that does not show improvement after a few days of home treatment, contact your doctor for advice.

- If you develop a new, severe pain in your low back that does not change with movement and is not related to stress or muscle tension.

- If you cannot walk or stand.

- If back pain does not improve after two weeks of home treatment.

Medical Doctors or Nurse Practitioners

In addition to diagnosing the cause of back pain and evaluating back injuries, a doctor (MD or DO) or nurse practitioner may also:

- Help you develop an individualized exercise and home care plan or modified work plan if needed.

- Prescribe muscle relaxants, anti-inflammatory drugs, and pain relievers. Note: If you do get a strong painkiller or muscle relaxer, avoid postures and activities that could reinjure your back.

- Refer you to physical therapy.

- Recommend back surgery.

Doctors of osteopathy (DO) may also do spinal manipulation.

Physical Therapists

After the initial first-aid actions, a physical therapist with training in orthopedic treatment can help you in either a group or individual setting by:

- Identifying specific muscle or disc problems.

- Providing other therapies, such as manual therapy, if you aren't improving.

- Helping you improve your posture and customizing an exercise program for recovery and long-term protection.

Other Professionals

Chiropractors can provide relief from some types of back pain through spinal manipulation. Acupuncturists, massage therapists, and others may also provide short-term relief.

Neck Problems

 Neck pain and stiffness are usually caused by strain or spasm of the neck muscles or inflammation of the neck joints. They may occasionally be due to arthritis or damage to the discs between the neck (cervical) vertebrae. Neck movement may be limited, usually more to one side than the other. Neck problems often cause headaches or pain in the shoulder, upper back, or down the arm.

When you sit, stand, or move in a way that mistreats your neck, you may feel aches, pains, or discomfort in your neck, shoulders, upper back, head, ears, sinuses, jaw, chest, or arms. You may feel numbness, tingling, or weakness in your arms or hands. You may also feel dizzy.

Neck pain and headaches are sometimes related to tension in the trapezius muscles, which run from the back of the head across the back of the shoulder. When you have neck pain, these muscles may also feel tight and painful.

Neck muscle strain may be due to:

- Forward head posture

- Sleeping on a pillow that's too high, too flat, or doesn't support your head

- Sleeping on your stomach or with the neck twisted or bent

- Extended periods of the "thinker's pose" (resting your chin on your upright fist or arm)

- Watching TV or reading lying down with the neck in an awkward position

- Stress

- A workstation that puts the neck in an awkward position

- Other pressures on the neck muscles

- Injury that causes sudden movement of the head and neck (whiplash) or a direct blow to the neck

- Strenuous activity with the upper body and arms

Meningitis is a serious illness that causes a severe stiff neck with headache and fever (see page 141).

Prevention

Good posture, body mechanics, and exercise are important to preventing neck problems. Most neck problems that aren't due to arthritis or an injury are completely avoidable.

If pain is worse at the **end of the day**, evaluate your posture and body mechanics during the day.

- Sit straight in your chair with your low back supported. Avoid sitting for long periods without getting up or changing positions.

Take mini-breaks several times each hour to stretch your neck muscles.

• If you work at a computer, adjust the monitor so that the top of the screen is at eye level. Use a document holder that puts the copy at the same level as the screen.

• If you use the telephone a lot, consider a headset or speaker phone.

• Adjust your car seat to a more upright position that supports your head and low back.

• If neck stiffness is worse **in the morning**, check your sleeping posture (and your activities the day before).

• Improve your sleeping support. A hard mattress or special neck support pillow may solve the problem (try before buying). Or, you can fold a towel lengthwise into a four-inch-wide pad, wrap it around your neck, and pin it for good support.

• Avoid pillows that force your head forward when you are sleeping on your back.

• When sleeping on your side, make sure your nose is in line with the center of your body.

• If stress is a factor, practice the progressive muscle relaxation exercises on page 273.

• Strengthen and protect your neck by doing neck exercises once a day. See page 101.

Home Treatment

Much of the home treatment for back problems is also helpful for neck problems, including the guidelines on posture, body mechanics, ice, and moist heat. Also see page 95.

• If there has been a recent accident involving the neck, see page 62.

• Place a cold pack or moist heat over painful muscles for up to 20 minutes at a time, as often as once every two hours. It will help

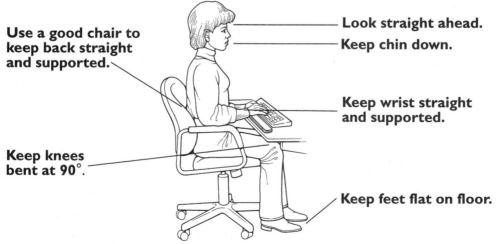

Use a good chair to keep back straight and supported.

Keep knees bent at 90°.

Look straight ahead.

Keep chin down.

Keep wrist straight and supported.

Keep feet flat on floor.

Good posture and support when you are seated can make any task more comfortable and will reduce strain on the eyes, neck, shoulders, arms, wrists, and back.

decrease any pain, muscle spasm, or swelling. If the problem is near the shoulder or upper back, it will usually help more to place ice or heat on the back of the neck.

• Keep your head and neck centered over your body. Avoid slouching or forward head posture.

• Use aspirin, ibuprofen, or acetaminophen to help relieve pain.

• Walking is also helpful in relieving and preventing neck problems. The gentle swinging motion of your arms often relieves pain. Start with short walks of 5 to 10 minutes, three to four times a day.

• If neck problems occur with headache, see Tension Headaches on page 170.

• Once the pain subsides, do the prevention exercises on page 101. Start with five repetitions twice a day. Gradually increase to 10 repetitions. Stop doing any exercise that causes pain.

• See Resource 56 on page 328.

When to Call Kaiser Permanente

Call your doctor *immediately*:

• If a stiff neck occurs together with headache and fever. Also see "Encephalitis and Meningitis" on page 141.

• If the pain extends or shoots down one arm, or you have numbness or tingling in your hands.

• If you develop new weakness in the arms or legs.

• If a blow or injury to the neck (whiplash) has caused new pain.

• If you are unable to manage the problem with home treatment.

• If the problem has lasted two weeks or longer without improvement despite home treatment.

Neck Exercises

You do not need to do every exercise. Stick with the ones that help you the most. Stop any exercise that increases pain. Start with five repetitions twice a day. Do each exercise slowly.

1. Dorsal glide: Sit or stand tall, looking straight ahead (a "palace guard" posture). Slowly tuck your chin as you glide your head backwards over your body. Hold for a count of five, then relax. Repeat 6 to 10 times. This stretches the back of the neck. If you feel pain, do not glide so far back. Some people find this exercise easier while lying on their back with ice on the neck.

2. Chest and shoulder stretch: Sit or stand tall and glide your head backward as in exercise 1. Raise both arms so that your hands are next to your ears. Relax your shoulders and, as you exhale, lower your elbows down toward your sides and backward. Feel your shoulder blades slide down and together. Hold for a few seconds. Relax and repeat.

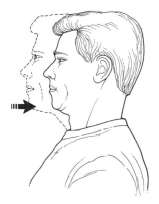

Dorsal glide

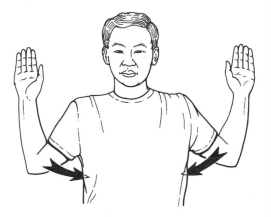

Chest and shoulder stretch: move elbows down toward your sides and backward.

*I don't deserve this award, but then I have arthritis
and I don't deserve that either.*
Jack Benny

6

Bone, Muscle, and Joint Problems

This chapter covers pain from arthritis to ankle sprains. The focus is less on reducing pain and more on limiting its impact on our quality of life. We hope these guidelines will make your life more comfortable.

Arthritis

 Arthritis refers to a variety of joint problems that cause pain, swelling, and stiffness. Simply put, arthritis means inflammation of a joint. Arthritis can occur at any age, but it affects older people the most.

There are over 100 different types of arthritis, each with its own specific symptoms. Little is known about what causes most types. Some seem to run in families; others seem to be related to imbalances in body chemistry or immune system problems.

The chart on page 104 describes the three most common kinds of arthritis. Osteoarthritis is the most common type and can usually be successfully managed at home. Rheumatoid arthritis and gout will improve with a combination of self-care and professional care.

Prevention

It may not be possible to prevent arthritis, but you can prevent a lot of pain by being kind to your joints. This is especially important if you already have arthritis.

• Modify activities that cause repeated jarring, such as high-impact aerobic activities, to low-impact activities if they cause pain.

• Exercise regularly.

• If you are experiencing back, hip, knee, or foot problems, controlling your weight may help.

While repeated jarring activities can increase joint pain, regular exercise can relieve or prevent it. Exercise is

 For more information, see the inside front cover.   **103**

needed to nourish the joint cartilage and remove waste products. It also strengthens the muscles around the joint. Strong muscles support the joint and reduce injuries caused by fatigue. Stretching maintains your range of pain-free motion.

Home Treatment

• A warm shower or bath may help relieve morning stiffness. Try to avoid sitting still after a warm shower or bath.

• If the joint is not swollen, apply moist heat for 20 to 30 minutes two to three times a day. Do not apply heat to a swollen, inflamed joint.

• Gently move the joint through as full a range of motion as possible without pain, several times a day, to prevent stiffness.

• When a joint is hurting, avoid activities that put unusual strain on it for a few days. Take short rest breaks from your regular activities throughout the day.

• Apply cold packs to inflamed, swollen joints for 10 to 15 minutes, once an hour. Cold will help relieve pain and reduce inflammation (although it may be uncomfortable for the first few minutes).

• Regular exercise is important to help maintain strength and flexibility in the muscles and joints. Strengthening exercises prevent the muscle decline that leads to loss of function. Try low-impact activities, such as swimming, water aerobics, biking, or walking.

Common Types of Arthritis

Type	Cause	Symptoms	Comments
Osteoarthritis	Breakdown of joint cartilage	Pain, stiffness, and swelling; common in fingers, hips, and knees.	Most common type in women and men between the ages of 45 and 90.
Rheumatoid Arthritis	Inflammation of the membrane lining the joint (synovium)	Pain, stiffness, swelling in multiple joints; joints may be "hot" and red; common in hands, wrists, and feet.	Occurs most often around age 30 to 40; more common in women.
Gout	Build-up of uric acid crystals in the joint fluid	Sudden onset of burning pain, stiffness, and swelling; common in big toe, ankle, knee, wrist, elbow.	Most common in men over 40; may be aggravated by drinking alcohol.

• Acetaminophen can provide safe pain relief for osteoarthritis. Aspirin, ibuprofen, naproxen, or ketoprofen can also help ease pain but can cause stomach upset. Do not use more than one anti-inflammatory medication (aspirin, ibuprofen, naproxen, etc.) at the same time. See page 317 for the symptoms of aspirin overdose.

• Enroll in an arthritis self-management program. Participants usually have less pain and fewer limitations on their activities. See Resource 16 on page 326.

• Call your local Arthritis Foundation office for more information.

When to Call Kaiser Permanente

• If you have fever or skin rash along with severe joint pain.

• If the joint is so painful that you cannot use it.

• If there is sudden, unexplained swelling, redness, or pain in any joint.

• If there is severe pain and swelling in multiple joints.

• If you experience sudden back pain that occurs with weakness in the legs or loss of bowel or bladder control.

• If joint pain continues for over six weeks and home treatment is not helping.

• If you experience side effects from aspirin or other arthritis medication (stomach pain, nausea, persistent heartburn, or dark, tarry stools). Do not exceed recommended doses of over-the-counter medications without your doctor's advice.

Bunions and Hammertoes

A bunion is a swelling of the joint at the base of the big toe. The big toe may bend toward and overlap the other toes. A hammertoe is a toe that bends up permanently at the middle joint. Both conditions are usually irritated by wearing shoes that are too short or narrow. These problems sometimes run in families.

Prevention

Tight or high-heeled shoes increase the risk of bunions and hammertoes and irritate them if they are already

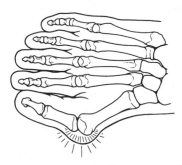

A bunion is a swelling caused by a misshapen joint at the base of the big toe.

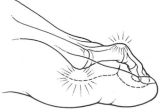

A hammertoe is a toe that bends up permanently at the middle joint.

 For more information, see the inside front cover. **105**

present. Wear shoes with no heel (or a low heel) and a roomy toe area. Tennis or basketball court shoes are often best. Make sure that your shoes fit properly.

Home Treatment

Once you have a bunion or hammertoe, there is usually no way to completely get rid of it. Home treatment will help keep it from getting worse.

- Wear low-heeled, roomy shoes that have good arch supports.

- Cushion the bunion or hammertoe with moleskin or doughnut-shaped pads to prevent rubbing and irritation.

- Cut out the area over the bunion or hammertoe from an old pair of shoes to wear around the house, or wear comfortable sandals that don't press on the area.

- Try aspirin, ibuprofen, or acetaminophen to relieve pain. Ice or cold packs may also help.

When to Call Kaiser Permanente

- If severe pain in the big toe came on suddenly, and you have not been diagnosed with gout.

- If severe pain interferes with walking or daily activities.

- If the big toe begins to overlap the second toe.

- If you have diabetes, poor circulation, or peripheral vascular disease. Irritated skin over a bunion or hammertoe can easily become

infected in people with these conditions.

- If pain does not respond to home treatment in two to three weeks.

Bursitis and Tendinitis

 A bursa is a small sac of fluid that helps the muscles slide easily over other muscles or bones. Injury or overuse of a joint or tendon may result in pain, redness, heat, and inflammation of the bursa, a condition known as bursitis. Bursitis often develops quickly, over just a few days, often after a specific injury or overuse.

Tendons are tough, rope-like fibers that connect muscles to bones. Injury or overuse may cause pain, tenderness, and inflammation in the tendons or the tissues surrounding them, a condition known as tendinitis. Both bursitis and tendinitis can also be related to job, sports, or household activities that require repeated twisting or rapid joint movements.

Bursitis and tendinitis can occur at several different places in the body and can occur together in one place. The same home treatment is good for both problems.

Prevention

Regular warm-ups and stretching may help prevent bursitis or tendinitis. Warm up well before exercising, gradually increase the intensity of the activity, and stretch afterwards. See pages 108 and 109 for additional, joint-specific prevention tips.

Home Treatment

Bursitis or tendinitis will usually go away or at least subside in a few days or weeks if you avoid the activity that caused it.

The most common mistake in recovery is thinking that the problem is gone when the pain is gone. Chances are, bursitis or tendinitis will recur if you do not take steps to strengthen and stretch the muscles around the joint and change the way you do some activities.

- When a joint or tendon is hurting, change the way you do the activity that causes pain so that you can do it without pain. See pages 108 and 109 for joint-specific guidelines. To maintain fitness, substitute activities that don't stress the inflamed area.

- As soon as you notice pain, apply ice or cold packs for 10-minute periods, once an hour for the first 72 hours. After that, continue applying ice (15 to 20 minutes, three times a day) as long as it relieves pain. See page 120. Although heating pads or hot baths may feel good, ice or cold packs will relieve inflammation and speed healing.

- Aspirin, ibuprofen, or naproxen may help ease pain and inflammation, but don't use medication to relieve pain while you continue overusing a joint. See page 317 for dosage.

- Gently move the joint through as full a range of motion as you can without pain several times a day to prevent stiffness. As the pain subsides, continue stretching and add exercises to strengthen the affected muscles.

- Warm up before and stretch after the activity. Apply ice to the injured area after exercise to prevent pain and swelling.

- Gradually resume the activity at a lower intensity. Increase slowly and only if pain does not recur.

In addition to the general prevention and home treatment information for bursitis and tendinitis above, the following tips will be useful if you have a specific joint problem.

Wrist pain may be due to tendinitis. Though this is not the same as carpal tunnel syndrome, the same home care may help. See page 110.

Elbow pain is often due to one of the following common types of tendinitis in the forearm muscle tendons. The inside or outside of the elbow is defined by holding the arm at your side with the palm facing forward.

Tennis elbow causes pain on the outside of the elbow where the muscles that bend the wrist back are attached.

Golfer's elbow causes pain on the inside of the elbow where the muscles that bend the wrist down are attached.

- Strengthen the wrist, arm, shoulder, and back muscles to help protect the elbow.

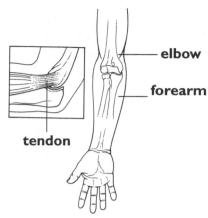

Elbow pain is often caused by inflammation of a tendon in the forearm.

- A brace or elbow sleeve may help relieve pain.

- Use tools with larger handles.

- Use a two-handed tennis backhand and a midsize, more flexible racquet.

- Avoid activities that put a strain on the elbow.

- Avoid sidearm pitching and throwing curve balls.

Shoulder pain that occurs on the outside of the upper arm is often due to impingement (caused by tendinitis or bursitis) in the shoulder joint. Pain on the top of the shoulder or in the neck is often due to tension in the trapezius muscles, which run from the back of the head across the back of the shoulders. See Neck Problems on page 98.

Common symptoms of impingement are pain, pinching, and stiffness in your shoulder when you raise your arm. It is often caused by repeated overhead movements. Problems develop when the shoulder continues to be used without getting time to rest. This leads to further swelling and pain.

For home treatment of shoulder pain, see the information on page 107. In addition, keep the following tips in mind:

- Avoid overhead activities, but continue to use your shoulder.

- Practice the pendulum exercise to help prevent stiffness (see below).

- Use proper throwing technique for baseball and football.

- Use a different swim stroke: breast stroke or sidestroke instead of the crawl or butterfly.

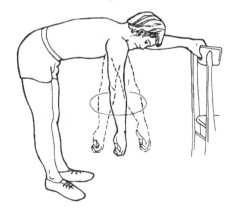

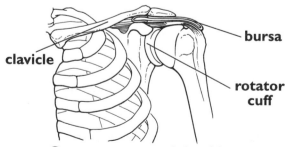

Common causes of shoulder pain are bursitis, tendinitis, and muscle tension.

Pendulum Exercise: Let your arm "dangle" freely. Move it clockwise and counterclockwise in increasingly large circles. Swing your arm forward, backward, and side to side.

Hip pain: Tendinitis or bursitis in the hip can cause pain at the side of the hip when rising from a chair and taking the first few steps, while climbing stairs, or while driving. If pain is severe, sleeping on your side may also be painful. Pain in the front of the hip may also be due to arthritis. See page 103.

- Wear well-cushioned shoes and avoid high heels.

- Walk up and down stairs one at a time, leading with your strong leg, until the pain is gone.

- Avoid activities that force one side of the pelvis higher than the other, such as running in only one direction on a track or working sideways on a slope. Keep the pelvis level.

- Sleep on your uninjured side with a pillow between your knees, or on your back with pillows beneath your knees.

- See the hip stretches on pages 94 and 268. Stretch after activity, when your muscles are warm.

Knee pain may be caused by bursitis or tendinitis. See Knee Problems on page 111.

Heel or foot pain may be due to plantar fasciitis or to Achilles tendinitis. See page 115. Pain in the front of the lower leg may be due to shinsplints. See page 112.

When to Call Kaiser Permanente

- If there is fever, rapid swelling, redness, or an inability to use a joint.

- If severe pain continues when the joint is at rest and you have applied ice.

- If the problem is severe and you can think of no injury or activity that might have caused it.

- If the pain persists for two weeks or longer despite home treatment. Your doctor or physical therapist can help you develop a specific exercise and home treatment plan.

Carpal Tunnel Syndrome

 The carpal tunnel is a narrow passageway between the bones and ligaments in your wrist. The median nerve, which controls sensation in your fingers and some muscles in the hand, passes through this tunnel along with some of the finger tendons. Carpal tunnel syndrome (CTS) occurs when there is pressure on the nerve where it goes through this tunnel, causing symptoms. A common cause is repeated motion or use of the hand or wrist that may cause the tendons to become inflamed and press the nerve against the bone.

Pressure on the nerve causes the following symptoms of CTS:

- Numbness or tingling in one or both hands except for the little finger.

- Wrist pain that may also affect your fingers and radiate up your arm. The pain is often greater at night and early in the morning.

Carpal tunnel syndrome can be caused by anything that causes pressure on the nerve, such as being overweight, swelling due to repetitive use of the hand and wrist, a cyst on the tendon, rheumatoid arthritis, or other conditions. Pregnancy, diabetes, an underactive thyroid, and taking birth control pills also may increase the risk of CTS.

Prevention

- Take frequent breaks (five minutes each hour) from repetitive hand motions. Stretch your fingers and thumb and change your grip often.

- Avoid repetitive hand motions with a bent wrist. Keep your wrist straight for the following activities:

  ° Writing, typing, drawing, knitting, crocheting, needlepoint, painting

  ° Driving

  ° Using power tools, pliers, or scissors

  ° Playing piano or other musical instruments

- Learn to type with a soft touch.

- Maintain good posture. Avoid rounding your shoulders or slouching. See pages 90 and 98.

Home Treatment

- Don't ignore wrist pain or numbness in the hand. If possible, stop the activity that triggered the problem. If you cannot stop the activity, try to change the way you do it so that your wrist is not stressed. If the symptoms decrease, resume the activity gradually with a greater effort to keep your wrist straight.

- Alternate tasks so that you don't spend more than one to two hours doing an activity involving your hands.

- Gently warm up your hands before starting work. Do some wrist circles and stretch your fingers and wrists. Repeat every hour.

- Have your keyboard at the correct height. Use a wrist rest pad with your computer keyboard to help maintain the straight alignment of your wrist, but don't lean on it continuously.

- Use aspirin, ibuprofen, or acetaminophen to relieve pain.

- Apply ice or a cold pack to the palm side of the wrist. See "Ice and Cold Packs" on page 120.

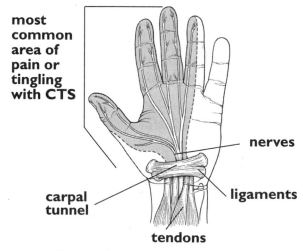

most common area of pain or tingling with CTS

nerves

carpal tunnel

ligaments

tendons

Pain and tingling in the hand may be caused by pressure on a nerve in the wrist.

• A wrist splint that keeps your wrist straight may help relieve pain. Try to combine a splint with a real effort to change the activities that cause you pain. Wear the splint at night and when doing heavy lifting or activities that cause you discomfort without the support. You can buy a splint at a pharmacy or hospital supply store.

• Some people find that 50 mg of vitamin B₆ taken twice a day helps relieve wrist pain. (Talk with your doctor before taking B_6.) The scientific proof of this is not clear, but it may help.

• Reducing the salt in your diet (see page 284) may help reduce water retention and relieve swelling in the wrist.

• When sleeping, try to keep your wrists straight and avoid sleeping on your hands.

When to Call Kaiser Permanente

• If the pain or numbness is severe and is not relieved by rest, changing positions, ice, or a normal dose of aspirin, ibuprofen, or acetaminophen.

• If your hand grip becomes weak.

• If minor symptoms do not improve after one month of prevention and home treatment.

• If any numbness remains after one month of home treatment. Long-term numbness can lead to *permanent* loss of some hand function.

Knee Problems

The knee is a vulnerable joint. It is basically just two long leg bones held together with ligaments and muscles. Problems develop when we put too much stress on the joint. The three most common knee problems are:

• Strained or sprained ligaments and muscles caused by a blow to the knee, forcing it in a direction that it does not normally bend. See Strains, Sprains, and Fractures on page 117.

• **Kneecap pain**, also known as patellofemoral pain. This problem causes pain around or behind the kneecap when running downhill, going up or down stairs, or after sitting for long periods of time.

• **Patellar tendinitis**, also known as jumper's knee, is an inflammation of the tendon that attaches the kneecap (patella) to the shinbone (tibia). It is common among basketball and volleyball players.

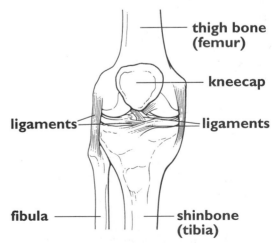

Knee problems can develop when too much stress is put on the joint.

Prevention

- The best way to prevent knee problems is to stay active and strengthen and stretch the leg muscles, especially the front and back of the thigh (quadriceps and hamstring). See page 268.

- Avoid deep knee bends.

- Avoid running downhill unless you are fully conditioned.

- Avoid wearing shoes with cleats in contact sports.

- Wear shoes with good arch supports. Replace running shoes every 300 to 500 miles.

- Avoid high-heeled shoes.

- Also see Bursitis and Tendinitis on page 106.

Home Treatment

- Apply ice to your knee. See "Ice and Cold Packs" on page 120.

- Reduce by at least half the activities that cause pain.

- A brace or elastic or neoprene sleeve or a band with a hole for the kneecap that holds the kneecap in place may help ease pain during activity. You can buy one at a pharmacy or sporting goods store.

- Warm up well before vigorous activities.

- Stretch the front and back of your thigh (quadriceps and hamstring) muscles after exercise, when they are warm. See pages 94 and 268.

- Also see Strains, Sprains, and Fractures on page 117 and Bursitis and Tendinitis on page 106.

- If knee pain is not related to exercise or due to a recent or past injury, see Arthritis on page 103.

When to Call Kaiser Permanente

- If the knee wobbles from side to side or "gives out."

- If you felt or heard a "pop" during a knee injury that was followed by immediate swelling.

- If you are unable to straighten the knee, or if the joint "locks."

- If knee is red, hot, swollen, or painful to touch.

- If pain is severe enough that you are limping, or if it does not improve substantially within two to five days.

Muscle Cramps and Leg Pain

Leg and muscle cramps ("charley horse" or "stitch") are common. They often occur during exercise, especially during hot weather, or at night. Dehydration or low levels of potassium in the body and using a muscle that is not stretched well may cause cramps.

Pain in the front of the lower leg may be due to shinsplints, especially if you have recently increased your exercise.

Arthritis can also cause leg pain (see page 103). Leg pain that runs from the buttocks down the back of the leg and into the foot may be due to sciatica. See page 89.

Phlebitis, an inflammation of a vein, also causes leg pain, usually in the calf of one leg. This condition can be serious if blood clots formed in the vein break loose and lodge in the lungs. It is most common after surgery or prolonged bed rest. Hardening of the arteries atherosclerosis) in the leg can also cause pain that is worse during activity and is relieved by rest.

Prevention

- Warm up well and stretch before any activity. Stretch after exercise to keep hot muscles from shortening and cramping.

- Drink extra water before and during exercise, especially during hot or humid weather.

- Include plenty of potassium in your diet. Bananas, orange juice, and potatoes are good sources.

- To avoid stomach muscle cramps ("stitches") during exercise, do side stretches before exercising and learn to breathe with your lower lungs. See page 272.

- If cramps wake you at night, take a warm bath and do some stretching exercises before going to bed. Keep your legs warm while sleeping.

Growing Pains

Children age 6 to 12 often develop harmless "growing pains" in their legs at night. The cause is unknown. A heating pad, acetaminophen, or gentle massage of the legs may help.

Home Treatment

If there is pain, swelling, or heaviness in the calf of one leg only, or other symptoms that cause you to suspect phlebitis (see When to Call Kaiser Permanente), call your doctor before attempting home treatment.

- Follow the prevention guidelines.

- Gently stretch the cramping muscle. Rub or massage the cramp.

- To stretch the calf, straighten your leg, grab your foot, and pull it toward you.

- Drink some extra water. Cramps are often related to dehydration.

- The best treatment for shinsplints is ice, aspirin, ibuprofen, or acetaminophen, and a week or two of rest followed by a gradual return to exercise. Try to identify the cause (shoes, exercise surface) and correct it.

When to Call Kaiser Permanente

- If you have the following symptoms:

  ° Pain deep in the leg or calf

  ° Heat, redness, or pain along the course of a leg vein

° Swelling of one leg

° Leg is cold and looks white or blue

° Shortness of breath, or chest pain

• If leg cramps worsen or persist in spite of prevention and home treatment.

• If cramps or leg pain occur repeatedly during even mild exercise, such as walking, even if relieved by rest.

Osteoporosis

 Osteoporosis or "brittle bones" is a condition that affects 25 percent of women over age 60. It is much less common and not as severe in men. It is more common after menopause, when estrogen levels decline. Osteoporosis is caused by loss of bone mass and strength. Bones weakened by osteoporosis are easily broken. Risk factors for osteoporosis include:

• Current smoker

• Thin, small-boned frame

• Family history of osteoporosis (especially hip fracture)

• History of fracture (other than spine) after age 50

Osteoporosis is a silent disease; there may be no symptoms until a bone breaks and the condition is recognized after X-rays. The first sign may be back pain, or fracture of a wrist after a fall.

Prevention

It is best to start to build sturdy bones in childhood, but the steps given here will help anytime. Peak bone mass is reached during your twenties and thirties. These steps can help you build and keep strong bones throughout your life.

• Get regular weight-bearing exercise, such as walking. Exercise helps keep bones strong. See Chapter 17.

• Get plenty of calcium in your diet. The average American diet contains about 500 mg per day, but 1,300 mg are recommended for teenagers and 1,000 mg for adults until age 50. After age 50 both men and women need 1,200 mg of calcium daily. Pregnant women and breast-feeding mothers should get about 1,200 mg per day. The best source of calcium is low-fat dairy products. See page 283.

• If you are unable to get all the calcium you need from your diet, take two to three calcium carbonate tablets (Tums or other calcium supplements) each day with meals or with milk. Don't take more than four to six tablets per day, and drink lots of water, because they can cause constipation. Too much calcium also increases the risk for kidney stones.

• Don't smoke, and drink alcohol only in moderation (one drink per day), if at all.

• Getting enough vitamin D is also important. Children and adults need 200 IU per day. After age 50, 400 IU are recommended, and adults over age 65 need 600 to 800 IU daily.

- Most of the vitamin D we need comes from our skin absorbing sunlight and from drinking vitamin D fortified milk (each 8-ounce serving has 100 IU). Older adults may need to take supplemental vitamin D. A good way to do this is to take a multivitamin with vitamin D every day.

When to Call Kaiser Permanente

- If you are at risk of osteoporosis and are nearing menopause, talk with your doctor about estrogen or hormone replacement therapy. It is the most effective way to prevent osteoporosis. See page 238.

- If a fall causes hip pain or if you are unable to get up after a fall.

- If you have sudden, unexplained back pain that does not improve after two to three days of home treatment.

Plantar Fasciitis

Plantar fasciitis is a condition that occurs when the thick, fibrous tissue that covers the bottom of your foot (plantar fascia) becomes inflamed and painful. Athletes (especially runners), middle-aged people, and those who are overweight tend to develop plantar fasciitis. Repetitive exercises such as running and jumping sports can lead to heel pain and plantar fasciitis.

An excessive inward rolling of the foot during walking or running (called pronation) can also cause

heel pain and plantar fasciitis. Pronation can be due to poor arch support, worn-out shoes, tight calf muscles, or by running downhill or on uneven surfaces.

Achilles tendinitis can cause pain in the back of the heel.

A heel spur is a calcium build-up that may occur where the plantar fascia attaches to the heel. It does not change the treatment of plantar fasciitis.

Prevention

- Stretch your Achilles tendon and calf muscles several times a day (see page 268). Stretching is important for both athletes and nonathletes.

- Maintain a reasonable weight for your height.

- Wear shoes with well-cushioned soles and good arch supports. Replace athletic shoes every few months because padding wears out.

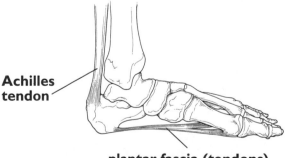

Achilles tendon

plantar fascia (tendons)

Foot or heel pain is often caused by inflammation of the Achilles tendon or the plantar fascia.

• Establish good exercise habits. Increase mileage slowly, limit your running and training on hilly terrain, and run on softer surfaces (grass or dirt) rather than concrete. Cross-train by alternating running with different sports.

Home Treatment

Treat heel pain when it first appears to keep plantar fasciitis or other problems from becoming chronic.

• Reduce all weight-bearing activities to a pain-free level.

• Apply ice to your heel. See "Ice and Cold Packs" on page 120.

• You may wish to try an over-the-counter arch support .

• Do not go barefoot until the pain is completely gone. Wear shoes or arch-supporting sandals during all weight-bearing activities, even going to the bathroom during the night.

• Take aspirin, ibuprofen, naproxen, or ketoprofen to relieve pain.

• Stretch the calf muscles. See page 268.

• For achilles tendinitis, try putting heel lifts or heel cups in both shoes. Use them only until the pain is gone (continue other self-care).

• Avoid "running through the pain." Reduce your activity to a level that does not cause pain. Try low-impact activities such as cycling or swimming to speed healing.

• Do not return to high-impact activity until you have been pain-free for one week. When you do return, start slowly and ice your heel afterward. If the pain recurs, start home treatment again.

When to Call Kaiser Permanente

• If heel pain occurs with fever, redness, or heat in your heel, or if there is numbness or tingling in your heel.

• If pain continues when you are not standing or bearing any weight on your heel.

• If heel pain persists for one to two weeks despite home treatment.

Sports Injuries

Injuries are common among physically active people. Most sports injuries are due to either traumatic injury or overuse and can be avoided by proper conditioning, training, and equipment.

Prevention

• Warm up before exercise. Cold, stiff muscles and ligaments are more susceptible to injury. Cool down and stretch after activities. See page 267.

• Increase the intensity and duration of activities and exercise gradually. As your fitness level improves, you will be able to do increasingly strenuous exercise without injury.

• Use proper sports techniques and equipment. For example, wear supportive, well-cushioned shoes for running, aerobics, and walking; use a two-handed tennis backhand stroke; wear protective pads for rollerskating. Make sure that your bicycle's seat and handlebars are adjusted properly for your body.

• Alternate hard workouts with easier ones to let your body rest. For example, if you run, alternate long or hard runs with shorter or easier ones. If you lift weights, don't work the same muscles two days in a row.

• Cross-train (do several activities regularly) to rest your muscles. Alternate days of walking with biking, running, or swimming.

• Don't ignore aches and pains. A few days of reduced activity or rest, ice, and other home treatment when you feel the first twinge of pain may help you avoid more serious problems.

Home Treatment

The biggest home treatment challenge for most sports injuries is to get enough rest to allow healing without losing overall conditioning. This approach is called relative rest.

• Keep the rest of your body fit by cross-training with activities that don't stress the injured area: swimming or biking for sore ankles or feet; walking or biking for sore shoulders or elbows. Don't hurry the return to the activity that caused the injury. Cross-training can maintain your level of fitness.

• Resume your regular activity gradually. Start with a slow, easy pace and increase only if you have no pain.

• Break your sport down into components. If you can throw a ball a short distance without pain, try increasing the distance. If you can walk comfortably, try jogging. If you can jog without pain, try running.

When to Call Kaiser Permanente

For information on when to call about specific injuries (for example, golfer's elbow), check the index and go to the page indicated. Then look under When to Call Kaiser Permanente in that section.

Strains, Sprains, and Fractures

A **strain** is an injury caused by over-stretching a muscle.

A **sprain** is an injury to the muscle and the ligaments, tendons, or soft tissues around a joint.

A **fracture** is a broken bone.

All three injuries cause pain and swelling. Unless a broken bone is obvious, it may be difficult to tell if an injury is a strain, sprain, or fracture. Injuries often involve all three. Rapid swelling often indicates a more serious injury. If a bone is poking through the skin, or if a limb below the injury is white, cold, or numb, immediate medical care is needed.

Most minor strains and sprains can be treated at home, but severe sprains and fractures need professional care. Apply home treatment while you wait to see your doctor.

You may have a severe sprain or broken bone if:

- The injured area is visibly swollen.

- The injured area is twisted or bent out of shape or a bone is poking through the skin.

Splinting

Splinting immobilizes a suspected fracture to prevent further injury. There are two ways to immobilize a fracture: tie the injured limb to a stiff object, or fasten it to some other part of the body. Do not tie too tight.

For the first method, tie rolled-up newspapers or magazines, a stick, a cane, or anything that is stiff to the injured limb with a rope, a belt, or anything else that will work.

Position the splint so the injured limb cannot bend. A general rule is to splint from a joint above the fracture to a joint below it. For example, splint a broken forearm from above the elbow to below the wrist.

For the second method, tape a broken toe to the next toe or immobilize an arm by tying it across the victim's chest.

- The injured area is black and blue.

- The pain from the injury prevents normal use of the limb, such as walking.

A **stress fracture** is a weak spot or small crack in a bone caused by repeated overuse. Stress fractures in the small bones of the foot are common during intensive training for basketball, running, and other sports. The main symptom is persistent foot pain and tenderness that increases during use. There may be no visible swelling.

Prevention

- Make sure you can always see where you are walking. To avoid falling, don't climb stairs with both hands full.

- To avoid falling, use a stepstool when reaching for high objects. Do not stand on chairs or other objects.

- Get help to carry heavy or awkward objects.

- See prevention tips for Sports Injuries on page 116.

Home Treatment

Generally speaking, if the injury is to a muscle, ligament, tendon, or bone, the basic treatment is the same. It is a two-part process: **RICE** (rest, ice, compression, elevation) to treat the acute pain or injury; and **MSA** (movement, strength, alternate activity) to help the injury heal completely and to prevent further problems.

Begin the RICE process immediately for most injuries. If you suspect a fracture, splint the affected limb to prevent further injury (see page 118).

If the sprain is to a finger or part of the hand, remove all rings immediately. See the box at right.

R. Rest. Do not put weight on the injured joint for at least 24 to 48 hours.

- Use crutches to support a badly sprained knee or ankle.

- Rest a sprained finger or toe by taping it to a healthy one next to it.

Injured muscle, ligament, or tendon tissue needs time and rest to heal. Stress fractures need rest for two to four months.

I. Ice. Cold will reduce pain and swelling and promote healing. Heat feels nice, but it may do more harm than good, since it may increase the swelling after an injury.

- Apply ice or cold packs immediately to prevent or minimize swelling. For difficult-to-reach injuries, a cold pack works best. See "Ice and Cold Packs" on page 120.

C. Compression. Wrap the injury with an elastic (Ace) bandage or compression sleeve to immobilize and compress the sprain. Don't wrap it too tightly, which can cause more swelling. Loosen the bandage if it gets too tight. A tightly wrapped sprain may fool you into thinking you can keep using the joint. With or without a wrap, the joint needs total rest for one to two days.

Removing a Ring

If you did not remove a ring before a sprained finger started to swell, try the following method to remove it:

- Stick the end of a slick piece of string, such as dental floss, under the ring toward the hand.

- Starting at the knuckle side of the ring, wrap the string snugly around the finger toward the end of the finger, wrapping beyond the knuckle. Each wrap should be right next to the one before.

- Grasp the end of the string that is stretched under the ring and start unwrapping it. Push the ring along ahead of the unwrapped string as you unwrap it until the ring passes the knuckle.

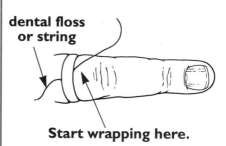

Start wrapping here.

Pull the ring over the wrapped joint.

E. Elevation. Elevate the injured area on pillows while you apply ice and anytime you are sitting or lying down. Try to keep the injury at or above the level of your heart to help minimize swelling.

• Aspirin, ibuprofen, naproxen, or Orudis may help ease inflammation and pain. Do not use drugs to mask the pain while you continue to use the injured joint. Do not give aspirin to children or teens under age 20. Review aspirin guidelines on pages 316 and 317.

• The use of heat (hot water bottle, warm towel, heating pad) after 48 hours of cold treatments is controversial. Some experts think it will increase swelling; others think it may speed healing. If you use heat, do not apply anything that is uncomfortably warm.

Begin the **MSA** process as soon as the initial pain and swelling have subsided. This may be in two days or up to a week or longer, depending on the location and severity of the injury. Resume sports and activities slowly. Any increased pain may be a sign that you need to rest a while longer.

M. Movement. After one to two days of rest, begin moving the joint. Move your joint gently through its full range of motion. If an activity causes pain, stop it and give the joint more rest. Gentle stretching will prevent scar tissue (formed as the injury heals) from limiting movement later.

Ice and Cold Packs

Ice can relieve pain, swelling, and inflammation from injuries and other conditions such as arthritis. Apply ice consistently and thoroughly as long as you have symptoms. Use either a commercial cold pack or one of the following:

• Ice towel: Wet a towel with cold water and squeeze it until it is just damp. Fold the towel, place it in a plastic bag, and freeze it for 15 minutes. Remove the towel from the bag and place it on the affected area.

• Ice pack: Put about a pound of ice in a plastic bag. Add water to barely cover the ice. Squeeze the air out of the bag and seal it. Wrap the bag in a wet towel and apply to the affected area.

• Homemade cold pack: See instructions on page 307.

Ice the area at least three times a day. For the first 72 hours, ice for 10 minutes once an hour. After that, a good pattern is to ice for 15 to 20 minutes three times a day: in the morning, in the late afternoon after work or school, and about one-half hour before bedtime. Also ice after any prolonged activity or vigorous exercise.

Always keep a damp cloth between your skin and the cold pack, and press firmly against all the curves of the affected area. Do not apply ice for longer than 15 to 20 minutes at a time, and do not fall asleep with the ice on your skin.

S. Strength. Once the swelling is gone and range of motion is restored, begin gradual efforts to strengthen the injured area. This may require specific exercises.

A. Alternate activities. After the first few days, but while the injury is still healing, phase in regular exercise using activities or sports that do not place a strain on the injured part. See page 117.

When to Call Kaiser Permanente

- If a bone is poking through the skin, or if a limb below the injury is white, cold, or numb.

- If you suspect a severe sprain or fracture (see page 118). After you have stopped weight-bearing activities, splinted the injury, and applied ice, a short delay in receiving professional care will not affect the outcome.

- If a sprained joint is very unstable, won't support your weight, or wobbles from side to side.

- If you cannot bear weight on a sprained ankle after 24 hours, or if it hurts to bear weight after three days.

- If pain is still severe after two days of home treatment.

- If a sprain does not improve after four days of home treatment.

Weakness and Fatigue

Weakness is a lack of physical strength that causes difficulty in moving or inability to move arms, legs, or other muscles.

Fatigue is a feeling of being tired or exhausted, or a lack of energy.

Unexplained muscle weakness is usually more serious than fatigue. It may be due to metabolic problems such as diabetes (see page 219), thyroid problems, kidney problems, or stroke. Call your doctor immediately.

Fatigue, on the other hand, can usually be treated with self-care. Most fatigue is caused by lack of exercise, stress or overwork, poor sleep, depression, worry, or boredom. Colds and flu may sometimes cause fatigue and weakness, but the symptoms disappear as the illness runs its course.

Prevention

- Regular exercise is your best defense against fatigue. If you feel too tired to exercise vigorously, try a short walk.

- Eat a well-balanced diet. See Chapter 18.

- Make sure you are getting enough sleep. See page 300.

- Deal with feelings of depression. See page 296.

Home Treatment

- Follow the prevention guidelines above and be patient. It may take a while to feel energetic again.

- Listen to your body. Alternate rest with exercise.

- Limit drugs that might contribute to fatigue. Tranquilizers and cold and allergy medications are particularly suspect.

- Reduce your use of caffeine, nicotine, and alcohol.

- Cut back on watching television. Spend that time with friends, new activities, or travel to break the fatigue cycle.

When to Call Kaiser Permanente

- If you have unexplained muscle weakness in one area of your body.

- If severe fatigue causes you to limit your usual activities for longer than two weeks despite home treatment.

- If you experience sudden, unplanned weight loss.

- If you do not feel more energetic after six weeks of home treatment.

Chronic Fatigue Syndrome

Chronic fatigue syndrome (CFS) is a flu-like illness that causes severe fatigue lasting longer than six months. Other symptoms include mild fever, sore throat, painful lymph glands, muscle weakness and pain, headaches, and sleep problems.

CFS is difficult to diagnose. There is no definitive lab test. Many other illnesses, such as depression, thyroid disorders, or mononucleosis, cause similar symptoms. A CFS diagnosis is made only after fatigue and other symptoms continue for at least six months and other possible causes have been ruled out.

The fatigue and other symptoms usually develop quickly in a previously healthy person. Treatment is focused on adequate rest, balanced diet, and mild exercise. No medications are known to cure CFS. Treatment of the individual symptoms can be effective. For treatment of depression, which develops in about half of CFS patients, see page 298.

Call your doctor if unexplained fatigue is severe, persistent, and interferes with your activities for more than two weeks despite home treatment.

Life is made up of sobs, sniffles, and smiles,
with sniffles predominating.
O. Henry

7

Chest and Respiratory Problems

Chest and respiratory problems can be as simple as a minor cold or as life-threatening as a heart attack. For most respiratory problems, including allergies, colds, sore throats, sinusitis, and tonsillitis, this chapter will help you decide what to do at home and when to call your doctor.

Start this chapter with a look at the chart on the next page. From asthma to pneumonia and from heart attack to heartburn, the chart will lead you to the information you need the most. If you don't find what you are looking for, please check the index.

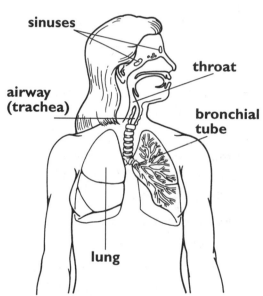

Respiratory problems can occur in the nose, sinuses, throat, or trachea (upper respiratory tract) or in the bronchial tubes or lungs (lower respiratory tract).

Allergies

Allergies come in many forms. Symptoms include itchy, watery eyes; sneezing; runny, stuffy, or itchy nose; temporary loss of smell; headache; and fatigue. Dark circles under the eyes ("allergic shiners") or postnasal drip may also accompany hay fever. A child with allergies may snore, wake with a sore throat, breathe through the mouth, and frequently rub his or her nose. Allergy symptoms are often like cold symptoms, but usually last longer.

Chest, Respiratory, Nose, and Throat Problems

Chest and Respiratory Symptoms	Possible Causes
Wheezing or difficult (rapid, shallow, labored) breathing	See Allergies, p. 123; Asthma, p. 127; Bronchitis, p. 132;
Cough, fever, yellow-green or rusty sputum, and difficulty breathing (possibly with chest-wall pain)	See Bronchitis, p. 132; Pneumonia, p. 142.
Chest pain with sweating or rapid pulse	Chest Pain, p. 133.
Burning, pain, or discomfort behind the breastbone	See Heartburn, p. 74; Chest Pain, p. 133.
Coughing	See Coughs, p. 137.

Nose and Throat Symptoms	Possible Causes
Stuffy or runny nose with watery eyes, sneezing	See Allergies, p. 123; Colds, p. 135.
Cold symptoms with fever, headache, severe body aches, fatigue	See Influenza, p. 140.
Thick green, yellow, or gray nasal discharge with fever and facial pain	See Sinusitis, p. 143.
Foul odor from nose; swollen, inflamed nasal tissue	See Objects in the Nose, p. 53; Sinusitis, p. 143.
Sore throat	See Sore Throat, p. 145; Tonsillitis, p. 148.
Sore throat with white spots on tonsils, swollen glands, fever of 101° or higher	See Strep Throat, p. 145.
Swollen tonsils, sore throat, fever	See Tonsillitis, p. 148.
Swollen lymph nodes in the neck	See Swollen Glands, p. 147; Tonsillitis, p. 148.
Hoarseness, loss of voice	See Laryngitis, p. 142.

The most common causes of allergies are particles in the air, such as pollen, house dust mites, mold or mildew, and animal dander.

Allergies seem to run in families. Hay fever is the most common allergy. Parents with hay fever often have children with allergies. Hay fever usually develops in childhood, but can occur at any age.

You can often discover the cause of an allergy by noting when symptoms occur. Symptoms that occur at the same time each year (especially during spring, early summer, or early fall) are often due to tree, grass, or weed pollen. Allergies that persist all year long may be due to dust mites in household dust, mold spores, or animal dander. Animal allergy is often easy to detect: symptoms clear up when you stay away from the animal.

Life-Threatening Allergic Reactions

A few people have severe allergies to insect stings or certain foods or drugs, especially penicillin. For these people, the allergic reaction is sudden and severe and may cause difficulty breathing and a drop in blood pressure (anaphylactic shock).

An anaphylactic reaction is a medical emergency, and prompt care is needed. If you have had a severe allergic reaction, doctors suggest that you carry an epinephrine syringe (EpiPen, Ana-Kit) designed for self-administering a shot that will decrease the severity of the reaction. If you have had an allergic reaction to a drug, wear a medical identification bracelet that will tell health professionals about your allergy if you cannot.

Prevention

- If practical, avoiding the substance that causes allergy attacks will help. See page 287 for more information on food allergies.

- If you or your spouse has a history of allergies, consider breast-feeding your infants. There is some evidence that feeding only breast milk during the first six months of life may reduce a child's risk of developing food allergies.

Home Treatment

If you can discover the source of your allergies, avoiding that substance is the best treatment. Keep a record of your symptoms and the plants, animals, foods, or chemicals that seem to trigger them.

If your symptoms are seasonal and seem to be related to pollen:

- Keep your house and car windows closed. Keep bedroom windows closed at night.

- Limit the time you spend outside when pollen counts are high. Dogs and other pets may bring large amounts of pollen into your house.

If your symptoms are year-round and seem to be related to dust:

- Keep the bedroom as dust-free as possible, because most of your time is spent there.

- Avoid carpeting, upholstered furniture, and heavy draperies that collect dust. Vacuuming doesn't pick up dust mites.

- Cover your mattress and box spring with dust-proof cases and wipe them clean weekly. Avoid wool or down blankets and feather pillows. Wash all bedding weekly in hot water.

- Consider using an air conditioner or air purifier with a special HEPA filter. Rent one before buying, to see if it helps.

If your symptoms are year-round and worse during damp weather, they may be related to mold or mildew:

- Keep the house well-ventilated and dry. Keep the humidity below 50 percent. Use a dehumidifier during humid weather.

- Use an air conditioner, which removes mold spores from the air. Change or clean heating and cooling system filters regularly.

- Clean bathroom and kitchen surfaces often with bleach to reduce mold growth.

If you are allergic to a pet:

- Keep the animal outside, or at least out of the bedroom.

- If your symptoms are severe, the best solution may be to find a new home for the pet.

General information on avoiding irritants:

- Avoid yardwork (raking, mowing), which stirs up both pollen and mold. If you must do it, wear a mask and take an antihistamine beforehand.

- Avoid smoking and inhaling other people's smoke.

What About Immunotherapy?

Immunotherapy involves a series of shots given to desensitize your body to an allergen. It requires regular treatments lasting up to three to five years. Because of the time and expense involved, you need a realistic idea of the benefits before agreeing to the treatment.

Immunotherapy is effective only if the specific allergen has been identified by sensitivity testing. It is 98 percent effective for allergies to bee stings and other insect venoms. For most people, it is effective against grass, tree, and weed pollens, as well as house dust, the house dust mite, and dog and cat dander.

The following factors make it more likely that immunotherapy will be worthwhile for you:

1. Your symptoms have bothered you a lot for at least two years.

2. You have tried home treatment without success.

3. You have tried both prescription and nonprescription medications without relief.

4. Immunotherapy is effective for the allergens identified by your skin tests.

- Eliminate aerosol sprays, perfumes, room deodorizers, cleaning products, and other substances that may add to the problem.

- Antihistamines and decongestants may relieve some allergy symptoms. Use caution when taking these drugs. See pages 313 and 315.

- For more information on allergies, including immunotherapy, ask your health care professional, or call LungLine, a service of the National Jewish Center for Immunology and Respiratory Medicine at 1-800-222-LUNG (5864).

When to Call Kaiser Permanente

- Call 911 or seek emergency services if signs of a severe allergic reaction develop, especially soon after taking a drug, eating a certain food, or being stung by an insect:

  ° Wheezing or difficulty breathing

  ° Swelling around the lips, tongue, or face, or significant swelling around the site of the insect sting (e.g., entire arm or leg is swollen)

  ° Rapidly spreading skin rash or hives

- If symptoms worsen over time, and your home treatment doesn't help. Your doctor can recommend stronger medication or desensitizing shots. Allergy shots may help reduce sensitivity to some allergens. See page 126.

Asthma

Asthma is the Greek word for panting. A person having an asthma flare-up is literally panting for breath. Asthma is a condition that causes inflammation and obstruction of the airways. The muscles surrounding the air tubes (bronchial tubes) of the lungs go into spasm, the mucous lining swells, and secretions build up, making breathing quite difficult.

Asthma usually occurs in flare-ups or episodes. During a flare-up, the person may make a wheezing or whistling sound while breathing, cough a great deal, or spit up mucus. A chronic dry cough may be the only symptom of mild asthma.

Many things can trigger asthma, including allergens, such as dust, pollen, mold, and animal dander. In general, infections are the most common triggers of asthma. Other triggers include exercise, cold air, cigarette or wood smoke, changes in weather, colds or the flu, chemical vapors from household or workplace products, analgesics (especially aspirin), food preservatives and dyes, and emotional stress.

Asthma usually develops in childhood but may also begin later in life. The first episode often follows a cold or the flu. It is more common in children who are exposed to cigarette smoke in the home. Many children outgrow asthma as they get older but will still be at risk for it in adulthood.

Most children and adults can control their asthma by avoiding triggers that cause flare-ups and using medications to manage symptoms. Severe flare-ups can usually be treated with inhaled or injected medications. Asthma flare-ups are rarely fatal if they are treated promptly and appropriately.

Prevention

Discover and avoid the things that cause your asthma flare-ups:

- Review the home treatment for allergies on pages 125 to 127.

- Avoid smoke of all kinds. Stop smoking and avoid secondhand smoke. Eat, work, travel, and relax in smoke-free areas. Stay away from wood-burning stoves.

- Avoid air pollution. Stay indoors when the air pollution is high.

- Avoid strong odors, fumes, and perfume.

- Avoid breathing cold air. In cold weather, breathe through your nose and cover your nose and mouth with a scarf or cold weather mask (available at most drug stores).

- Avoid indoor pets with fur or feathers. Outdoor pets or pets such as fish or turtles may cause less trouble.

- Reduce your risk of colds and flu by washing your hands often and getting a flu shot each year.

Build up the strength of your lungs and airways:

- Get regular exercise. Swimming or water aerobics may be good choices because the moist air is less likely to trigger a flare-up. If vigorous exercise triggers asthma flare-ups, talk with your doctor. Adjusting your medication and your exercise routine may help.

- Practice belly breathing as described on page 272.

Home Treatment

- Learn to use a peak flow meter to monitor your ability to exhale. Used regularly, this device measures your progress as you improve your ability to breathe. It can also provide an early warning that a flare-up may be coming on, so you can take appropriate steps.

- Ask your doctor or health care professional for a written care plan to guide you in adding medication as needed.

- If your child has an asthma flare-up, remain calm. Give the recommended medication and help the child relax. Make sure your child and his or her teachers or child care providers know what to do in case of a flare-up.

- Learn to use a metered-dose inhaler. Inhalers help get the right amount of medication to the airways. However, it takes some skill to use the inhaler correctly. A device called a spacer is now recommended for use with an inhaler (see page 129). Ask your doctor to watch you use your inhaler and spacer to make sure you are doing it right.

- Ask your doctor about anti-inflammatory inhalers.

- Increase your fluid intake to help thin bronchial mucus.

- Anti-inflammatory medications, such as aspirin, naproxen sodium, and ibuprofen, can cause severe reactions in some people with asthma. Use them with caution and discuss them with your doctor. If you find that these medications bother you, avoid using them.

- Do not use over-the-counter cold and cough medicines unless your doctor tells you to do so.

- Practice the relaxation exercises on pages 272 to 274.

- Follow the prevention tips on page 128.

- Work in partnership with your doctor to maximize your control over your asthma.

- To get information on managing asthma, ask your health care professional or contact the National Asthma Center at 1-800-222-5864, or your local chapter of the American Lung Association.

When to Call Kaiser Permanente

- If acute asthma symptoms have occurred for the first time.

- If asthma symptoms fail to respond to your usual treatment, or if the flare-up is severe (i.e., peak flow is less than 50 percent of best).

How to Use an Inhaler and Spacer

1. Shake the inhaler well for five seconds. Remove the protective cap and insert the mouthpiece of the inhaler into one end of the spacer. Hold the inhaler with your index finger on top and your thumb supporting the bottom.

2. Breathe out as much as possible to empty the lungs. Tilt your head back, place the mouthpiece of the spacer tube in your mouth, and close your lips around it.

3. Press down on the top of the inhaler to release a puff of medication. Breathe in slowly and deeply, filling your lungs with as much air as possible. If you hear a musical sound, you are inhaling too fast. Hold your breath for at least 10 seconds; then breathe out.

4. With your lips still closed around the mouthpiece, take two or three more deep breaths, holding each one for 10 seconds. For maximum effectiveness, wait a minute or two before taking the next puff.

5. Wash the inhaler mouthpiece, spacer, and protective caps weekly with mild soapy water and allow to air dry.

- If sputum becomes discolored, particularly green, yellow, or bloody. This may be a sign of a bacterial infection (see below).

- If a person with asthma or other family members have not been educated about treatment, or if the medication required is not available.

- To learn exactly what to do when a flare-up begins. With proper training, medication, and confidence, you can often handle acute episodes without professional help.

- If you begin to use your asthma medication more often than usual, which may be a sign that your asthma is getting worse.

- To discuss allergy shots, which are sometimes helpful in preventing asthma flare-ups. See page 126.

- To get a referral to a support group. Talking with others who have asthma can give you information and confidence in dealing with prevention and treatment.

Bacterial Infections

Respiratory infections caused by bacteria are often hard to distinguish from those caused by viruses. In particular, a bad case of the flu may be hard to distinguish from a bacterial infection. Bacteria will sometimes attack the weakened system of a person with a cold or the flu. Because of this, bacterial infections sometimes follow viral infections.

Bacterial or Viral?

Bacterial Infections

- May follow a viral infection that does not improve.

- Usually localized at a single point in the body: sinuses, ear, lungs.

- Typical bacterial infections: strep throat, ear infection.

- Antibiotics do help.

Viral Infections

- Usually involve different parts of the body: sore throat, runny nose, headaches, muscle aches. In the abdominal area, viruses cause nausea and/or diarrhea.

- Typical viral infections: cold, flu, stomach flu.

- Antibiotics do not help.

The most common bacterial infections are ear infections and strep throat. Bronchitis, sinusitis, and pneumonia may also be caused by bacteria.

Symptoms of a bacterial infection may include:

- Fever of 104° or higher that does not reduce with two hours of home treatment.

- Fever over 101° with shaking chills and productive cough.

- Persistent fever. Many viral illnesses cause fevers of 102° or higher for short periods of time (up to 12 to 24 hours). Call a doctor if the fever stays high:

  ° 102° or higher for two full days

  ° 101° or higher for three full days

  ° 100° or higher for four full days

- If you think you may have the flu, see page 140.

- Labored, shallow, rapid breathing with shortness of breath.

- Sputum (mucus coughed up from lungs) that is yellow, green, rust-colored, or bloody, and other symptoms (fever, productive cough, severe fatigue) that are worsening. Sputum that is coughed up from the lungs is more significant than mucus that has drained down the back of the throat (postnasal drip).

- Nasal discharge that changes from clear to colored (yellow or green) after five to seven days of a cold, and other symptoms (such as sinus pain or fever) that are worsening. If nasal discharge is colored from the start of a cold, call if it lasts longer than 7 to 10 days.

- Cough that lingers more than 7 to 10 days after other symptoms have cleared, especially if it is productive (bringing up sputum). A dry, hacking cough may last several weeks after a viral illness such as a cold.

- Ear pain that lasts more than 24 hours, or severe ear pain that lasts longer than one hour. If the pain is severe at night, call the next morning even if the pain has stopped. See page 159.

- Localized sinus pain that persists despite two to four days of home treatment, especially if nasal discharge is colored rather than clear. See Sinusitis, page 143.

- Sore throat that lasts longer than two to three days despite home treatment and does not "act" like a cold. See page 145.

Antibiotics are effective against bacterial infections only after the infection has developed, so most doctors will not prescribe them until a bacterial infection is confirmed. However, antibiotics are sometimes used to prevent recurrent sinus and ear infections. They cannot prevent complications of a viral infection. For important information about antibiotics, see page 319.

When to Call Kaiser Permanente

Call if symptoms of a bacterial infection develop. Bacterial infections need to be diagnosed and treated by a doctor.

Bronchitis

Bronchitis is an inflammation and irritation of the bronchial tubes in the lungs. It is caused most often by viruses or bacteria but may also be caused by cigarette smoke or air pollution. It often occurs after a cold or an upper respiratory infection that does not heal completely.

The inflamed bronchial tubes secrete a sticky mucus (called sputum), which is difficult for the hairs (cilia) on the bronchi to clear out of the lungs. The productive cough that comes with bronchitis is the body's attempt to get rid of the mucus. Other symptoms include discomfort or tightness in the chest, fatigue, low fever, sore throat, runny nose, and sometimes wheezing. Severe cases may lead to pneumonia.

Bronchitis can become chronic, especially among people who smoke or who work in polluted air. Seventy-five percent of people with chronic bronchitis have a history of heavy smoking.

Chronic bronchitis may occur with emphysema or chronic asthma. Any combination of these conditions is known as chronic obstructive pulmonary disease (COPD).

Prevention

• Give proper home care to minor respiratory problems such as colds and flu. See pages 135 and 140.

• Stop smoking. People who smoke and those who live with them have more frequent bouts of bronchitis.

• Avoid polluted air.

Home Treatment

Self-care for bronchitis focuses on getting rid of the mucus in your lungs. Here is what you can do at home to speed healing.

• Increase your fluid intake to as much as 8 to 12 glasses per day (until you are urinating more than usual). Liquids help thin the mucus in the lungs so your cough can clear it out.

• Stop smoking and avoid others' smoke. Smoke irritates the lungs and slows healing.

• Breathe moist air from a humidifier, hot shower, or a sink filled with hot water. The heat and moisture will thin mucus and help the cough bring it up.

• Get some extra rest. Let your energy go to healing.

• Have someone massage your chest and back muscles. The massage helps sore chest muscles and helps you relax.

• Take aspirin, ibuprofen, or acetaminophen to relieve fever and body aches. Do not give aspirin to children and teens younger than 20.

• If a dry, nonproductive cough keeps you awake, take a cough syrup containing dextromethorphan and guaifenesin. Avoid products containing more than one active ingredient. See page 315.

When to Call Kaiser Permanente

If the following signs of a bacterial infection develop:

• Fever of 104° or higher that does not reduce with two hours of home treatment.

• Fever over 101° with shaking chills and productive cough.

• Persistent fever. Many viral illnesses cause fevers of 102° or higher for short periods of time (up to 12 to 24 hours). Call a doctor if the fever stays high:

° 102° or higher for two full days

° 101° or higher for three full days

° 100° or higher for four full days

• If you think you may have the flu, see page 140.

• Labored, shallow, rapid breathing with shortness of breath.

• Sputum (mucus coughed up from lungs) is yellow, green, rust-colored, or bloody, and other symptoms (fever, productive cough, severe fatigue) are worsening. Sputum that is coughed up from the lungs is more significant than mucus that has drained down the back of the throat (postnasal drip).

• Cough that lingers more than 7 to 10 days after other symptoms have cleared, especially if it is productive (bringing up sputum). A dry, hacking cough may last several weeks after a viral illness such as a cold.

• If the sick person is an infant, an older adult, or is chronically ill, especially with lung problems.

Chest Pain

CALL 911 OR OTHER EMERGENCY SERVICES IMMEDIATELY if chest pain is crushing or squeezing, increases in intensity, or occurs with any of the symptoms of a heart attack:

• **Sweating**

• **Shortness of breath**

• **Pain radiating to the arm, neck, or jaw**

• **Nausea or vomiting**

• **Dizziness**

• **Rapid and/or irregular pulse**

After calling for emergency medical help, see CPR on page 56, if necessary.

 Chest pain is a key warning sign of a heart attack, but it may also be caused by other problems.

Pain that increases when you press on the site is probably chest-wall pain, which may be caused by strained muscles or ligaments in the chest wall. A shooting pain that lasts a few seconds, or a quick pain at the end of a deep breath, is usually not a cause for concern. Hyperventilation (see page 47) can also cause chest pain.

Chest pain can be associated with other disorders. With pleurisy or pneumonia (see page 142), the pain will get worse with a deep breath or cough. An ulcer (see page 83) can cause chest pain that is worse on an empty stomach. Gallbladder pain may worsen after a meal or in the middle of the night. Heartburn or indigestion can also cause chest pain. See page 74.

Angina is pain, pressure, heaviness, or numbness behind the breastbone or across the chest. It is caused by poor circulation to the heart muscle due to arteriosclerosis (hardening of the arteries) in the arteries that supply blood to the heart. It is a symptom of coronary artery disease. The symptoms of angina may radiate to the neck, jaws, shoulders, arms, or back. Angina may be brought on by exertion or stress and is usually relieved by rest and use of prescribed medication.

A **heart attack** (myocardial infarction) is caused by blocked blood flow to the heart muscle. The pain of a heart attack is usually more severe than angina, lasts longer, and does not go away with rest or with medicine that was previously effective for angina. It may be accompanied by other symptoms such as sweating, nausea, shortness of breath, weakness, or indigestion. However, the symptoms of a heart attack are varied and may be considerably milder.

Lifestyle and other factors that may increase your risk of a heart attack include:

- Smoking
- High blood pressure
- High cholesterol
- Inactive lifestyle
- Family history of early heart disease
- High stress levels
- Diabetes

Ask your health care professional for more information about these risk factors.

Home Treatment

For chest-wall pain caused by strained muscles or ligaments:

- Use pain relievers such as aspirin, ibuprofen, or acetaminophen.
- Ben-Gay or Vicks VapoRub may soothe sore muscles.
- Avoid the activity that strains the chest area.

When to Call Kaiser Permanente

- **CALL 911 OR OTHER EMERGENCY SERVICES IMMEDIATELY IF SYMPTOMS OF A HEART ATTACK ARE PRESENT (see page 133).**

- If your chest pain has been diagnosed by a doctor and he or she has prescribed a home treatment plan, follow it. Call 911 or emergency services if the pain worsens or if you develop any of the heart attack symptoms on page 133.

• If you suspect angina and your symptoms have not been diagnosed.

• If symptoms of angina do not respond to your prescribed treatment, or if the pattern of your angina changes.

Call a health professional if minor chest pain occurs without the symptoms of a heart attack and any of the following apply:

• If the person has a history of heart disease or blood clots in the lungs.

• If chest pain is constant, nagging, and not relieved by rest.

• If chest pain occurs with symptoms of pneumonia. See page 142.

• If any chest pain lasts 48 hours without improvement.

Colds

 The common cold is caused by any one of 200 viruses. The symptoms of a cold are a runny nose, red eyes, sneezing, sore throat, dry cough, headache, and general body aches. There is a gradual one- or two-day onset. As a cold progresses, the nasal mucus may thicken. This is the stage just before a cold dries up. A cold may last up to two weeks.

Colds occur throughout the year but are most common in late winter and early spring. The average child has six colds a year; adults have fewer.

Using a mouthwash will not prevent a cold, and antibiotics will not cure one. There is no cure for the common cold. If you catch a cold, treat the symptoms.

Sometimes a cold will lead to a bacterial infection (see page 130) such as bronchitis or pneumonia. Good home treatment of colds can help prevent complications.

If someone seems to have a cold all the time, or if cold symptoms last two weeks or more, suspect allergies (see page 123) or sinusitis (see page 143).

Prevention

• Eat well and get plenty of sleep and exercise to keep up your resistance.

• Keep your hands away from your nose, eyes, and mouth, but cover your mouth when you cough or sneeze.

• Wash your hands often, particularly when you are around people who have colds.

• Stop smoking.

• Consider breast-feeding your baby. Breast-fed babies seem to have fewer, milder colds.

Home Treatment

Home treatment for a cold will help relieve symptoms and prevent complications.

• Get extra rest after work or school. Slow down just a little from your usual routine. It isn't necessary to stay home in bed, but take care not to expose others.

- Drink plenty of liquids. Hot water, herbal tea, or chicken soup may help relieve congestion.

- Take aspirin, ibuprofen, or acetaminophen to relieve aches. Do not give aspirin to children and teens under age 20.

- Humidify the bedroom and take hot showers to relieve nasal stuffiness.

- Watch the back of your throat for postnasal drip. If streaks of mucus appear, gargle to prevent a sore throat.

- Use disposable tissues, not handkerchiefs, to reduce spreading the virus to others.

- If your nose is red and raw from rubbing with tissues, put a bit of petroleum jelly on the sore area.

- Avoid cold remedies that combine drugs such as decongestants, antihistamines, and pain relievers to treat many different symptoms. Treat each symptom separately. Take a decongestant for stuffiness, a cough medicine for a cough. See Home Treatment for coughs on page 138.

- Avoid antihistamines. They are not an effective treatment for colds.

- Use a mucus-thinning agent to improve mucus drainage.

- Use nasal decongestant sprays for only three days or less. Continued use may lead to a "rebound" effect, when the mucous membranes swell up more than before using the spray. See page 314 for nose drops you can make at home.

When to Call Kaiser Permanente

If the following signs of a bacterial infection develop:

- Fever of 104° or higher that does not reduce with two hours of home treatment.

- Fever over 101° with shaking chills and productive cough.

- Persistent fever. Many viral illnesses, especially the flu, cause fevers of 102° or higher for short periods of time (up to 12 to 24 hours). Call a doctor if the fever stays high:

  ° 102° or higher for two full days

  ° 101° or higher for three full days

  ° 100° or higher for four full days

- If you think you may have the flu, see page 140.

- Labored, shallow, rapid breathing with shortness of breath.

- Sputum (mucus coughed up from lungs) is yellow, green, rust-colored, or bloody, and other symptoms (fever, productive cough, severe fatigue) are worsening. Sputum that is coughed up from the lungs is more significant than mucus that has drained down the back of the throat (postnasal drip).

- If facial pain, fever, and other signs of sinusitis develop. See page 143.

• Nasal discharge changes from clear to colored (yellow or green) after five to seven days of a cold, and other symptoms (such as sinus pain or fever) are worsening. If nasal discharge is colored from the start of a cold, call if it lasts longer than 7 to 10 days.

• Cough that lingers more than 7 to 10 days after other symptoms have cleared, especially if it is productive (bringing up sputum). A dry, hacking cough may last several weeks after a viral illness such as a cold.

Coughs

Coughing is the body's way of removing foreign material or mucus from the lungs. Coughs have distinctive traits that you can learn to recognize.

Productive coughs produce phlegm or mucus (sputum) that comes up from the lungs. This kind of cough generally should not be suppressed; it is needed to clear mucus from the lungs.

Nonproductive coughs are dry coughs that do not produce sputum. A dry, hacking cough may develop toward the end of a cold or after exposure to an irritant, such as dust

Description and Treatment of Coughs

Type of Cough	Possible Causes
Loud cough like a seal's bark	See Croup, p. 208.
Dry cough in the morning that gets better as day goes on	Dry air; cigarette smoking. Increase fluids. Humidify the bedroom. Stop smoking. See Coughs, above.
Hacking, dry, nonproductive cough; may be worse at night	Common for several weeks following a viral illness. May be due to postnasal drip, smoking, or mild asthma. Increase fluids. Try a decongestant. Stop smoking. See Coughs, above; Asthma, p. 127.
Productive cough following a cold or flu	See Bronchitis, p. 132; Pneumonia, p. 142; Sinusitis, p. 143.
Dry, sudden-onset cough after a choking episode, most often in an infant or toddler	Foreign object in the throat. See Choking, p. 37.

or smoke. Dry coughs that follow viral illnesses may last up to several weeks and often get worse at night.

A chronic dry cough may be a sign of mild asthma. See page 127.

Prevention

• Don't smoke. A dry, hacking "smoker's cough" means your lungs are constantly irritated.

• Increase fluid intake to as much as 8 to 10 glasses of water every day. You are drinking enough if you are urinating more often than usual.

• Cover your mouth when you cough to avoid spreading infection.

Home Treatment

• Drink lots of water. Water helps loosen phlegm and soothe an irritated throat. Dry, hacking coughs respond to honey in hot water, tea, or lemon juice. (Do not give honey to children under one year of age.)

• Cough drops can soothe irritated throats, but most have no effect on the cough-producing mechanism. Expensive medicine-flavored cough drops are not any better than inexpensive candy-flavored ones or hard candy.

• Elevate your head with extra pillows at night to ease a dry cough.

• Use an over-the-counter cough suppressant containing dextromethorphan to help quiet a dry, hacking cough so you can sleep. If you have a productive cough,

don't suppress it so much that you are no longer bringing up mucus. See Cough Preparations on page 314.

• For coughs caused by inhaled irritants (smoke, dust, or other pollutants), avoid exposure or wear a face mask.

When to Call Kaiser Permanente

If the following signs of a bacterial infection develop:

• Fever of 104° or higher that does not reduce with two hours of home treatment.

• Fever over 101° with shaking chills and productive cough.

• Persistent fever. Many viral illnesses, especially the flu, cause fevers of 102° or higher for short periods of time (up to 12 to 24 hours). Call a doctor if the fever stays high:

° 102° or higher for two full days

° 101° or higher for three full days

° 100° or higher for four full days

• If you think you may have the flu, see page 140.

• Labored, shallow, rapid breathing with shortness of breath.

• Sputum (mucus coughed up from lungs) is yellow, green, rust-colored, or bloody, and other symptoms (fever, productive cough, fatigue) are worsening. Sputum that is coughed up from the lungs is more significant than mucus that has drained down the back of the throat (postnasal drip).

• Cough that lingers more than 7 to 10 days after other symptoms have cleared, especially if it is productive (bringing up sputum). A dry, hacking cough may last several weeks after a viral illness such as a cold.

• If any cough lasts more than four weeks.

Fever

A fever is an abnormally high body temperature. It is a symptom, not a disease. A fever is one way your body fights illness. A temperature of up to 102° is generally beneficial, though it may be uncomfortable. Most healthy adults can tolerate a fever as high as 103° to 104° for short periods of time without problems.

For specific fever guidelines for children under age four, see page 212.

Home Treatment

• Drink more liquids, especially water.

• Take and record your temperature every two hours and whenever symptoms change.

• For fevers that cause discomfort, sponge with lukewarm water and take acetaminophen, aspirin, or ibuprofen to lower fever. Do not give aspirin to children or teens under age 20.

• Watch for signs of dehydration. See page 72.

When to Call Kaiser Permanente

• Fever over 104° does not go down after two hours of home treatment.

• Persistent fever. Many viral illnesses, especially the flu, cause fevers of 102° or higher for short periods of time (up to 12 to 24 hours). Call a doctor if the fever stays high:

° 102° or higher for two full days

° 101° or higher for three full days

° 100° or higher for four full days

• If you think you may have the flu, see page 140.

• Fever over 103° with dry skin, even under the armpits (possible heat stroke, see page 46).

• If fever occurs with other signs of a bacterial infection. See page 130.

• If fever occurs with the following symptoms:

° Very stiff neck and headache. See "Encephalitis and Meningitis" on page 141.

° Shortness of breath and cough. See Bronchitis on page 132 and Pneumonia on page 142.

° Pain over eyes or cheekbone. See Sinusitis on page 143.

° Painful or burning urination. See Urinary Tract Infections on page 243.

° Abdominal pain, nausea, and vomiting. See Stomach Flu and Food Poisoning on page 81, or Appendicitis on page 69.

• If fever is associated with disturbing or unexplained symptoms.

Influenza (Flu)

 Influenza, or flu, is a viral illness that commonly occurs in the winter and affects many people at once (epidemic). (The name "influenza" comes from the Italian word for "influence.")

Influenza has symptoms similar to a cold, but they are usually more severe and come on quite suddenly.

The flu is commonly thought of as a respiratory illness, but the whole body can be affected. Symptoms include fever (101° to 104°), chills, muscle aches, headache, pain in the muscles around the eyes, fatigue and weakness, sneezing, and runny nose. Symptoms may last five to seven days. Most other viruses, such as colds, have milder symptoms that don't last as long.

Although a person with the flu feels very sick, the illness seldom leads to more serious complications. It is usually dangerous only for infants, older adults, and people with chronic diseases.

Prevention

• Get a flu shot each autumn if you are over 65, if you have a chronic illness, such as asthma, heart disease, or diabetes, or if you are a health care worker who might expose others to the disease.

• Keep up your resistance to infection with a good diet, plenty of rest, and regular exercise.

• Avoid exposure to the virus. Wash your hands often and keep your hands away from your nose, eyes, and mouth.

Home Treatment

• Get plenty of rest.

• Drink extra fluids, at least one glass of water or juice every waking hour.

• Take acetaminophen, aspirin, or ibuprofen to relieve fever, headache, and muscle aches. (Do not give aspirin to children and teens under age 20.)

When to Call Kaiser Permanente

It is common for adults with influenza to have high fevers (up to 103°) for three to four days. When trying to decide if you need to see a doctor, consider the likelihood that you have the flu versus a possible bacterial infection. If it is the flu season, and many people in your community have similar symptoms, it is likely that you have the flu. However, if you have any concerns or any of the following signs of a

Encephalitis and Meningitis

Encephalitis is an inflammation of the brain that may occur following a viral infection, such as chicken-pox, flu, measles, mumps, or cold sores (herpes simplex). A serious type of encephalitis is spread by mosquitoes in the eastern and southeastern U.S.

Meningitis is a viral or bacterial illness that causes inflammation around the tissues surrounding the brain and spinal cord. It may follow an infection, such as an ear or sinus infection, or a viral illness.

Encephalitis and meningitis are serious illnesses with similar symptoms. Call a health professional *immediately* if the following symptoms develop, especially following a viral illness or a mosquito bite:

- Severe headache with stiff neck, fever, nausea, and vomiting

- Drowsiness, lethargy, confusion, or delirium

- Bulging soft spot on an infant's head (when the baby is not crying)

bacterial infection, contact your doctor.

- Fever of 104° or higher that does not reduce with two hours of home treatment.

- Fever over 101° with shaking chills and productive cough.

- Persistent fever. Flu may cause fevers of 102° or higher for three to four days. However, unless you are sure you have flu, it may be wise to call your doctor if a fever stays high:

  ° 102° or higher for two full days

  ° 101° or higher for three full days

  ° 100° or higher for four full days

- Labored, shallow, rapid breathing with shortness of breath.

- Sputum (mucus coughed up from lungs) is yellow, green, rust-colored, or bloody, and other symptoms (fever, productive cough, severe fatigue) are worsening. Sputum that is coughed up from the lungs is more significant than mucus that has drained down the back of the throat (postnasal drip).

- Cough that lingers more than 7 to 10 days after other symptoms have cleared, especially if it is productive (bringing up sputum). A dry, hacking cough may last several weeks after a viral illness such as a cold.

- If facial pain, fever, and other signs of sinusitis develop. See page 143.

- If the person seems to get better, then gets worse again.

- If a red rash or flu-like symptoms occur four days to three weeks after a tick bite. See page 64.

Laryngitis

Laryngitis is an infection or irritation of the voice box (larynx). The most common cause is a viral infection or a cold. It can also be caused by allergy; excessive talking, singing, or yelling; cigarette smoke; or reflux of acid from the stomach into the throat. Heavy drinking or smoking can lead to chronic laryngitis.

Symptoms include hoarseness or loss of voice, the urge to clear your throat, fever, tiredness, pain in the throat, and coughing.

Prevention

To prevent hoarseness, stop shouting as soon as you feel minor pain. Give your vocal cords a rest.

Home Treatment

- Laryngitis will usually heal in 5 to 10 days. Medication does little to speed recovery.

- If hoarseness is caused by a cold, treat the cold (see page 135). Hoarseness may last up to a week after a cold.

- Rest your voice by not shouting and by talking as little as possible. Do not whisper, and avoid clearing your throat.

- Stop smoking and avoid other people's smoke.

- Humidify the air with a humidifier, or take a hot shower.

- Drink lots of liquids.

- To soothe the throat, gargle with warm salt water (one teaspoon in eight ounces of water) or drink honey in hot water, lemon juice, or weak tea.

- If you suspect stomach acid problems may be contributing to your laryngitis, refer to the remedies for heartburn on page 75.

When to Call Kaiser Permanente

- If signs of a bacterial infection develop. See page 130.

- If hoarseness persists for three to four weeks.

Pneumonia

Pneumonia is an infection or inflammation of the smallest air passages in the lungs (alveoli). These passages fill up with pus or mucus, preventing oxygen from reaching the blood. Pneumonia can be caused by a variety of bacteria or viruses.

Pneumonia may follow or accompany a cold, flu, or bronchitis. Someone who has bacterial pneumonia is usually very sick, and symptoms may include:

- Fever (101° to 106°) and shaking chills

- Productive cough with yellow, green, rust-colored, or bloody sputum (mucus coughed up from lungs)

- Pain in the chest wall, especially when coughing or taking a deep breath

- Labored, shallow, or rapid breathing
- Fatigue that is worse than you would expect from a cold
- Sweating and flushed appearance
- Loss of appetite or upset stomach

Prevention

- Keep up your resistance to infection with a good diet, plenty of rest, and regular exercise.
- Take care of minor illnesses. Don't try to "tough them out." See home treatment for colds on page 135 and flu on page 140.
- Avoid smoke and other irritants.
- If you are over 65, or if you have a chronic lung disease (except asthma), get a pneumococcal vaccination. See page 20.

Home Treatment

Call a health professional if you suspect pneumonia. If pneumonia is diagnosed, follow the home treatment below.

- Increase your fluid intake to 8 to 12 glasses of water a day (until you are urinating more than usual). Extra fluids help thin the mucus.
- Get lots of rest. Don't try to rush recovery.
- Take the entire course of all prescribed medications.
- Stop smoking.

When to Call Kaiser Permanente

- If you suspect pneumonia.
- If there is rapid or labored breathing during any respiratory illness.

Sinusitis

Sinusitis is an inflammation or infection of the sinuses. The sinuses are cavities, or hollow spaces, in the head that are lined with mucous membranes. The sinuses usually drain easily unless there is an inflammation or infection. Sinusitis may follow a cold and is often associated with hay fever, asthma, or any air pollution that causes inflammation. It can occur in infants and children but is more common in adults.

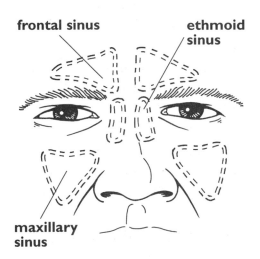

Sinusitis can cause pain in the cheekbones, in the forehead, or around the eyes.

The key symptom of acute sinusitis in adults is pain in the cheekbones and upper teeth, in the forehead over the eyebrows, or around and behind the eye. In children, a chronic stuffy nose is a common symptom. There may also be headache, fever (if the sinuses are infected), or mucus running down the back of the throat (postnasal drip). Sore throat and cough are common in both acute and chronic sinusitis. Sinus headaches may occur on rising and get worse in the afternoon or when bending over.

If there is a bacterial infection, antibiotics may be needed.

Prevention

• Treat colds promptly. Blow your nose gently. Do not close one nostril when blowing your nose.

• Drink plenty of extra fluids when you have a cold, to help keep mucus thin and draining.

• Stop smoking. Smokers are more prone to sinusitis.

Home Treatment

Some nasal stuffiness and facial pressure are common with a cold. Home treatment will often get your sinuses draining normally again.

• Drink extra fluids to keep mucus thin. Drink a glass of water or juice every waking hour.

• Breathe moist air from a humidifier, hot shower, or sink filled with hot water.

• Increase home humidity, especially in the bedrooms.

• Take an oral decongestant, use a decongestant nasal spray, or use a mucus-thinning agent (see page 314). Do not use a nasal spray for more than three days. Avoid products containing antihistamines.

• Take aspirin, acetaminophen, or ibuprofen for headache.

• Check the back of your throat for postnasal drip. If streaks of mucus appear, gargle with warm water to prevent a sore throat.

• Elevate your head at night.

• Salt water (saline) irrigation helps wash mucus and bacteria out of the nasal passages. Use an over-the-counter saline nasal spray or a homemade solution (see page 314):

  ° Use a bulb syringe and gently squirt the solution into the nose, or snuff the solution from the palm of your hand one nostril at a time.

  ° Blow the nose gently afterward. Repeat two to four times a day.

When to Call Kaiser Permanente

• If cold symptoms last longer than 10 to 14 days or worsen over time.

• If there is a severe headache, different from a "normal" headache, that is not relieved by acetaminophen, aspirin, or ibuprofen.

- If there is increased facial swelling, or blurring or changes in vision.

- If nasal discharge changes from clear to colored (yellow or green) after five to seven days of a cold, and other symptoms (such as sinus pain or fever) are worsening. If nasal discharge is colored from the start of a cold, call if it lasts longer than 7 to 10 days.

- If facial pain, especially in one sinus area or along the ridge between the nose and lower eyelid, persists after two to four days of home treatment. If you also have a fever and colored nasal discharge, call in one to two days.

- If sinusitis symptoms persist after you have taken a full course of antibiotics.

Sore Throat and Strep Throat

Most sore throats are caused by viruses and sometimes accompany a cold. A mild sore throat is often due to low humidity, smoking, air pollution, or perhaps yelling. People who have allergies or stuffy noses may breathe through their mouths while sleeping, causing a mild sore throat.

Another common cause of sore throat is stomach acid that refluxes into the throat. Although reflux is often associated with heartburn or an "acid" taste in the mouth, sometimes a sore throat is the only symptom.

Strep throat is a sore throat caused by streptococcal bacteria. It is more common in children ages 4 to 11 and is less common in older children and adults. Symptoms of strep throat include sore throat with two of these three:

- Fever of 101° or higher (fever may be lower in adults)

- White or yellow coating on the tonsils

- Swollen, tender glands in the neck

In children, other symptoms may include general body aches, headache, stomachache, nausea, vomiting, runny nose, or listlessness. Strep throat is treated with antibiotics to prevent rheumatic fever. Antibiotics are effective in preventing rheumatic fever if started within nine days of the sore throat.

If a sore throat is accompanied by runny or stuffy nose and cough, it is probably due to a virus, and antibiotics will not help.

Another cause of persistent sore throat is **mononucleosis** (mono or "the kissing disease"), a viral infection. It is most common in older teens and young adults. In addition to a severe sore throat and fatigue, mono symptoms often include weakness, aches, dizziness, swollen lymph nodes in the neck, and an enlarged spleen. It is diagnosed by a blood test for the Epstein-Barr virus.

Mono may last for several weeks and is usually not severe. Symptoms can recur for several months, and it is normal for the lymph nodes to remain enlarged for up to a month. There is no specific treatment except rest, plenty of fluids, and aspirin or acetaminophen for body aches.

Prevention

- Increase your fluid intake to as much as 8 to 12 glasses of water a day (until you are urinating more often than usual).

- Identify and avoid irritants that cause sore throat (smoke, fumes, yelling, etc.). Don't smoke.

- Avoid contact with people who have strep throat.

- If you have mono, don't share eating or drinking utensils and avoid kissing, to keep from spreading the virus.

Home Treatment

Home care is usually all that is needed for viral sore throats. If you are taking antibiotics for strep throat, these tips will also help you feel better.

- Gargle with warm salt water (one teaspoon of salt in eight ounces of water). The salt reduces swelling and discomfort.

- If you have postnasal drip, gargle frequently to prevent more throat irritation.

- Drink more fluids to soothe a sore throat. Honey and lemon in weak tea may help.

- Stop smoking and avoid others' smoke.

- Acetaminophen, aspirin, or ibuprofen will relieve pain and reduce fever. Do not give aspirin to children and teens under age 20.

- Some over-the-counter throat lozenges have a local anesthetic to deaden pain. Dyclonine hydrochloride (Sucrets Maximum Strength) and benzocaine (Spec-T and Tyrobenz) are safe and effective. Regular cough drops or hard candy may also help.

- If you suspect problems with stomach acid may be contributing to your sore throat, refer to the remedies for heartburn on page 75.

When to Call Kaiser Permanente

- If the following symptoms develop:
  - Excessive drooling in a small child (more than the usual amount)
  - Difficulty swallowing
  - Labored or difficult breathing

- If sore throat develops after exposure to strep throat.

- If a sore throat occurs with two of these three symptoms of strep throat:

  ° Fever of 101° or higher (may be lower in adults)

  ° White or yellow coating on the tonsils

  ° Swollen, tender glands in the neck

- If a rash occurs with sore throat. Scarlet fever is a rash that may occur when there is a strep throat infection. Like strep throat, scarlet fever is treated with antibiotics.

- If you cannot trace the cause of a sore throat to a cold, allergy, smoking, overuse of your voice, or other irritation.

- If a mild sore throat lasts longer than two weeks.

Swollen Glands

The lymph nodes are small glands in the body. The most noticeable nodes are those in the neck. The lymph nodes swell as the body fights minor infections from colds, insect bites, or small cuts. More serious infections may cause the glands to greatly enlarge and become very firm and tender.

Swelling in the glands on either side of the neck is common with a cold or sore throat. The lymph nodes in the groin may swell if there is a vaginal or other pelvic infection, or if there is a cut or sore on the leg or foot.

Lymph nodes may remain hard long after the initial infection is gone. This is especially true in children, whose glands may get smaller but remain hard and visible for several weeks.

Home Treatment

- There is no specific home treatment for swollen lymph glands. Continue treating the cold or other infection that is causing the glands to swell.

- If small hardened glands following a child's cold or minor infection are not tender and are not getting larger, you can monitor them at home and report them at the child's next regular doctor visit.

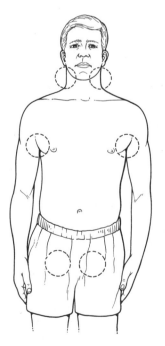

Swollen lymph nodes can occur in the areas shown.

When to Call Kaiser Permanente

- If the glands are large, very firm, red, and very tender.

- If swollen glands are associated with other signs of infection in a nearby cut or sore:

  ° Fever of 100° or higher with no other cause

  ° Swelling and tenderness

  ° Discharge from the cut or sore

  ° Red streaks extending from the area

- If swollen glands continue to get bigger, or appear without apparent cause and persist two weeks or longer.

- If swollen glands appear in areas other than the ones shown on page 147.

Tonsillitis

The tonsils and adenoids are lymph tissues in the throat. They assist in the production of antibodies to fight infections. The tonsils can be seen on either side of the throat at the back of the mouth. The adenoids are higher in the throat and usually cannot be seen.

Inflammation of the tonsils (tonsillitis) or adenoids (adenoiditis) is common in children and may occur separately or together. Symptoms of tonsillitis or adenoiditis are sore throat, fever, and tiredness. It may be painful to swallow, and the tonsils are often bright red, spotted with pus, and swollen. The lymph glands in the neck may also swell. Adenoiditis can also cause headache and vomiting.

If the adenoids are chronically inflamed, the child may breathe through the mouth, snore, and have a nasal or muffled voice. Inflamed adenoids can block the eustachian tubes, contributing to ear infections. See page 159.

Tonsillitis and adenoiditis are sometimes caused by a virus. It is common to have mildly swollen and painful tonsils with a sore throat and other cold symptoms such as runny nose and cough.

A severe sore throat with very swollen tonsils, fever, and swollen glands in the neck can be due to a

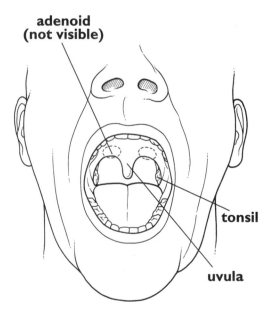

The tonsils and adenoids are at the back of the throat.

Tonsillectomy and Adenoidectomy

It was once common to remove children's tonsils and adenoids. Today, in recognition of the risks, costs, and limited benefits, tonsillectomy and adenoidectomy are done less often, and only when the benefits greatly outweigh the risk, inconvenience, and pain.

Tonsillectomy may be recommended if at least one of the following criteria is met:

• If there have been *at least* four to six severe strep tonsillitis infections in the past year despite treatment with at least two different antibiotics.

• If the enlarged tonsils cause severe breathing difficulty or sleep disturbance.

• If there are deep pockets of infection in the tonsils that haven't responded to drug treatment.

Adenoidectomy may be recommended if at least one of the following criteria is met:

• If the enlarged adenoids are obstructing the airway, causing breathing difficulty and sleep disturbance.

• If the adenoids are believed to cause persistent ear infections despite antibiotic treatment.

If surgery is recommended without meeting one of the above criteria, a second opinion may be advisable.

strep or other bacterial throat infection. See page 145 for signs of strep throat, which needs antibiotic treatment.

Surgical removal of the tonsils (tonsillectomy) or adenoids (adenoidectomy) used to be common operations for children who had frequent sore throats. Now it is thought that this lymph tissue may be helpful in fighting infection and should not be removed unless necessary. These surgeries have some risk and should be done only for valid reasons and after discussion with your doctor.

Home Treatment

Home treatment is usually all that is needed for mildly swollen and painful tonsils with other cold symptoms. See page 135.

When to Call Kaiser Permanente

• If sore throat occurs with two of these three signs, which may indicate a bacterial tonsillitis infection:

  ° Fever of 101° or higher (may be lower in adults)

  ° White or yellow coating on the tonsils or swollen, tender tonsils

  ° Swollen glands in the neck

• If sore throat or tonsillitis develops after exposure to strep.

• If there are repeated bouts of tonsillitis, especially more than four or five per year.

- If a child has persistent mouth breathing, snoring, or very nasal or muffled voice.

- If a person is unable to swallow or open his or her mouth without pain.

Quitting Smoking

Quitting smoking is one of the most important things you can do for your own health and the health of those around you. Smoking is a risk factor for many health problems, including heart disease, stroke, and cancer. Children who are exposed to cigarette smoke in the home have more ear infections and are more prone to other health problems. When you quit smoking, it doesn't take long for your body to start to heal and reduce your risk of health problems.

- Your risk of heart disease goes down almost immediately and after 10 years is close to that of a nonsmoker.

- Your lungs begin to heal, and after 10 to 15 years your risk of lung cancer is almost as low as that of a nonsmoker.

It isn't easy to stop smoking. No single method works for everyone–some people can quit "cold turkey," and others succeed by gradually cutting down over several months. No matter which method you choose, the following tips will help you get started.

The Nicotine Patch

The nicotine patch is an adhesive patch that releases nicotine into the bloodstream through the skin. Used together with a smoking cessation program, there is strong evidence that using patches helps smokers quit. Patches help some smokers gradually withdraw from nicotine addiction by supplying smaller and smaller amounts of nicotine.

While many smokers quit without nicotine replacement, the patch can be helpful for some. Generally, it is used by those who smoke more than a pack a day. In order to be successful, it is essential that you not smoke at all while using the patch.

By combining the patch with a good smoking cessation program, your chances of success can be greatly increased.

There are other promising medications that appear to be effective in helping quit smoking. Some of these medications can be taken as a pill. Talk with your doctor about them.

Tips for Quitting

Preparation

• Decide how and when you will quit. About half of ex-smokers quit "cold turkey"; the other half cut down gradually, over a brief period of time (i.e., one to three weeks).

• Figure out why you smoke. Do you smoke to pep yourself up? To relax? Do you like the ritual of smoking? Does smoking help you deal with anger or negative feelings? Do you smoke out of habit, often without realizing you're doing it?

• Find a healthy alternative that accomplishes what smoking does for you. For example, if you like to have something to do with your hands, pick up something else: coins, worry beads, pen or pencil. If you like to have something in your mouth, substitute sugarless gum or minted toothpicks.

• List your reasons for quitting: for your own and your family's health, to save money, to prevent wrinkles, or whatever. Keep reminding yourself of your goal.

• Plan a healthful reward for yourself when you have stopped smoking. Take the money you save by not buying cigarettes and spend it on yourself.

• Plan things to do for when you get the urge to smoke. Urges don't last long—take a walk, brush your teeth, have a mint, or chew gum.

• Choose a reliable smoking cessation program. Good programs have at least a 20 percent success rate after one year. Higher numbers may be too good to be true.

• Set a quit date and stick to it. Try to choose a time that will be busy but not stressful.

• Your doctor may bring up your smoking at regular visits. He or she is doing this because it has been shown to help you quit successfully. If you are interested in quitting and are unsure how to go about it, you can talk with your doctor, as well as contact your local chapter of the American Lung Association for more resources.

Action

• Know what to expect. The worst will be over in just a few days, but physical withdrawal symptoms may last one to three weeks. See Chapter 17 for relaxation tips.

• Remove all reminders of smoking from your surroundings. Do things that are incompatible with smoking, like bicycling or going to a movie.

• For the first few weeks, avoid situations and settings that you associate with smoking.

• Drink plenty of water to help flush the nicotine out of your system. Keep alcohol to a minimum, if any.

 For more information, see the inside front cover.

• Keep low-calorie snacks handy for when the urge to munch hits. Your appetite may perk up, but most people gain less than 10 pounds when they quit smoking. A healthy, low-fat diet and regular exercise will help you resist the urge to smoke and avoid unwanted pounds. The health benefits of quitting outweigh a few extra pounds.

• Get help and support. Ask an ex-smoker to help you.

• Think of yourself as an ex-smoker. Be positive.

• Be prepared for slip-ups. It often takes several tries to quit smoking permanently. If you do smoke, forgive yourself and learn from the experience. You will not fail as long as you keep trying.

• **Good luck!**

See Resource 68 on page 328.

Tuberculosis

Tuberculosis (TB) is a contagious disease caused by bacteria that primarily infect the lungs. TB is spread when infected people cough or sneeze the bacteria into the air and others inhale the organisms. After infection, it can take up to two years to develop active TB, and many never do. Symptoms of active infection include a persistent cough, weight loss, fatigue, and fever.

Since 1985, TB has increased in the U.S., primarily due to the increased number of people who are infected with the human immunodeficiency virus (HIV), which makes them more susceptible to TB. Other groups at higher risk include IV-drug users, the homeless, immigrants from countries with high rates of TB, health care workers, and older adults.

Drug treatment can cure TB, but it may take up to 6 to 12 months. Many patients become discouraged and stop their treatment, increasing the risk that they will spread the infection.

To prevent TB, avoid close contact with someone who has an active infection, especially spending a long time together in a stuffy room. You cannot get TB by handling things an infected person has touched.

If you think you've had close contact with someone with active TB, contact your doctor or local health department about a tuberculin skin test (see page 21).

You can observe a lot just by watching.
Yogi Berra (naturally)

8

Eye and Ear Problems

From dry eyes to pinkeye and earaches to earwax, your eyes and ears can cause you trouble. With home care and patience, most of these problems will clear up. This chapter will explain what you can do at home and when to get professional help.

Dry Eyes

Eyes that don't have enough moisture in them may feel dry, hot, sandy, or gritty. Dry eyes may be due to low humidity, smoke, the natural aging process, certain diseases or certain medications such as antihistamines, decongestants, and birth control pills.

Home Treatment

• Try an over-the-counter artificial tear solution, such as Akwa Tears, Duratears, or HypoTears. These are different from drops like Visine, which reduce eye redness rather than dryness.

• Call a health professional if dry eyes are persistent and artificial tears do not help.

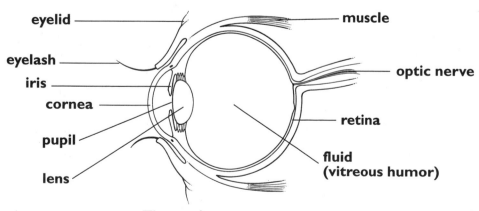

The eye has many parts.

Eye Problems

Eye Symptoms	Possible Causes
Red, itchy, watery eyes	See Allergies, p. 123. Think about allergy to eye care products, make-up, smoke; or contact lens irritation. Remove lenses. See p. 155.
Excessive discharge from eye; red, swollen eyelids; scratchy, sandy feeling	See Eye Infections, below. Possible contact lens irritation, p. 155.
Pimple or swelling on eyelid	See Styes, p. 157.
Pain in the eye	See Chemical Burns, p. 36; Migraine Headaches, p. 168; Cluster Headaches, p. 168; Objects in the Eye, p. 53; consider contact lens irritation, p. 155; Eye Infections, below.
Severe eye pain, blurred vision, reddened eyeball	Possible iritis or acute glaucoma. See a doctor now!
Red spot on white of eye	See Blood in the Eye, p. 156.
Blow to eye	See Bruises (black eye), p. 33.
Dry, scratchy eyes	See Dry Eyes, p. 153.

Eye Infections

Conjunctivitis, or pinkeye, is an inflammation of the delicate membrane (conjunctiva) that lines the inside of the eyelid and the surface of the eye. It can be caused by bacteria or viruses (which can be very contagious), allergies, pollution, or other irritants.

The symptoms are redness in the whites of the eyes, red and swollen eyelids, lots of tears, and a sandy feeling in the eyes. There may be a discharge that causes the eyelids to stick together during sleep and occasional sensitivity to light.

Prevention

• Wash your hands thoroughly after treating pinkeye.

Eye Twitches

Eye twitches or muscle spasms around the eye are most often associated with fatigue or stress. Twitches will usually stop on their own in a short time, and they will improve with rest or reduced stress.

Call a health professional if twitches occur with redness, swelling, discharge from the eye, or fever, or if the eye twitch lasts longer than one to two weeks.

• Do not share towels, handkerchiefs, or washcloths with an infected person.

• If a chemical or object gets into your eye, immediately flush the eye with water. See page 36 or page 53.

Home Treatment

Although most cases of conjunctivitis will clear up in five to seven days on their own, viral pinkeye can last many weeks. Conjunctivitis due to allergies or pollution will last as long as you are exposed to the irritating substance. Good home care will speed healing and bring relief.

• Apply cold or warm compresses several times a day to relieve discomfort.

• Gently wipe the edge of the eyelid with moist cotton or a clean wet washcloth to remove encrusted matter.

• Don't wear contact lenses or eye makeup until the infection or inflammation is gone. Discard eye makeup after an eye infection.

• If eyedrops are prescribed, insert as follows:

° For older children and adults, pull the lower lid down with two fingers to create a little pouch. Put the drops there. Close the eye for several minutes to let the drops move around.

° For younger children, ask the child to lie down with eyes closed. Put a drop in the inner corner of

---

Contact Lenses

If you wear contact lenses, these tips will help you avoid problems.

• Follow the cleaning instructions for your lenses. Keep your lenses and anything that touches them (hands, storage containers, solution bottles, makeup) very clean. Wash your hands before handling your contacts.

• Use a commercial saline solution. (Generic brands are just as good as name brands.) Homemade solution is easily contaminated with bacteria.

• Insert your contacts *before* applying eye makeup. Do not apply makeup to the inner rim of the eyelid. Replace eye makeup every three to six months to reduce the risk of contamination.

• When worn for long periods of time, extended-wear lenses are more likely to cause severe eye infections. If you choose to wear them, follow the wearing and cleaning schedule your doctor recommends.

• Symptoms of a possible problem with your contacts include unusual redness, pain or burning in the eye, discharge, blurred vision, or extreme sensitivity to light. Remove your lenses and disinfect them. If symptoms persist longer than two to three hours after removing your contacts, call your eye care professional.

• Visit your eye care professional once a year to check the condition of your lenses and the health of your eyes.

 For more information, see the inside front cover.

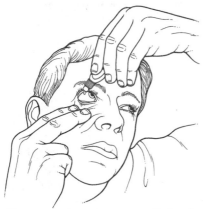

To insert eyedrops, pull the lower lid down to make a pouch. Look away from the dropper as you put the drops in the pouch, then close the eye to spread the drops.

the eye. When the child opens the eye, the drop will run in.

° Be sure the dropper is clean and does not touch the eye, eyelid, or any surface. Eyedrops are washed out by normal tearing, so they will need to be replaced at least three times a day.

Floaters and Flashes

Floaters are spots, specks, and lines that "float" across your field of vision. They are caused by stray cells or strands of tissue that float in the vitreous humor, the gel-like substance that fills the eyeball. Floaters can be annoying but are not usually serious. However, if you see floaters or flashes of light for the first time, call your eye doctor or family doctor. If you have had floaters for some time, or if you have occasional flashes, mention it at your next routine eye exam.

Blood in the Eye

Sometimes, blood vessels in the whites of the eyes break and cause a red spot or speck. This is called a subconjunctival hemorrhage. The blood may look alarming, especially if the spot is large. It is usually not a cause for concern and will clear up in two to three weeks.

However, if your eye is bloody and painful, if there is blood in the colored part of the eye, or if the bleeding followed a blow to the eye, call a health professional *immediately*. Also call if bleeding in the eye occurs often, occurs after you begin taking blood thinners (anticoagulants), or covers more than $\frac{1}{4}$ of the white of the eye.

• Putting antibiotic ointment in the eye can be tricky, especially with children. If you can get it on the eyelashes, it will melt and get into the eye.

• Make sure any over-the-counter medicine you use is ophthalmic (for eyes), not otic (for ears).

When to Call Kaiser Permanente

• If there is pain in the eye (rather than irritation), blurring, or loss of vision, not cleared even momentarily with blinking.

• If the eye is painfully sensitive to light.

• If the skin around the eye or the eyelid is red.

Cataracts and Glaucoma

Cataracts are cloudy areas in the lens of the eye. They may cause vision problems such as cloudy, foggy, or filmy vision; glare from lamps, sunlight, or car headlights; and double vision. They are common in older adults. Risk factors for cataracts include:

• Diabetes

• Native American or African-American race

• Use of steroids

• Smoking

• Ultraviolet light exposure (it isn't clear whether protecting the eyes from sunlight reduces the risk)

Glaucoma is an eye disorder that results when there is excess pressure in the eyeball. If the pressure is not relieved, the optic nerve may be damaged, causing blindness. It rarely has symptoms and develops slowly over several years. Risk factors for glaucoma include:

• Family history of glaucoma

• African-American race

• Diabetes or nearsightedness

Cataracts and glaucoma are easy to detect during routine eye exams and respond well to medical treatment. Talk with your doctor about the best schedule of eye exams for you, based on your age and risk factors for these eye problems.

Call your health professional immediately if you have sudden blurry vision, loss of vision, or pain in the eye.

• If you feel there is a foreign object in the eye.

• If the eye is red and there is a greenish yellow discharge that does not begin to improve in 24 hours.

• If there is an abnormal difference between the sizes of the pupils.

• If the problem continues for more than seven days.

Styes

A sty is a noncontagious infection of the eyelash follicle. It looks like a small, red bump, much like a pimple, either in the eyelid or on the edge of the lid. It comes to a head and breaks open after a few days.

Styes are very common and are not a serious problem. Most will resolve with some home treatment and don't require removal.

Home Treatment

• Do not rub the eye, and do not squeeze the sty.

• Apply warm, moist compresses for 10 minutes, five to six times a day, until the sty comes to a head and drains.

When to Call Kaiser Permanente

• If the sty interferes with vision.

• If the sty gets worse despite your home treatment.

• If the redness centered on the sty spreads to involve the entire lid.

 For more information, see the inside front cover.

Ear Problems

Ear Symptoms	Possible Causes
Earache and fever; pulling at ears by infants and small children, especially with inconsolable crying	See Ear Infections, p. 159.
Pain while chewing; headache	See TMJ Syndrome, p. 179.
Pain when ear is wiggled; itching or burning in ear	See Swimmer's Ear, p. 163.
Discharge from ear	See Swimmer's Ear, p. 163; eardrum rupture, p. 159.
Feeling of fullness in ear; with runny or stuffy nose, cough, fever	See Colds, p. 135; Ear Infections, p. 159.
Feeling of something in ear; as if ear is "bumping around"	See Objects in the Ear, p. 52.
Hearing loss; inattentiveness	See Earwax, p. 162; serous otitis media, p. 160.
Ringing or noise in the ears	See Ringing in the Ears, p. 163.

Dizziness

Dizziness or **lightheadedness** is usually not due to a serious problem; in fact, it is common to feel lightheaded occasionally. It is often due to a momentary drop in blood pressure and blood flow to the head that occurs when you get up too quickly from a seated or lying position. This is called orthostatic hypotension, and it is most commonly caused by medications or dehydration.

Other causes of dizziness include side effects of medications, stress, anxiety, or drinking alcohol. Another less common cause is an abnormality in your heart rhythm, which usually causes recurrent spells of lightheadedness over a period of a few days.

Vertigo is a sensation that your body or the world around you is spinning. It may occur with nausea and vomiting. It may be impossible to walk when you have severe vertigo. Benign positional vertigo, the most common form, is triggered by changes in the position of the head, such as when you move your head from side to side or bend your head back to look up. Vertigo may also be caused by inflammation (called labyrinthitis) in the part of the inner ear that controls balance. Labyrinthitis may be caused by a viral infection and sometimes occurs following a cold or the flu.

Home Treatment

Dizziness is not usually a cause for concern unless it is severe, persistent, or occurs with other symptoms.

- When you feel dizzy, sit down for a minute or two and take some deep breaths. Stand up again slowly.

- Sit up or stand up slowly to avoid the changes in blood flow to the head that can make you feel dizzy.

- Avoid head positions or changes in position that bring on vertigo. However, some experts suggest that practicing these positions may help overcome the problem.

- If you have vertigo, avoid lying flat on your back. Prop yourself up slightly to relieve the spinning sensation.

When to Call Kaiser Permanente

- If dizziness is accompanied by chest pain, headache, confusion, loss of hearing, changes in vision, weakness in the arms or legs, or numbness in any part of the body.

- If you feel like you might faint or if there is a complete loss of consciousness.

- If you have vertigo that is severe (often causing vomiting) or occurs with hearing loss or significant ear pain.

- If you suspect dizziness may be a side effect of a medication.

- If dizziness lasts more than three to five days and interferes with your daily activities.

- If you experience vertigo (sensation that the room is spinning around you) that is severe or persists for more than three days, has not been diagnosed, or is significantly different from previous episodes.

- If you have repeated spells of lightheadedness over a few days.

- If your pulse is less than 50 or more than 130 beats per minute when you are feeling lightheaded.

Ear Infections

 Ear infections can occur in the middle ear or the ear canal (see Swimmer's Ear, page 163).

A middle ear infection (otitis media) usually starts when a cold causes the eustachian tube between the ear and throat to swell and close. When the tube closes, fluid seeps into the ear and bacteria or a virus can start to grow. As the body fights the infection, pressure builds up, causing pain. Antibiotic treatment stops bacterial growth, relieving pressure and pain.

Left untreated, the pressure can cause the eardrum to rupture. A single eardrum rupture (perforation) is not serious and does not cause hearing loss. Repeated ruptures may cause hearing loss.

Young children get more ear infections because they get more colds and their eustachian tubes are more easily blocked.

Symptoms of a bacterial or viral ear infection include earache, dizziness, ringing or fullness in the ears, hearing loss, drainage from the ear, fever, headache, and runny nose. In children who can't yet talk, tugging on the ear may be a sign of pain, especially if they are sick.

Otitis media with effusion (**serous otitis**) is a collection of fluid in the ear that often remains after an ear infection. There are often no symptoms, or there may be a feeling of fullness in the ear and some minor hearing loss. Effusion is not a cause for concern and may not require treatment unless it lasts longer than three months or causes significant hearing loss.

Prevention

- Teach your children to blow their noses gently. This is a good idea for adults, too.

- Breast-feed your baby. Breast-fed babies have fewer ear infections.

- Feed infants in a relatively upright position to prevent milk from getting into the eustachian tubes. Do not allow infants to fall asleep with a bottle. (Nursing infants may fall asleep at the breast.)

- Avoid exposing children to cigarette smoke, which is associated with more frequent ear infections.

- If possible, limit your child's contact with other children who have colds. Teach your children to wash their hands before eating.

Home Treatment

- Apply heat to the ear to ease the pain. Use a warm washcloth or a heating pad set on low. Don't leave a child alone with a heating pad.

- Rest. Let your energy go to fighting the infection.

- Increase clear liquids.

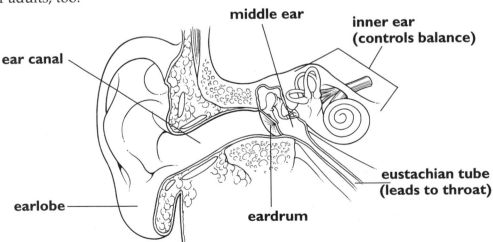

Ear infections can occur in the ear canal or middle ear.
Dizziness can be caused by an inflammation of the inner ear.

Recurrent Ear Infections and Persistent Effusion

If your child has at least three ear infections in a six-month period, or has more than two infections before age six months, prophylactic antibiotics may be recommended. This is a low dose of antibiotics taken daily throughout the season when the child is prone to ear infections. It may reduce the frequency of ear infections but may not always prevent fluid in the ear (effusion). However, there is increasing concern that such antibiotic use may promote the spread of more dangerous antibiotic-resistant bacteria.

If infection persists after one month of continuous treatment (with at least two different antibiotics), your doctor may suggest inserting ear tubes (tympanostomy) through the eardrum to help prevent ear infections. The tubes remain in the eardrum for 6 to 18 months.

In some children, effusion (fluid behind the eardrum) persists longer than three months after an ear infection. Since this can affect your child's hearing, he or she should have a hearing test. If the child still has effusion and significant hearing loss after four to six months, your doctor may recommend ear tubes. Ask your child's doctor about the long-term risks and benefits of all treatment options.

- Acetaminophen, aspirin, or ibuprofen will help relieve earache. See dosage on page 317. Do not give aspirin to a child or a teen under 20.

- Oral nasal decongestants may help relieve earache pain. Avoid products that contain antihistamines.

- If dizziness occurs, see page 158.

When to Call Kaiser Permanente

- Anytime an ear infection is suspected. If the exam confirms an infection, antibiotics will be needed.

- If a severe earache lasts longer than one hour or any earache lasts longer than 12 to 24 hours. If the pain is severe at night, call the next morning even if the pain has stopped. The infection may still be present.

- If an infant repeatedly rubs or pulls on the ear and is not just playing with the ear.

- If a child has an earache and fever and appears ill.

- If a headache, fever, and stiff neck are also present, which may be signs of meningitis (see page 141).

- If home otoscope exam shows redness in the ear of a small child who cannot describe ear pain. See page 309.

- If there is a white or yellow discharge that is not wax, or a bloody discharge from the ear. This may indicate a ruptured eardrum.

- If there is no improvement after three to four days of antibiotics.

- If stuffy ears or hearing loss persist without other symptoms for more than 10 days after a cold has cleared up.

Earwax

Earwax is a protective secretion, similar to mucus or tears, that filters dust and keeps the ear clean. Normally, earwax is liquid, self-draining, and does not cause problems. Occasionally, the wax will build up, harden, and cause some hearing loss. Poking at the wax with cotton swabs, fingers, or other objects will only further compact the wax against the eardrum. Professional help is needed to remove tightly packed wax. You can handle most earwax problems by avoiding cotton swabs and following the home treatment tips below.

Children have a lot of earwax, which seems to taper off as they grow older. You should be concerned only if the earwax causes ringing or a full feeling in the ears, or some hearing loss.

Home Treatment

- Use drops of warm mineral oil to help loosen wax. Wash the wax out with an ear syringe and warm water. (Cold fluid may make you dizzy.) Use very gentle force. Do not do this if there is discharge from the ear, if you suspect an ear infection or a ruptured eardrum, or if you have ear tubes.

- If the warm mineral oil does not work, use an over-the-counter wax softener, followed by gentle flushing with an ear syringe, each night for a week or two. Do not use it if you suspect infection or eardrum rupture.

When to Call Kaiser Permanente

- If home treatment does not work and the wax build-up is hard, dry, and compacted.

- If you suspect that earwax is causing a hearing problem.

- If the ear is sore or bleeding.

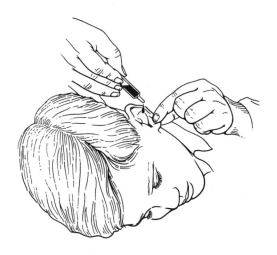

Let eardrops flow gently into the opening of the ear canal.

Ringing in the Ears

Almost everyone has experienced an occasional ringing (or hissing, buzzing, or tinkling) in their ears. The sound usually lasts only a few minutes. Persistent ringing in the ear is called tinnitus.

Tinnitus is usually caused by damage to the nerves in the inner ear from prolonged exposure to loud noise. Other, more treatable causes include excess earwax, ear infection, dental problems, and medications, especially antibiotics and large amounts of aspirin. Drinking excessive alcohol can also cause tinnitus.

Home Treatment

• Limit or avoid exposure to loud noises, such as music, power tools, gunshots, and industrial machinery.

• Cut back or eliminate caffeine, nicotine, and alcohol.

• Try to relax. Stress and fatigue seem to make it worse.

• Limit your use of aspirin and products containing aspirin.

When to Call Kaiser Permanente

• If tinnitus becomes persistent and interferes with your daily activities or sleep.

• If ringing occurs with dizziness, loss of balance, vertigo, nausea, or vomiting.

• If tinnitus persistently affects only one ear.

Swimmer's Ear

Swimmer's ear (otitis externa) is an infection of the outer ear canal. It often develops after water has gotten into the ear, especially after swimming. Sand or other debris that get into the ear canal may also cause swimmer's ear. Scratching the ear or injury from a cotton swab or other object may also irritate the ear canal.

Symptoms include pain, itching, and a feeling of fullness in the ear. The ear canal may be swollen. A more severe bacterial infection may cause increased pain, a discharge from the ear, and possibly some hearing loss. Unlike a middle ear infection (otitis media), swimmer's ear pain is worse when you chew and when you press on the "tag" in front of the ear or wiggle the earlobe.

Prevention

• Keep your ears dry. After swimming or showering, shake your head to remove water from the ear canal. Gently dry your ears with the corner of a tissue or towel, or use a blow-dryer on its lowest setting held several inches from the ear.

• Put a few drops of rubbing alcohol or alcohol mixed with an equal amount of white vinegar in the ear after swimming or showering. Wiggle the outside of the ear to let the liquid enter the ear canal; then tilt your head and let it drain out.

You can also use over-the-counter drops (Star-Otic, Swim-Ear) to prevent swimmer's ear.

• Avoid cleaning the ears with cotton swabs or other objects. See page 162 for tips on removing excess earwax. Remove dirt or sand that gets into the ear while swimming by using a bulb syringe or a gentle warm shower directed into the ear; then tip your head to let it drain out.

Home Treatment

• Make sure there isn't an object or insect in the ear. See Objects in the Ear on page 52.

• Gently rinse the ear using a bulb syringe and saline solution or a half-and-half solution of white vinegar and warm water.

• Avoid getting water in the ear until the irritation clears up. Cotton coated with petroleum jelly can be used as an earplug. Do not use plastic earplugs.

• If your ear is itchy, try over-the-counter swimmer's eardrops (see Prevention). Use them before and after swimming or getting your ears wet.

• To insert eardrops, have the person lie down, ear facing up. Warm the drops first by rolling the container between your hands. Place drops on the wall of the ear canal in small quantities so air can escape and drops can get into the ear. Wiggling the outer ear will help.

• You may find it easier to insert eardrops in a small child by holding the child on your lap with his or her legs around your waist and head down on your knees.

• Apply heat to the outer ear with a warm towel or heating pad set on low to relieve discomfort. Don't leave a child alone with a heating pad. Acetaminophen or aspirin may also help. Don't give aspirin to children or to teens under age 20.

When to Call Kaiser Permanente

• If ear pain and itching persist or worsen despite five days of home treatment.

• If the ear canal is swollen, red, and very painful, or if there is a discharge from the ear.

• If redness extends to the outer ear.

• If the earache follows a cold. See pages 159 and 160.

*I'm very brave generally, only today I happen
to have a headache.*
Tweedledum in Alice in Wonderland

9

Headaches

Headaches are one of the most common health complaints. Some possible causes include tension, infection, allergy, injury, hunger, changes in the flow of blood in the vessels of the head, or exposure to chemicals.

Most headaches that occur without other symptoms will respond well to self-care.

The majority of headaches—over 90 percent—are caused by tension and respond well to prevention and home care. See page 170.

An unusual headache that is very different from any you have had before, or a change in the usual pattern of your headaches, is a cause for concern. See "Headache Emergencies." However, if you have had similar headaches before and your doctor has recommended a treatment plan for them, emergency care may not be needed.

Headache Emergencies

Call your doctor now if you have:

- A very sudden, "thunderclap" headache.

- A sudden, severe headache unlike any you have had before.

- Headache with stiff neck, fever, nausea, vomiting, drowsiness, confusion.

- Sudden, severe headache with stiff neck developing soon after the headache starts.

- Headache with weakness, paralysis, numbness, visual disturbances, slurred speech, confusion, or behavior changes.

- Headaches following a recent fall or blow to the head. See page 44 for information on head injuries.

Possible Headache Causes

If headache occurs:	Possible causes
On awakening.	See Tension Headaches, p. 170; Allergies, p. 123; Sinusitis, p. 143; Neck Problems, p. 98; TMJ Syndrome, p. 179.
In jaw muscles or in both temples.	See TMJ Syndrome, p. 179; Tension Headaches, p. 170.
Each afternoon or evening; after hours of desk work; with sore neck and shoulders.	See Tension Headaches, p. 170; Neck Problems, p. 98.
On one side of the head.	See Migraine Headaches, p. 168; Cluster Headaches, p. 168.
After a blow to the head.	See Head Injuries, p. 44.
After exposure to chemicals (paint, varnish, insect spray, cigarette smoke).	Chemical headache. Get into fresh air. Drink water to flush poisons.
With fever, runny nose, or sore throat.	Flu, p. 140; Sore Throat, p. 145; Colds, p. 135.
With fever, stiff neck, nausea, and vomiting.	See Encephalitis and Meningitis, p. 141.
With runny nose, watery eyes, and sneezing.	See Allergies, p. 123.
With fever and pain in the cheek or over the eyes.	See Sinusitis, p. 143.
On mornings when you drink less caffeine than usual.	Caffeine-withdrawal headache. Cut back slowly. See p. 170.
Following a stressful event.	See Tension Headaches, p. 170.
At the same time during menstrual cycle.	See Premenstrual Syndrome, p. 241.
With new medication.	Drug allergy. Contact doctor.
With severe eye pain.	Possible acute glaucoma. See doctor now!

Headaches in Children

Children's headaches rarely indicate a serious problem. They are more frequent in children whose parents often discuss their own headaches. Children tend to imitate their parents, so mention headaches as little as possible.

Emotional tension is the most common cause of headaches in children. A parent can often discover the cause of stress and help relieve it. Many times, just talking about a problem may help a child relax. Some children try to do too much or are pushed to do too much at home or at school. Even fun activities can be overdone and cause fatigue and headaches. Encourage your children to talk openly about problems and stress at school.

Tension headaches (see page 170) are common in teenagers and are generally caused by emotional stress related to school, sports, or relationships. Migraine headaches (see page 168) sometimes begin during the teen years.

Hunger can also cause headaches in children. A daily breakfast and a nutritious after-school snack may prevent them. Eyestrain may also cause headaches. Headaches are also common with viral illnesses that cause fever, such as colds and flu.

Home Treatment

• Talk to your child. If the headache seems to be due to emotional tension, try to discover the source of the headache and deal with it. Let the child know you care. Tension headaches are sometimes "attention" headaches. In these cases, quiet time and extra attention can manage the headaches without pain relievers.

• Play quietly with the child, or read stories together.

• If the headache is still present, have the child lie down in a darkened room with a cool cloth on the forehead.

• If nondrug treatments do not relieve the pain, try acetaminophen. See page 317 for the dose. Avoid creating the pattern of using a pill for every pain. Do not give aspirin to children.

When to Call Kaiser Permanente

• If a headache is severe and is not relieved by relaxation or acetaminophen.

• If a severe headache occurs with signs of encephalitis or meningitis (see page 141), especially following a viral illness.

• If a child's headaches occur two to three times a week or more, or if you are using pain relievers to control a child's headaches more than once a week.

- If you cannot discover a reasonable cause. A child may share problems with someone other than a parent.

- If headaches awaken the child at night or are worse early in the morning.

- Also see "Headache Emergencies" on page 165.

Cluster Headaches

Cluster headaches are sudden, very severe, sharp, stabbing headaches that occur on one side of the head, usually in the temple or behind the eye. The eye and nostril on the affected side may be runny. The eye may also become red.

The pain often begins at night and may last from 30 minutes to a few hours. The headache may recur several times a day. Attacks may last 4 to 12 weeks, then disappear for months or years.

Cluster headaches are five times more common in men. Many men who get them are heavy smokers and drinkers. Avoid alcohol and cigarettes during an attack.

See your doctor if you think you have cluster headaches or if you have persistent, severe headaches with no apparent cause.

Also see "Headache Emergencies" on page 165.

Migraine Headaches

Migraine headaches have very specific symptoms including throbbing pain on one or both sides of the head and sensitivity to light or noise. Because migraines may also cause nausea or vomiting, they are sometimes called "sick" headaches. Migraines are also called vascular headaches, because they were once believed to be caused by changes in the flow of blood in the vessels of the head.

Although a migraine headache comes on quite suddenly, it is sometimes preceded by visual disturbances, such as zig-zagged lines, called an aura. Dizziness and numbness on one side of the body may also precede a migraine. The headaches last from a few hours to a few days and recur from several times a week to once every few years.

Migraines are more common in women. The headaches may begin during childhood, but most begin during the teens and early twenties.

Prevention

Keep a diary of your headache symptoms. See "Tracking Your Headaches" on page 169. Once you know what events, foods, medications, or activities bring on a headache, you may be able to prevent or limit their recurrence.

Some women find that their headaches improve if they stop taking
birth control pills. If you are taking
birth control pills and having
migraine headaches, consult with
your doctor.

Tracking Your Headaches

If you have recurring headaches,
keep a record of your symptoms.
This record will help your doctor
if medical evaluation is needed.

1. The date and time each headache started and stopped.

2. Any factors that seem to trigger the headache: food, smoke,
bright light, stress, activity.

3. The location and nature of the
pain: throbbing, aching, stabbing, dull.

4. The severity of the pain.

5. Other physical symptoms:
nausea, vomiting, visual disturbances, sensitivity to light or
noise.

6. If you are a woman, note any
association between headaches
and your menstrual cycle or use
of birth control pills or hormone
replacement therapy.

Home Treatment

• At the first sign of a migraine, lie
down in a darkened room with a
cool cloth on your forehead. Relax
your entire body, starting with the
forehead and eyes and working
down to the toes (see page 273).
Sleeping can relieve migraines.

• Many people find aspirin, acetaminophen, or ibuprofen helps
relieve a migraine.

• If a doctor has prescribed medication for your migraines, take the
recommended dose at the first sign
that a migraine is starting.

• If you use over-the-counter or
prescription headache medications
daily or several times a week, they
may actually make the headaches
more frequent or severe. These are
called "analgesic rebound"
headaches.

When to Call Kaiser Permanente

• If you suspect your headaches are
migraines. Professional diagnosis
and treatment, combined with
your self-care, can help decrease
the impact of migraines on your
life. Discuss relaxation and
biofeedback techniques, which
help many people prevent
migraines.

• If headaches are becoming more
frequent or more severe.

• Also see "Headache Emergencies"
on page 165.

Tension Headaches

More than 90 percent of headaches are tension headaches, which become more frequent and severe during times of physical or emotional stress. A tension headache may be accompanied by tightness or pain in the muscles of the neck, back, and shoulders. A previous neck injury or arthritis in the neck can also cause tension headaches.

A tension headache may cause pain all over the head, pressure, or a feeling of having a band around the head. The head may feel like it is in a vise. Some people feel a dull, pressing, burning sensation above the eyes.

The pain may also affect the jaw, neck, and shoulder muscles. You can rarely pinpoint the center or source of pain.

Prevention

- Reduce emotional stress. Take time to relax before and after you do something that causes a headache. See page 272 for good ways to cope with stress.

- Reduce physical stress. Change positions often during desk work and stretch for 30 seconds each hour. Make a conscious effort to relax your jaw, neck, shoulder, and upper back muscles.

- Evaluate your neck and shoulder posture at work and make adjustments if needed. See pages 98 and 99.

- Daily exercise helps relieve the muscle tension related to tension headaches.

- Treat yourself to a massage. Some people find regular massages very helpful in relieving tension.

- Limit your caffeine intake to one to two cups per day. People who drink a lot of caffeinated beverages often develop a headache several hours after they have their last beverage or may wake with a headache that is relieved by drinking caffeine. Cut down slowly to avoid caffeine-withdrawal headaches.

Home Treatment

- Stop whatever you are doing and sit quietly for a moment. Close your eyes and inhale and exhale slowly. Try to relax your head and neck muscles.

- Take a stretching break or try a relaxation exercise. See page 272 or Resources 56 and 70 on page 328.

- Gently and firmly massage the neck muscles. See page 101 for neck exercises.

- Apply heat with a heating pad, hot water bottle, or a warm shower.

- Lie down in a dark room with a cool cloth on your forehead.

- Aspirin, acetaminophen, or ibuprofen often helps relieve a tension headache. However, using over-the-counter or prescription headache medications too often may make headaches more frequent or severe.

When to Call Kaiser Permanente

- If a headache is severe and cannot be relieved with home treatment.

- If unexplained headaches continue to occur more than three times a week.

- If headaches become more frequent and severe.

- If headaches awaken you out of a sound sleep or are worse first thing in the morning.

- If you need help discovering or eliminating the source of your tension headaches, talking with a health professional may be helpful.

- Also see "Headache Emergencies" on page 165.

Be true to your teeth or your teeth will be false to you.
Dental Proverb

10

Mouth and Dental Problems

Your teeth will last a lifetime if you care for them properly. Regular brushing, flossing, and visits to a dentist will help keep your teeth healthy.

Choose a dentist as carefully as you choose any other doctor. See pages 5 and 6 for tips on finding a dentist who meets your needs and is concerned about preventive care.

Canker Sores

Canker sores are painful open sores on the inside of the mouth and cheek. Possible causes of canker sores include injury to the inside of the mouth, infection, stress, genetic predisposition, and female hormones. The sores usually heal in 7 to 10 days.

Prevention

• Avoid injury to the inside of your mouth:

  ° Chew food slowly and carefully.

  ° Use a soft-bristle toothbrush and brush your teeth thoroughly but gently.

• Avoid foods that seem to cause sores.

Home Treatment

• Avoid coffee, spicy and salty foods, and citrus fruits.

• Apply an oral paste, like Orabase, to the canker sore. It will protect the sore, ease pain, and speed healing. Other over-the-counter canker sore medications include Gly-Oxide, Amosan, and Cankaid. Anbesol may help relieve pain.

• Rinse your mouth with a mixture of one tablespoon of hydrogen peroxide in eight ounces of water.

Mouth and Dental Problems

Problem	Possible Causes
White spots, sores, or bleeding in mouth	See Canker Sores, p. 173; may be a sign of thrush, p. 189. If unexplained sores last longer than 14 days, call a health professional.
Bleeding gums	Gum disease. See Dental Problems, p. 175.
Toothache	See p. 179.
Sores on the lips	See Cold Sores, below.
Bad breath	May be a sign of dental problems, p. 176; indigestion, p. 74; or upper respiratory infection, p. 135, 140, 142.
Pain and stiffness in jaw, with headache	See TMJ Syndrome, p. 179; Tension Headaches, p. 170.

• A thin paste of baking soda and water applied to the sore may bring relief.

When to Call Kaiser Permanente

• If mouth sores develop after you start taking a medication.

• If a canker sore, or any sore, does not heal in 14 days.

• If a sore is very painful or recurs frequently.

• If white spots that are not canker sores appear in the mouth and are not improving in one to two weeks.

Cold Sores

Cold sores (fever blisters) are small red blisters that usually appear on the lip and outer edge of the mouth. They often weep a clear fluid and form scabs after a few days. They are sometimes confused with impetigo (see page 215), which usually develops between the nose and upper lip. The fluid that weeps from impetigo is cloudy and honey-colored, not clear.

Cold sores are caused by a herpes virus. Herpes viruses (chickenpox is another kind) stay in the body after the first infection. Later, something that triggers the virus causes it to become active again. Cold sores may appear after colds, fevers, exposure to the sun, stressful times, or during menstruation. Sometimes, they appear for no apparent reason.

Prevention

- Avoid kissing someone who has a cold sore and avoid direct skin contact with genital herpes sores (see page 260). Both types of herpes can affect either the mouth or genitals. Condoms help reduce the risk.

- Use a sunscreen on your lips and wear a hat if exposure to the sun seems to trigger cold sores.

- Reducing stress may help in some cases. Practice relaxation exercises often. See page 272.

Home Treatment

- At the first sign of a cold sore (tingling or prickling at the site where the sore will appear), apply ice to the area. This may help reduce the severity of the sore.

- Apply petroleum jelly (Vaseline) to ease cracking and dryness.

- Apply a paste made of cornstarch and a little water.

- Blistex or Campho-Phenique may ease the pain. Don't share them with others.

- Be patient. Cold sores usually go away in 7 to 10 days.

When to Call Kaiser Permanente

Call if sores last longer than two weeks or you have many or frequent cold sores. A prescription medication may reduce the frequency and severity of outbreaks.

Dental Problems

Dental disease is preventable. You can keep all of your teeth by practicing good home care and having regular professional checkups. Brush and floss regularly. Both tooth decay and gum disease are the result of bacterial growth that forms plaque.

Plaque and Tooth Decay

Bacteria are always present in the mouth. When they are not removed by brushing and flossing, bacteria stick to the teeth and multiply into larger and larger colonies called plaque. Plaque forms as a sticky, colorless film on your teeth.

This sticky plaque damages teeth in two ways. First, food particles, especially refined sugars, stick to it. The plaque uses that food to grow more bacteria and to produce acid. Second, the plaque holds the acid against the tooth surface. If not removed, the acid will eventually eat through the tooth enamel, causing tooth decay.

If you eat only at mealtimes, it takes about 24 hours for bacteria and acid to harm your teeth. This is enough time for you to brush the plaque off and wash away the acid. If you eat a lot of between-meal snacks, plaque builds up faster and you need to brush more often.

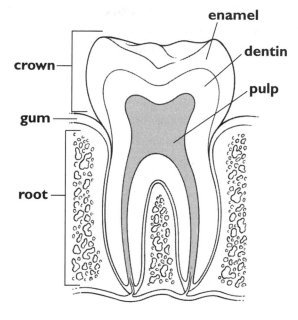

crown

enamel

dentin

pulp

gum

root

Proper dental care will help keep the structures that support your teeth healthy.

Plaque and Gum (Periodontal) Disease

Periodontal disease, an inflammation of the gums and in the bone supporting them, is a major cause of tooth loss. It is caused by bacterial plaque that builds up and sticks to the teeth at and below the gum line.

The first stage of the disease, called **gingivitis**, is marked by swollen, bleeding gums and bad breath. This stage is painless and, unfortunately, many people do not seek treatment.

As the disease progresses, the supporting bones and ligaments are affected. The gums recede, creating gaps between the teeth, which eventually fall out.

People with diabetes and those who smoke or chew tobacco are at increased risk of gum disease.

However, everyone is at risk; an estimated 75 to 80 percent of Americans have some form of gum disease.

Occasional bleeding when you brush or floss is an early sign of gum disease. However, with good care, it won't take long to get your gums back to normal. Brush and floss your teeth every day, and follow the prevention guidelines.

Prevention

- Have your teeth checked and cleaned at least twice a year by a dentist or dental hygienist.

- Eat crunchy foods that naturally clean the teeth (apples, carrots, and other raw vegetables) and foods with ample vitamin C, like citrus fruits and broccoli.

Brushing

Brush and floss properly to remove plaque. Brush at least twice a day for three to five minutes each time. Clean every surface of every tooth.

1. Use a toothbrush with soft, rounded-end bristles and a head that allows you to reach all parts of your mouth. Replace your toothbrush every three to four months.

2. Use a fluoride toothpaste and use only a small dab (pea-sized or smaller). Tartar-control toothpastes may help slow the formation of hard plaque build-up (tartar) on the teeth, but daily brushing with any toothpaste and flossing are the best tartar-control methods.

3. Place the brush at a 45° angle where the teeth meet the gums. Press firmly, and gently rock the brush back and forth using small circular movements. Do not scrub if you have a stiff-bristled brush. Vigorous brushing can make the gums recede and scratch your tooth enamel.

4. Brush all surfaces of the teeth, tongue side and cheek side. Pay special attention to the front teeth and behind the back teeth.

5. Brush the chewing surfaces vigorously with short back-and-forth strokes.

6. Brush the tongue. Plaque on the tongue can cause bad breath and is an ideal environment for bacteria to grow.

7. Use disclosing tablets periodically to see if any plaque is left on the teeth. Disclosing tablets are chewable tablets that will color any plaque left on the teeth after brushing. They are available at most drugstores.

Flossing

Brushing properly can remove most dental plaque. Regular flossing is the best way to remove plaque that forms between the teeth and below the gum line. Floss once a day using one of the following methods:

1. The finger-wrap method: Cut off a piece of floss 18 to 20 inches long. Wrap one end around the left middle finger and the other end around the right middle finger, until your hands are about two to three inches apart.

2. The circle method: Use a piece of floss about 12 inches long. Tie the ends together, forming a loop. If the loop is too large, wrap the floss around the middle fingers to make it smaller.

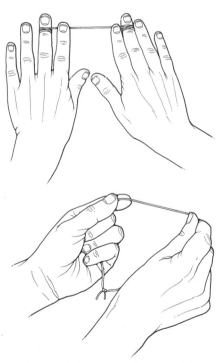

Dental floss can be used by wrapping it around your fingers or by tying the ends together.

To floss the upper teeth, use the thumb of one hand and forefinger of the other as shown in the illustration.

To floss the lower teeth, use both forefingers to guide the floss (see illustration). The fingers should be about ½ inch apart.

Curve the floss around each tooth and gently slide it under the gum line. Move the floss firmly up and down several times to scrape off the plaque. Popping the floss in and out without scraping will not remove much plaque.

Flossing tools may be especially helpful for adults who are flossing a child's teeth. Use the same scraping motion to remove plaque.

With practice, flossing will become easy. Any bleeding should subside as gums become healthy.

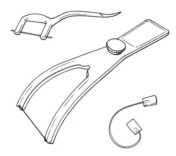

There are many kinds of tools to help you floss your teeth.

Dental Care for Children

Children should have their first dental visit by age two to three. Visits every six months for checkups and cleaning are usually recommended for children and adults.

• Start caring for your children's teeth early, before permanent teeth have come in. Do not put an infant or small child to bed with a bottle of juice or milk. Prolonged contact with the sugar in these liquids can cause tooth decay. Nursing an infant to sleep is fine, however.

• Start toothbrushing as soon as the teeth come in. Brush your children's teeth for the first four to five years, until they have enough dexterity to take over the job. A good teaching method is to have your child brush in the morning and you brush at night until they master the skill. Use disclosing tablets to see if the child is removing all the plaque.

• Start flossing as soon as the child has teeth that touch each other. As with brushing, you will have to help with flossing until the child is old enough to manage it. Flossing tools can help.

Sealants and Fluoride

Sealants are a plastic coating applied to the chewing surfaces of the back teeth to protect them from developing cavities. Sealants are especially good for the permanent molars when they first emerge in the mouth, usually between age 6 and age 11. Even with sealants, regular brushing and flossing are essential.

Fluoride is a mineral that strengthens tooth enamel and reduces the harmful effects of plaque. Children and adults need fluoride to build and keep strong teeth. Talk with your dentist about the amount of fluoride in your area's drinking water, and discuss fluoride treatments if needed.

When to Call the Dentist

• See your dentist for regular cleanings and exams. Every six months is the recommended schedule.

• If your gums bleed when you press on them or bleed often when you brush your teeth.

• If teeth are loose or moving apart or if there are changes in the way your teeth fit together when you bite.

• If gums are very red, swollen, or tender, or if pus is present.

• If you have a toothache. Toothaches are caused when the inside of the tooth (dentin) is exposed. The pain may go away temporarily, but the problem will not. Take aspirin, ibuprofen, or acetaminophen for pain relief until you can get an appointment. A cold pack on your jaw may also help.

TMJ Syndrome

 The olive-sized joint in front of your ear that connects your jawbone to your skull is called the temporomandibular joint (TMJ). TMJ syndrome is a set of symptoms that relate to damage, wear and tear, or unusual stress to the joint. The symptoms can include:

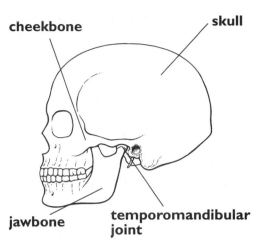

cheekbone   skull

jawbone   temporomandibular joint

TMJ syndrome can be caused by damage or stress on the joint that moves the jaw.

• Pain in and around the joint

• Noises such as clicking, popping, or snapping in the joint

• Inability to "open wide"

• Muscle pain and spasms where the jaw muscles attach to the bone

• Headache, neck and shoulder pain, ear or eye pain, and difficulty swallowing

The cause of TMJ syndrome is difficult to determine. The most likely causes include:

• Injury, such as a direct blow to the jaw, whiplash, or forceful stretching of the jaw during dental work

• Chronic tooth grinding, clenching, or gum chewing

• Arthritis in the joint

• Chronic muscle tension due to stress, anxiety, depression, or poor posture (usually affects the jaw muscles more than the joint)

- Teeth that do not fit together when you bite (malocclusion)

Home treatment and nonsurgical treatments will successfully relieve most TMJ symptoms. Your doctor may recommend use of a plastic mouth plate (splint), physical therapy, or prescription pain relievers. Surgery is needed for a very small percentage of TMJ problems.

Prevention

- Regularly practice progressive muscle relaxation, particularly before going to sleep. See page 273.

- Stop chewing gum or tough foods at the first sign of pain or discomfort in your jaw muscles.

- Avoid biting your nails and nibbling on pencils or other objects, because doing so forces your jaw into an awkward position and may cause pain.

- Maintain good posture with your ear, shoulder, and hip in a straight line. See page 90.

Home Treatment

- Continue the prevention tips.

- Avoid chewing gum and hard or chewy foods.

- Avoid opening your mouth too wide.

- Avoid cradling a telephone receiver between your shoulder and jaw.

- Rest your jaw, keeping your teeth apart and your lips closed. (Keep your tongue on the roof of your mouth, not between your teeth.)

- Put an ice pack on the joint for five minutes, three times a day. Gently open and close your mouth occasionally while the ice pack is on. If the jaw muscle is swollen, apply ice six times a day.

- Take aspirin or ibuprofen to reduce swelling and pain.

- If there is no swelling, use moist heat on the jaw muscle three times a day. Gently open and close your mouth while the heat is on. Alternate with the cold pack treatments.

- If you are under severe stress or suffer from anxiety or depression, see Chapter 19.

When to Call Kaiser Permanente

- If the pain is severe.

- If TMJ symptoms occur after an injury to the jaw.

- If your jaw locks in certain positions.

- If any jaw problem or pain continues more than two weeks without improvement.

- If other mild TMJ symptoms do not improve after four weeks of home treatment.

I have a simple philosophy… scratch where it itches.
Alice Roosevelt Longworth

11

Skin Problems

Skin problems can be a nuisance, but they are rarely life-threatening. Diagnosing skin problems may require a doctor's help, especially the first time you have a particular ailment. Use the chart on the next page and the index to find the skin problem you're interested in. Also see "Childhood Rashes" on page 205.

Acne

 Acne is the term for pimples or black-heads that commonly form on the face, chest, upper back, or shoulders. A pimple forms when an oil gland in the skin is blocked and secretions and bacteria build up

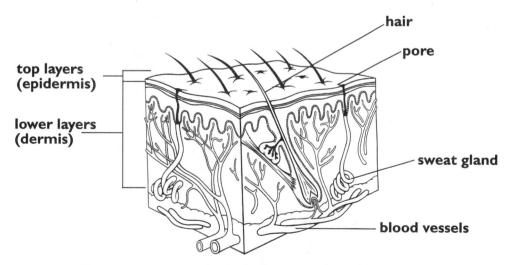

Skin protects your body from dirt and germs and helps you maintain a steady body temperature.

Skin Problems

Skin Symptoms	Possible Causes
Raised, red, itchy welt or fluid-filled bumps after an insect bite or taking a drug	See Hives, p. 191; Insect and Spider Bites and Stings, p. 49.
Red, painful, swollen bump under the skin	See Boils, p. 185.
Red, flaky, itchy skin	See Dry Skin, p. 187; Atopic Dermatitis, p. 183; Fungal Infections, p. 188; Rashes, p. 193.
Crusty, honey-colored rash	See Impetigo, p. 215.
Rash that develops after wearing new jewelry or clothing, exposure to poisonous plants, eating a new food, or taking a new drug	See Rashes, p. 193; Allergies, p. 123.
Red, itchy, blistered rash	Possible poison ivy, oak, sumac. See Rashes, p. 193; Chickenpox, p. 204.
Painful blisters in a band around one side of the body	See Shingles, p. 190.
Change in shape, size, or color of a mole, or persistently irritated mole	See Skin Cancer, p. 195.
Cracked, blistered, itchy, peeling skin between the toes	See Fungal Infections (athlete's foot), p. 188.
Red, itchy, weeping rash on the groin or thighs	See Fungal Infections (jock itch), p. 188; Impetigo, p. 215.
Scaly, itchy, bald spots on scalp	See Fungal Infections (ringworm), p. 188.
Flaky, silvery patches of skin, especially on knees, elbows, or scalp	See Psoriasis, p. 189.
Sandpapery skin rash with sore throat, "strawberry" tongue	May be a sign of scarlet fever, p. 147.

under the skin. Acne usually starts during the teens and often persists into adulthood.

Many women get a few pimples just before their menstrual period. Stress and some oral contraceptives may make acne worse. Fatty foods such as chocolate and nuts are not considered a cause of acne.

Many cases of acne will respond to home treatment, especially if they are mild. For severe or persistent cases, your doctor can prescribe stronger topical medication, anti-biotics, or other drugs.

Prevention

• Wash your face with a mild soap, such as Dove, or one that contains benzoyl peroxide, such as Oxy Sensitive. Wash as often as neces-sary to keep it clean, but do not scrub or overdry.

• While foods are no longer consid-ered a significant cause of acne, avoid any food that seems to cause pimples.

Home Treatment

• Cleanliness is essential. Wash your face, shoulders, chest, and back with a very gentle soap such as Aveeno, Neutrogena, or Basis. Avoid drying soaps such as deodorant soaps. Always rinse well.

• Keep long hair off the face and shoulders, and wash it daily.

• Don't pop pimples and black-heads. This can cause infection and scarring.

• Benzoyl peroxide gel or cream, an over-the-counter medication, is one of the best treatments for acne. Start with the lowest strength and increase the strength if your skin is able to tolerate it. Apply the med-ication once a day, half an hour after washing. It may take several weeks to work and may cause mild redness and dryness. Never use more than 5 percent benzoyl peroxide except on the advice of a doctor.

• Use only water-based lotions and cosmetics that do not clog skin pores (noncomedogenic), and only if they don't aggravate acne.

• Controlling stress may help reduce acne flare-ups. See page 270.

When to Call Kaiser Permanente

• If acne gets worse despite several months of home treatment.

• If you have severe red or purple inflammation, cysts, or lumps under the skin.

• If scars develop as acne heals.

Atopic Dermatitis

Atopic dermatitis (eczema) is a chronic skin disorder common in people with asthma, hay fever, and other allergies. It causes an itchy, red, raised rash that may weep or ooze clear fluid. The rash may develop as tiny blisters, which break and crust over. The lesions are prone to infection, especially if scratching is not controlled.

In children, atopic dermatitis (AD) appears most often on the face, scalp, buttocks, thighs, and torso. In adults, it usually affects the neck, inside the elbows, and backs of the knees.

Adults whose hands or feet are often exposed to irritating substances may often have AD on those areas.

AD is often worse during infancy and greatly improves by early adulthood. Many children improve by age five or six.

Home Treatment

Helping the skin retain moisture is important to successful treatment.

- Take brief daily baths or showers with lukewarm (not hot) water. Use a gentle soap (Dove, Oil of Olay, Neutrogena) or non-soap cleanser (Cetaphil or Aveeno). If possible, bathe without soap.

- After bathing, pat skin dry and apply a lubricating cream (Lubriderm, Moisturel). The cream may help keep your skin from drying out. Reapply cream often.

- Use a humidifier in the bedroom.

- An oral antihistamine (Benadryl) may help relieve itching and relax you enough to allow sleep. Avoid antiseptic and antihistamine creams and sprays, because they irritate the skin.

- Avoid contact with any irritants or allergens that cause problems. Wear gloves when working with irritating substances.

- Wash clothes and bedding in mild detergent and rinse at least twice. Do not use fabric softener if it is irritating.

- For more tips on relieving itching, see page 188.

When to Call Kaiser Permanente

- If crusting or weeping sores appear, because a bacterial infection may be present.

- If itching interferes with sleep and home treatment is not working.

- If atopic dermatitis is not controlled with home treatment.

Blisters

Blisters are usually the result of persistent or repeated rubbing against the skin. Some illnesses, such as shingles, cause blister-like rashes (see page 190). Burns can also blister the skin. See page 34.

Prevention

- Avoid shoes that are too tight or that rub on your feet.

- Wear gloves to protect your hands when doing heavy chores.

Home Treatment

- If a blister is small and closed, leave it alone. Protect it from further rubbing with a loose bandage, and avoid the activity or shoes that caused it.

- If a small blister is in a weight-bearing area, protect it with a doughnut-shaped moleskin pad. Leave the area over the blister open.

- If a blister is larger than one inch across, it is usually best to drain it. The following is a safe method:

  ° Sterilize a needle with rubbing alcohol.

  ° Gently puncture the blister at the edge.

  ° Press the fluid in the blister toward the hole you have made to drain it.

- Once you have opened a blister, or if it has torn open, wash the area with soap and water.

- Do not remove the flap of skin covering the blister unless it is very dirty or torn, or if pus is forming under the blister. Gently smooth it flat over the tender skin underneath.

- Apply an antibiotic ointment and a sterile bandage. Do not use alcohol or iodine. They will delay healing.

- Change the bandage once a day to reduce the chance of infection.

- Remove the bandage at night to let the area dry.

When to Call Kaiser Permanente

- If blisters form often and you do not know the cause.

- If signs of infection develop:

  ° Increased pain, swelling, redness, or tenderness

  ° Heat or red streaks extending from the blister

  ° Discharge of pus

  ° Fever of 100° or higher with no other cause

- If you have diabetes or peripheral vascular disease and blisters are forming on hands, feet, or legs.

Boils

A boil is a red, swollen, painful bump under the skin, similar to an overgrown pimple. Boils are often caused by an infected hair follicle. Bacteria from the infection will form an abscess or pocket of pus. The abscess can become larger than a ping-pong ball and be extremely painful.

Boils occur most often in areas where there is hair and chafing. The face, neck, armpits, breasts, groin, and buttocks are common boil sites.

Prevention

- Wash boil-prone areas with soapy water. An antibacterial soap may help. Dry thoroughly.

- Avoid clothing that is too tight.

Home Treatment

- Do not squeeze, scratch, drain, or lance the boil. Squeezing can push the infection deeper into the skin. Scratching can spread the bacteria and form new boils.

- Wash yourself well with an antibacterial soap to prevent the boil from spreading.

- Use moist heat often. Apply hot, wet washcloths to the boil for 20 to 30 minutes, three to four times a day. Do this as soon as you notice a boil. The heat and moisture can help bring the boil to a head, but it may take five to seven days. A hot water bottle or waterproof heating pad applied over a damp towel may also help.

- Continue using warm compresses for three days after the boil opens. Apply a bandage to keep draining material from spreading, and change it daily.

When to Call Kaiser Permanente

If needed, your doctor can drain the boil and treat the infection. Call the doctor:

- If the boil is on your face, near your spine, or in the anal area.

- If signs of worsening infection develop:

  ° Increased pain, swelling, heat, redness, or tenderness

  ° Red streaks extending from the boil

Birthmarks

Birthmarks are relatively common. Those that are pigmented generally do not go away. Those due to blood vessels usually fade as the child grows.

Salmon patches ("stork bites") are light pink birthmarks that may appear on the upper lip, eyelids, forehead, and back of the neck. They usually fade within a few months.

Strawberry birthmarks are soft, red lumps formed by clusters of blood vessels. They may be present at birth or appear during the first few months. They may grow for up to six months, stabilize for a short time, and then usually begin to recede and fade. Sixty percent are gone by age five; nearly all have disappeared by age nine. No treatment is necessary unless they continue to grow.

Port-wine stains are light pink or wine-colored birthmarks that appear most often on the head and face. They are permanent and become darker as the child grows.

Birthmarks need to be removed if they interfere with breathing or vision, or if they disfigure the face. If surgery is desired for cosmetic reasons, it is best to wait until the child is older. Report any changes in birthmarks to your health professional.

° Continued discharge of pus

° Fever of 100° or higher with no other cause

- If any other lumps, particularly painful ones, develop near the infected area.

- If the pain limits your normal activities.

- If you have diabetes.

- If the boil is as large as a ping-pong ball.

- If the boil has not improved after five to seven days of home treatment.

- If many boils develop over several months.

Dandruff

Dandruff occurs when the skin cells of the scalp flake off. This flaking is natural and occurs all over your body. On the scalp, however, flakes can mix with oil and dust to form dandruff. Dandruff cannot be cured, but it can be controlled.

Home Treatment

- Try frequent and energetic shampooing with any shampoo. Wash hair daily if it controls dandruff.

- If dandruff is excessive and itchy, try a dandruff shampoo (Head & Shoulders, Sebulex, T-Gel, Tegrin). Work the dandruff shampoo into your scalp and leave it on for several minutes before rinsing. Experiment to find the one that works best for you.

When to Call Kaiser Permanente

Call if frequent shampooing or shampooing with a dandruff shampoo doesn't control dandruff.

Dry Skin

Dry, itchy, flaky skin is the most common skin problem, especially in the winter. It results when the skin loses water (not oil) to the air. Dry indoor air is a common cause, as is excessive bathing and hot water. Dry skin is often worse in the winter due to lower humidity and indoor heat.

Prevention

- Avoid showers. They strip the skin's natural oil, which helps hold in moisture. Baths are much kinder to the skin than showers.

- Use bath oils in the tub.

- Use mild soaps (Dove, Cetaphil), especially under the arms and in genital areas.

- Seal in moisture with a moisturizing lotion after your bath.

Home Treatment

- Follow the prevention guidelines above. Prevention is more important than treatment.

Relief From Itching

- Keep the itchy area well lubricated.

- An oatmeal bath may help relieve itching. Be careful not to dry out the skin, because doing so will increase the itching. Wrap one cup of oatmeal in a cotton cloth and boil as you would to cook it. Use this as a sponge and bathe in tepid water without soap. Or try an Aveeno colloidal oatmeal bath.

- Calamine lotion is helpful for poison ivy or oak rashes.

- Try an over-the-counter 1 percent hydrocortisone cream for small itchy areas. Use very sparingly on the face or genitals. If itching is severe, your doctor may prescribe a stronger cream.

- Try an over-the-counter oral antihistamine (Chlor-Trimeton, Benadryl).

- Cut nails short or wear gloves at night to prevent scratching.

- Wear cotton clothing. Avoid wool and acrylic fabrics next to the skin.

- For very dry hands, try this for a night: Apply a thin layer of petroleum jelly, and wear thin cotton gloves to bed. (Dry feet may benefit from similar treatment.)

- Avoid scratching, which damages the skin. If itching is a problem, see "Relief From Itching," above.

When to Call Kaiser Permanente

- If you itch all over your body without obvious cause or rash.

- If itching is so bad that you cannot sleep and home treatment is not helping.

- If the skin is badly broken due to scratching.

Fungal Infections

Fungal infections of the skin most commonly affect the feet, groin, scalp, or nails. Fungi grow best in warm, moist areas of the skin, such as between the toes, in the groin, and in the area beneath the breasts.

Athlete's foot (tinea pedis) is the most common fungal skin infection. Symptoms include cracked, blistered, and peeling areas between the toes, redness and scaling on the soles, and itching. It rarely affects children before puberty; if it does, it may resemble eczema. Athlete's foot often recurs and must be treated each time.

Jock itch (tinea cruris) causes severe itching and moistness on the skin of the groin and upper thighs. There may be red, scaly, raised areas on the skin that weep or ooze pus or clear fluid.

Ringworm is a contagious fungal infection of the scalp or body. It is not caused by worms. Its symptoms include round spots that may be scaly and itchy. It may appear on the torso as a small, red, scaly spot that itches and grows until it is about an inch across. It is more common in children than in adults.

Fungal infections of the **fingernails and toenails** cause discoloration, thickening, and often softening of the nails. They are difficult to treat and often cause permanent damage to the nails.

Thrush is a yeast infection that occurs in the mouth, especially in babies. It causes a white coating inside the mouth, often on the cheeks, that may look like milk but is hard to remove.

Prevention

• Keep the feet clean, cool, and dry. Dry well between the toes after swimming or bathing.

• Wear leather shoes or sandals that allow your feet to "breathe," and wear cotton socks to absorb sweat. Use powder on your feet and in your shoes. Give shoes 24 hours to dry between wearings.

• Wear thongs or shower sandals in public pools and showers.

• Keep the groin clean and dry. Wash and dry well, especially after exercise, and apply talcum powder to absorb moisture. Wear cotton underclothes and avoid tight pants and pantyhose.

• Teach children not to play with dogs or cats that have bald or mangy spots on their coats.

• Don't share hats, combs, or brushes.

Psoriasis

Psoriasis is a chronic skin condition that causes raised red patches topped with silvery, scaling skin, usually on the knees, elbows, scalp, and back. The fingernails, palms, and soles of the feet may also be affected. It is not contagious.

The patches, called plaques, are made up of dead skin cells that accumulate in thick layers. Normal skin cells are replaced every 30 days. In psoriasis, skin cells are replaced every three to four days.

Small patches of psoriasis can often be treated with regular use of hydrocortisone cream.

Tar products (lotions, gels, shampoos) may also be useful, although they may increase sensitivity to the sun. Limited exposure to the sun may also help (protect unaffected skin with sunscreen). If psoriasis affects the scalp, try a mild tar shampoo (Neutrogena, T-Gel, etc.).

Stress may contribute to psoriasis. Stress reduction may help in some cases. See page 270.

Call your doctor if psoriasis covers much of your body or is very red. More extensive cases often need professional care.

Home Treatment

- Follow the prevention guidelines above.

- For athlete's foot and jock itch, use an over-the-counter antifungal powder or lotion, such as Micatin or Lotrimin AF. Use the medication for a week or two after the symptoms clear up to prevent recurrence. Do not use hydrocortisone on a fungal infection.

- Consider wearing cotton socks, and change them twice a day to keep your feet dry. If possible, wear open sandals with cotton socks. When indoors, go in stocking feet.

- Ringworm on the body can be treated with one of the antifungals listed above.

When to Call Kaiser Permanente

- If signs of infection are present: increased swelling and redness or signs of pus.

- If you have diabetes and develop athlete's foot. People with diabetes are at increased risk of infection and may need professional care.

- If home treatment fails to improve a fungal infection after two weeks or clear it up after one month.

- If there is a sudden loss of patches of hair associated with flaking, broken hairs, and inflammation of the scalp; or if there are several household members with hair loss.

Shingles

Shingles (herpes zoster) is caused by the reactivation of the chickenpox virus in the body years after the initial illness. The virus usually affects one of the large nerves that spread outward from the spine, causing pain and a rash in a band around one side of the chest, abdomen, or face. The rash will blister and scab, then clear up over the course of a few weeks.

No one knows what makes the virus active again. Shingles can affect anyone who has had chickenpox. However, older adults and people with weakened immune systems are more likely to get shingles. People with weakened immune systems include those who:

- Have had a bone marrow or other organ transplant.

- Have cancer, especially of the lymph system.

- Are infected with HIV.

Shingles itself is not contagious, but exposure to the rash can cause chickenpox in a person who has not had it before.

If you suspect shingles, call your doctor or advice nurse, within a day after the rash starts if possible, to discuss medication that can limit the pain and rash.

• If ringworm is severe and spreading or is present on the scalp. Prescription medicine may be needed.

Hives

Hives are raised, red, itchy patches of skin (wheals or welts), often fluid-filled, that may appear and disappear at random. They range in size from less than a quarter-inch to an inch or more, and they may last a few minutes or a few days.

Acute hives are often due to an allergy, but chronic hives often have no known cause. Multiple hives often occur in response to a drug, food, or infection. A single hive commonly develops after an insect sting. Other possible causes include plants, inhaled allergens, stress, cosmetics, and exposure to heat, cold, sunlight, or pressure of clothing. Often a cause cannot be found. If possible, avoid foods, medications, and insects that have previously caused hives.

Home Treatment

• Avoid the substance that causes hives.

• Cool water compresses will help relieve itching. Also see page 188.

• An oral antihistamine (Benadryl, Chlor-Trimeton) may help treat the hives and relieve itching. Once the hives have disappeared, decrease the dose of the medication slowly over five to seven days.

When to Call Kaiser Permanente

• Call 911 or seek emergency services if spreading hives occur with dizziness, wheezing, difficulty breathing, tightness in the chest, or swelling of the tongue, lips, or face.

• If hives develop soon after a person takes a new drug.

• If hives persist for several days despite home treatment and avoiding the suspected irritants.

Ingrown Toenails

Ingrown toenails are usually caused when an improperly trimmed toenail cuts into the skin at the edge of the nail or by wearing shoes that are too tight. Because the cut can easily become infected, prompt care is needed.

Prevention

• Cut toenails straight across and leave the nails a little longer at the corners so that the sharp ends don't cut into the skin.

• Wear roomy shoes and keep your feet clean and dry.

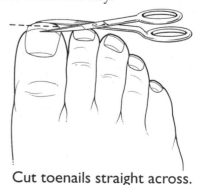

Cut toenails straight across.

  For more information, see the inside front cover.

Home Treatment

- Soak your foot in warm water.

- Wedge a small piece of wet cotton under the corner of the nail to cushion the nail and lift it slightly to keep it from cutting the skin.

- Repeat daily until the nail has grown out and can be trimmed.

- Soaking the feet in warm water for 15 minutes three to four times a day will help relieve swelling or tenderness while toenails grow out.

When to Call Kaiser Permanente

- If signs of infection develop:

  ° Increased pain, swelling, redness, or tenderness

  ° Heat or red streaks extending from the area

  ° Discharge of pus

  ° Fever of 100° or higher with no other cause

- If you have diabetes, circulatory problems, or impaired vision.

Lice and Scabies

Lice are tiny, dark brown, wingless insects that may live on the skin, hair, or clothing. They feed by biting the skin and sucking blood. The bites itch. Lice lay tiny, white eggs, called nits, which can often be seen on the hair. Head lice live in the hair on the head; body lice live on clothing; and pubic lice (also called crabs) live in the groin, underarms, and eyelashes. Lice are spread by close physical contact or contact with the clothing, bedding, brushes, or combs of an infected person. Pubic lice can be spread by sexual contact.

Scabies are tiny mites that burrow under the skin and lay eggs. This burrowing causes an allergic reaction with a rash that itches intensely. They are often found between folds of skin on the fingers and toes, wrists, underarms, and groin. They are usually treated with a medication that is applied over the entire body and left on overnight. Itching may last for several weeks after treatment.

Prevention

- Be alert for signs of lice: itching and lice or nits attached to the hair shafts of the head. Prompt treatment can help prevent spreading them to others.

- Don't share hairbrushes or hats.

Home Treatment

- Nix and RID are over-the-counter medications for lice. Follow the manufacturer's directions for use exactly. For head lice, comb the hair well with a fine-toothed comb after treatment to remove all nits.

- On the day you start treatment, wash all dirty clothing, bedding, and towels in hot water to help get rid of lice, nits, and mites. Iron things that cannot be washed.

- Don't use cream rinses, gel, hairspray, or other products immediately after treatment.

• Contact your pharmacist or health department for more information on treatment and preventing reinfestation.

When to Call Kaiser Permanente

Call if treatment with over-the-counter medication is not successful. Stronger prescription drugs are available.

Rashes

A rash (dermatitis) is any irritation or inflammation of the skin. Rashes can be caused by illness, allergy, or heat, and sometimes by emotional stress. For rashes related to childhood illnesses, see page 205. If the rash occurred after a tick bite, see page 64.

Poison ivy and other plant rashes are often red, blistered, and itchy and appear in lines where the leaves brushed against the skin.

When you first get a rash, ask yourself these questions to help determine the cause (also see pages 182 and 205):

• Did a localized rash follow contact with anything new that could have irritated your skin: poison ivy, oak, or sumac; soaps, detergents, shampoos, perfumes, cosmetics, or lotions; jewelry or fabrics; new tools, appliances, latex gloves, or other objects? The location of the rash is often a clue to the cause.

Bald Spots

Bald spots are not the same as baldness. Some men have a natural tendency toward baldness. This natural hair loss is largely hereditary. It poses no health risks other than sunburn (wear a hat and use sunscreen).

Bald spots may be caused by repeated pulling of the hair, such as tight braids or habitual tugging or twisting. Ringworm is a fungal infection that causes scaly bald spots. See page 188.

Bald spots that appear on a normal scalp may indicate a more significant problem. If hair loss is sudden, or if it develops after you begin taking a new medication, call your doctor.

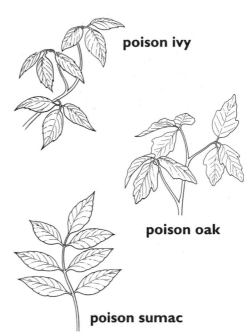

poison ivy

poison oak

poison sumac

The oil on the leaves of these plants can cause an uncomfortable, itchy, red skin rash with blisters or hives.

- Have you eaten anything new that you may be allergic to?

- Are you taking any new medications, either prescription or over-the-counter?

- Have you been unusually stressed or upset recently?

- Is there joint pain or fever with the rash?

- Is the rash spreading?

- Does the rash itch?

Prevention

- If you are exposed to poison ivy, oak, or sumac, wash the skin with dish soap and water within 30 minutes to get the irritating oil off the skin. This may help prevent or reduce the rash. Also wash your clothes, your dog, and anything that may have come in contact with the plant.

- Avoid products that cause the rash: detergents, cosmetics, lotions, clothing, jewelry, etc.

- Use fragrance- and preservative-free or hypoallergenic detergents, lotions, and cosmetics if you have frequent rashes.

Home Treatment

- Wash affected areas with water. Soap can be irritating. Pat dry thoroughly.

- Apply cold, wet compresses to reduce itching. Repeat frequently. Also see page 188.

- Leave the rash exposed to the air. Baby powder can help keep it dry. Avoid lotions and ointments until the rash heals. However, calamine lotion is helpful for plant rashes. Use it three to four times a day.

- Hydrocortisone cream can provide temporary relief of itching. Use very sparingly on facial and genital rashes.

- Rashes on the feet or groin may be due to fungal infections. See page 188.

When to Call Kaiser Permanente

- If signs of infection develop:

  ° Increased pain, swelling, redness, or tenderness

  ° Heat or red streaks extending from the area

  ° Discharge of pus or honey-colored crust

  ° Fever of 100° or higher with no other cause

- If you suspect a medication reaction caused the rash.

- If rash occurs with fever and joint pain.

- If rash occurs with sore throat. See page 147.

- If a rash appears and you aren't sure what is causing it.

- If rash continues after two to three weeks of home treatment.

Skin Cancer

Skin cancer is the most common type of cancer. Fortunately, many types of skin cancer are easy to cure.

Most skin cancer is caused by sun damage. Ninety percent of skin problems occur on the face, neck, and arms, where sun exposure is greatest. Light-skinned, blue-eyed people are more likely to develop skin cancer. Dark-skinned people have less risk.

Most skin cancers are generally slow-growing, easy to recognize, and easy to treat in a doctor's office. A small percentage of skin cancers are more serious.

Basal cell and squamous cell skin cancers tend to develop in sun-exposed areas. They differ from noncancerous growths in several important ways. Skin cancers:

- Tend to bleed more and are often open sores that do not heal.

- Tend to be slow-growing.

Most moles are harmless. However, malignant melanomas (one type of cancerous mole) can be fatal and should be promptly treated.

Prevention

Most skin cancers can be prevented by avoiding excessive exposure to the sun. Most damaging sun exposure has occurred by age 20, so keep your children protected (see page 63). Cumulative exposure to sun is a major factor in some types of skin cancers.

Home Treatment

Examine your skin with a mirror or another person's help. Look for unusual moles, spots, or bumps. Pay special attention to areas that get a lot of sun exposure: hands, arms, chest, neck (especially the back of the neck), face, ears, etc. Report any changes to your doctor.

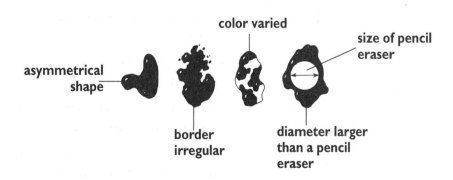

asymmetrical shape

color varied

size of pencil eraser

border irregular

diameter larger than a pencil eraser

Watch for these mole changes.

When to Call Kaiser Permanente

If your moles do not change over time, there is little cause for concern. If you have a family history of malignant melanoma, let your doctor know. You may be at higher risk. Call your doctor if you notice any of the following changes:

• Asymmetrical shape: One half does not match the other half.

• Border irregularity: The edges are ragged, notched, or blurred.

• Color: The color is not uniform. Watch for shades of red and black, or a red, white, and blue mottled appearance.

• Diameter: The mole is larger than a pencil eraser. (Harmless moles are usually smaller than this.)

• Scaliness, oozing, bleeding, or spreading of pigment into surrounding skin.

• Appearance of a bump or nodule on the mole, or any change in appearance of the mole.

• Itching, tenderness, or pain.

• Unusual skin changes or growths, especially if they bleed and keep growing.

Warts

Warts are skin growths that are caused by a virus. They can appear anywhere on the body. Warts are not dangerous, but they can be bothersome.

Little is known about warts. Most types are only slightly contagious. They can spread to other areas on the same person but rarely to other people. Genital and anal warts are an exception; they are easily transmitted through sexual contact and may increase the risk of cervical cancer. See page 260.

Plantar warts appear on the soles of the feet. Most of the wart lies under the skin surface and may make you feel like you are walking on a pebble.

Because warts seem to come and go for little reason, it's possible they are sensitive to slight changes in the immune system. Although there is no scientific explanation for why it works, in some cases you can "think" them away.

When necessary, your doctor can remove warts. Unfortunately, they often come back.

Home Treatment

• Warts appear and disappear spontaneously. They can last a week, a month, or even years. To get rid of your warts, it helps to believe in the treatment. If something works for you, stick with it.

• If the wart bleeds a little, cover it with a bandage and apply light pressure to stop the bleeding.

• If the wart is in the way, use a pumice stone or an over-the-counter salicylic acid ointment. This drug can be irritating in high concentrations; you may need to use a milder form for a longer period of time.

• If you have diabetes or peripheral vascular disease, do not use salicylic acid or irritate the wart without discussing it with a health professional.

• If you use a pumice stone, both the debris from the wart and the area of the pumice stone that touched the wart can be infectious. Do not handle this material. Discard both the wart debris and pumice stone promptly.

• For plantar warts, apply a doughnut-shaped pad to cushion the wart and relieve pain. Apply salicylic acid solution to the wart at night, and rub the whitened skin off in the morning.

• Try the least expensive method of treating warts first. You may save a trip to your doctor.

• Don't cut or burn off a wart.

When to Call Kaiser Permanente

• If a wart looks infected after being irritated or knocked off.

• If a plantar wart is painful when you walk and foam pads do not help.

• If you have warts in the anal or genital area. See page 260.

• If the wart causes continual discomfort.

• If a wart develops on the face and is a cosmetic concern.

Calluses and Corns

Calluses are hard, thickened skin on parts of the foot exposed to friction. Corns are caused by pressure on the skin from the inside, such as from a bone.

Soak your feet in warm water and rub the callus or corn with a pumice stone. You may need to do this for several days until the thickened skin is gone.

Do not try to cut or burn off corns or calluses. If you have diabetes or peripheral vascular disease, talk with your doctor before attempting to remove troublesome corns or calluses.

 For more information, see the inside front cover.

My mother had a great deal of trouble with me,
but I think she enjoyed it.
Mark Twain

12

Infant and Child Health

When your child gets sick or hurt, you are usually the first person to provide care. Your calmness, confidence, and competence in caring for your children's health problems will help them enjoy healthy childhoods and learn the importance of self-care for their own use as they mature.

Virtually every health problem in this book may affect children. However, a few are almost exclusively childhood concerns. For convenience, we have grouped these problems into this chapter. If the problem you are looking for is not in this chapter, please look for it in the index.

Facts About Infants and Young Children

The following brief notes are of particular concern to parents. This information may help dispel some unnecessary fears and give you some guidance.

For more information on child health, see Resources 21 to 28 on page 326.

Umbilical Cords and Bellybuttons

Clean the bellybutton (navel) three or four times a day with a bit of cotton moistened with a little rubbing alcohol. Pull the cord up gently but firmly to clean the base (try to avoid getting alcohol on the skin around the navel). Swabbing the bellybutton with alcohol will help it to dry and prevent infection. Keep the cord dry and do not give a tub or pan bath until the umbilical cord has fallen off and the navel is healed. Fold diapers below and shirts above the cord to promote drying.

The umbilical cord will drop off and the navel will heal in one to three weeks. After the cord comes off, there may be a moist or bloody oozing for a few days, less than the size of a quarter, between diaper changes. This does not need special treatment.

Call your doctor if there is redness or swelling around the navel or a large amount of foul-smelling discharge from the navel.

The appearance of the bellybutton is not affected by the way the cord is tied off. A small nodule of tissue sometimes remains after the cord falls off. If it is small, no treatment is usually needed. If it is larger or persists longer than two weeks, call your doctor.

Breast-Feeding

Breast milk is the ideal food for babies younger than four to six months. The American Academy of Pediatrics recommends that babies be breast-fed for the first year of life. Although breast-feeding is best, babies can also get good nutrition from formula. Most doctors do not recommend giving cow's milk to a baby less than one year old.

Breast-feeding has many advantages for both baby and mother. Breast milk contains substances that help your baby resist infections and other diseases. It protects against allergies and asthma and also is easier to digest than formula. Breast-fed babies have fewer colds and ear infections, less diarrhea, and less vomiting.

Some instruction helps ensure that you can breast-feed successfully. Try to take a breast-feeding class. Also see Resources 78 and 79 on page 329. The La Leche League and the Nursing Mother's Council are other

---

Child Car Seats

Infant and child car seats save lives. Many states require them for all children under age four and those weighing less than 40 pounds. Children who are not in car seats can be seriously injured or killed during crashes or even abrupt stops at low speeds. For maximum safety, follow the manufacturer's recommendations for car seat use.

All children under age 12 should be in the back seat, especially if the car has airbags.

Infants under 20 pounds: Use an infant car seat that reclines and faces the rear. Check the manufacturer's instructions.

Infants and children over 20 pounds: Use a toddler seat that faces the front and has a shield or harness. Some infant seats can be converted into toddler seats.

Children over age four and over 40 pounds: Use a booster seat that raises the child so he or she can see out of the window. Use regular lap and shoulder belts. Adjust the shoulder belt to fit across the shoulder, not the neck.

Set a good example for your children by always wearing your own seat belt, and always insist that they buckle up.

good sources of breast-feeding information, advice, and support.

Nursing mothers need 500 calories per day more than they needed before becoming pregnant. Although you don't need to drink milk to make milk, extra calcium and protein are important, and your doctor may prescribe a vitamin supplement. Avoid smoking and drinking alcohol, and limit caffeine to one or two beverages per day. Do not take any medication while breast-feeding unless it was prescribed by a health professional.

Circumcision

Circumcision is surgery to remove the foreskin of a newborn boy's penis. About 60 percent of boys in the U.S. are circumcised, down from over 80 percent in the late 1970s.

There are both benefits and risks associated with circumcision. Discuss the risks and benefits with your doctor. The decision is entirely up to you.

The major benefit is that circumcision makes it easier to keep the penis clean. Cleanliness reduces the risk of developing urinary tract infections.

The risks of circumcision are slight. Complications of local infection or bleeding occur in about one in every 250 cases. Local anesthetic will reduce the pain of circumcision. Generally, circumcision is not recommended for a sick infant.

After circumcision, apply petroleum jelly liberally to the head of the penis at each diaper change to prevent the scab from sticking to the diaper. Wash the penis by dripping

warm water over it (do not use alcohol or baby wipes). Pat dry with a soft towel.

If the circumcision site is red, apply an antibiotic ointment (Bacitracin or Polysporin). Call your doctor if the redness extends down the shaft of the penis.

If you choose not to have your son circumcised, clean the exposed foreskin gently during the first four years. Starting around age four, gently begin to retract the foreskin. Do not forcibly retract the foreskin; it may not be fully retractable until puberty. Teach your son to wash his penis well at every bath and to gently retract the foreskin when possible and clean beneath it.

Uniqueness

No two children are exactly alike. Each child has his own special way of approaching the world. Study your child's behavior and temperament. What is "normal" for him may be far different from the "normal" behavior of a sibling, neighbor, or friend of the same age. To learn more about child temperament programs, check with your child's pediatrician or at your local Kaiser Permanente facility for additional resources.

Discipline

Discipline is a way to help children develop self-control and responsible behavior. Children best accept discipline that is fair, firm, consistent, and loving. Focus on the child's behavior, not the child's personality. Set limits and offer the child choices within those limits. For older children and teens, be specific and firm in setting rules and expectations.

It is important to listen carefully when your child tells you how she feels. When she is finished, briefly repeat back to her what you heard her say. This lets her know that you are listening and helps her be clear about her feelings.

Look for and praise good behavior, and ignore bad behavior. If bad behavior doesn't get attention, a child will usually stop doing it.

When your child misbehaves:

- If you are angry, take a few minutes to calm down before disciplining him. Make it clear that you like the child, but you don't like the behavior.

- Use "time-outs" to interrupt problem behaviors and help the child build self-control.

- Discipline older children with loss of privileges or allowances.

- Do not use physical punishment, like spanking, to discipline your children.

Temper Tantrums

 Children often have temper tantrums when they are frustrated, want attention, or to get their own way. Children tend to have more temper tantrums when they are tired, hungry, or sick.

- Be supportive if the tantrum is due to frustration, fatigue, or hunger. Offer encouragement, suggest a nap, or provide a snack.

- Stay calm. Getting angry will prolong the tantrum. Avoid spanking, because it tells the child that you have lost control.

- Use "time-outs" to help the child calm down.

- Don't let tantrums change your behavior as a parent. Children will learn quickly that a tantrum is not the way to get their own way.

Toilet Training

Every child has a unique timetable for becoming toilet-trained. Most children are ready to begin toilet training between age 18 and 36 months. Look for these other signs of readiness in your child:

- Understands words referring to bowel movements and urination.

- Recognizes the sensation of a full bladder and the urge to have a bowel movement.

- Knows what the toilet is for and has watched others use it.

- Prefers clean, dry diapers to soiled ones.

- Understands that using the potty means having a dry diaper.

If you think your child is ready to begin toilet training, the following tips may make it go more smoothly:

- Get the child a potty chair. Make sure the child's feet can rest on the floor or on a footrest. Encourage the child to sit on the chair at least once a day at about the same time each day. Let the child use the chair for looking at books or watching TV.

- After the child has had a bowel movement in a diaper, put him or her on the chair, and put the contents of the diaper in the pot.

- Once the child is interested, let the child play for short periods without a diaper and have the chair nearby. Encourage the child to use the chair if he or she needs to "go potty."

- Reward every success with hugs and words of praise. Relapses are common in the first few weeks, but don't scold or punish when the child forgets. Keep a casual attitude.

- Bladder control may take longer than bowel control. If the child is aware of a full bladder, try putting him or her on the potty every 30 to 60 minutes. Praise the child for success and give gentle encouragement when the child wets his or her pants.

Sleep Habits

Babies have both deep and light sleep cycles. In each sleep cycle, there are 60 minutes of light sleep, 60 to 90 minutes of deep sleep, and another 30 minutes of light sleep. At the end of this cycle, the baby is semi-alert and can be wakened easily.

Parents can help the baby sleep through the night by helping the baby learn to soothe him- or herself back to sleep during the light sleep cycles.

For infants (birth to 2 months):

- Put the baby in the crib when he or she is drowsy but awake.

- Make middle-of-the-night feedings short and boring.

- As the baby gets older, delay the middle-of-the-night feeding, and discontinue it sometime after age four months.

- Also see Resource 26 on page 326.

It appears that it is safer for a baby to sleep on his or her back or side to prevent sudden infant death syndrome (SIDS). Do not force a baby into a sleeping position. Babies are capable of moving themselves.

Bed-Wetting

Bed-wetting (enuresis) in children who have never been dry is common, and most children will outgrow it by about age six to eight. In almost all cases, it is really not a disease, but rather a normal variation in development.

In some cases, a child who has been dry for several months or longer may begin bed-wetting again. This may happen without a clear cause, or may possibly be due to a urinary tract infection or to emotional problems.

Home Treatment

There are a number of ways to deal with bed-wetting that don't require medication. Ask your doctor for advice in managing bed-wetting until your child outgrows it.

- Do not punish, embarrass, or blame the child.

- Remind the child to get up during the night to urinate. Providing a bedside potty chair and night light may help.

- Let children over age five take control of the problem. Help them learn to wake themselves at night to go to the bathroom. Set an alarm for three to four hours after bedtime, and make sure the child has to get out of bed to turn it off.

- Do not force a child to wear diapers at night. However, some children may be more comfortable wearing adult diapers such as Attends or Depend. Waterproof, extra-absorbent underwear or thick pads to protect the mattress may also help avoid daily bed changes. Wash them with one-half cup of vinegar to eliminate odor.

When to Call Kaiser Permanente

Your doctor can rule out or treat any physical causes of bed-wetting and help you and your child manage the problem.

- If bed-wetting occurs with painful or burning urination or other signs of urinary tract infection. See page 243.

- If prevention and home treatment are not successful after four to six weeks in a child older than six.

- If bed-wetting becomes more frequent or severe.

- If bed-wetting occurs in a child who had previously been dry for several months.

- If bed-wetting occurs with soiling of the underwear with bowel movements after age three.

- If a child over age three has daytime bladder control problems.

Chickenpox

 Chickenpox (varicella) is a relatively minor illness. Almost all children will get it. The first couple of days, your child will be in generally ill health, with a cold, cough, fever, and abdominal pain; then a rash of red, pimple-like spots appears. A child may have just one or two spots, or the rash may cover the entire body, including the throat, mouth, ears, groin, and scalp.

The spots turn into clear blisters that become cloudy, break open, and crust over. This rash itches a lot. Spots continue to appear for one to five days and subside over a week or two.

Chickenpox is very contagious. After exposure, symptoms occur in 10 days to 3 weeks. It is contagious for one to two days before the rash appears and for up to five days after the spots appear. Children can generally return to school or day care when all the spots have scabbed, or on the sixth day after the rash appeared. Encephalitis (see page 141) is a rare complication of chickenpox.

Prevention

The chickenpox vaccine can be given to children age 12 months and older, and to teens and adults who have not had the illness. See page 19. It is especially important to immunize teens and adults who have not had chickenpox, because the disease is more severe in adulthood.

Adults who have not been vaccinated and who have not had chickenpox should avoid exposure to children who have it and avoid exposure to people who have shingles (see page 190). Pregnant women who have never had chickenpox and have not been vaccinated should also avoid exposure, since the illness can harm the developing fetus. The vaccine cannot be given during pregnancy.

Home Treatment

• Use acetaminophen to relieve fever. Do not give aspirin to children and teens under age 20 who may have chickenpox because

Childhood Rashes

Rashes that come with childhood illnesses are hard to tell apart. Review all symptoms before deciding what to do.

Description	Possible Illness
Red, pimple-like spots that turn to blisters; fever	Chickenpox, p. 204
Rash in diaper area only	Diaper Rash, p. 209
Red rash on face that looks like slapped cheeks; pink rash on torso that comes and goes; possible fever	Fifth Disease, p. 218
Red or pink dots on head, neck, shoulders; more common in infants	Prickly Heat, p. 217
Sudden high fever for 2–3 days followed by rose-pink rash on torso, arms, and neck after fever goes down	Roseola, p. 218
Fine pink rash; starts on face and covers whole body; swollen glands behind ears	Rubella (rare), p. 217
Fever, runny nose, hacking cough; red eyes 2–3 days before spotty red rash covers whole body	Rubeola (measles) (rare), p. 217
High fever, sore throat, sandpapery rash, and strawberry-textured tongue	Scarlet fever, p. 147

aspirin use is related to Reye's syndrome, a rare but often fatal condition.

- Control the itching (see page 188). Oral Benadryl and warm baths with some baking soda or Aveeno colloidal oatmeal added to the water will help. Avoid Benadryl creams because the medication can build up to toxic levels in the body.

- Cut the child's fingernails to prevent scratching. If scabs are scratched off too early, the sores may become infected.

When to Call Kaiser Permanente

- If your child is at risk of complications from chickenpox (is taking steroid medications or cancer chemotherapy, or has a weakened immune system).

- If a child age three months to three years has a fever of 103° or higher for 24 hours. See Fever on page 212.

- If severe itching cannot be controlled by Benadryl and warm baths.

- If bruising appears without injury.

- If sores appear in the eyes.

- If you notice signs of encephalitis (see page 141):

  ° Fever, severe headache, and stiff neck

  ° Unusual sleepiness or lethargy

  ° Persistent vomiting

Colic

Colic is not a disease; it is a condition that causes otherwise healthy babies to cry inconsolably, usually in the evening and at night. Doctors aren't sure what causes colic. The leading theory is that colic is caused by abdominal pain due to intestinal gas.

All babies cry, so how do you know if your baby has colic? Colic usually follows the "rule of three": Crying starts in the first three months after birth and continues more than three hours a day, more than three days a week.

Fortunately, colic goes away as the baby matures, almost always by the end of the third month, sooner for many babies. Although no single method always works to relieve colicky babies, there are a number of things you can try. Unfortunately, what works one time may not work the next. Be creative and persistent.

Home Treatment

- Most important: Stay calm and try to relax. If you start to lose control, take a minute to calm down. Never shake a baby; it can cause permanent brain damage and even death.

- Make sure your baby is getting enough to eat and not too much. The problem may be hunger, not colic.

- Make sure your baby isn't swallowing too much air while eating. Feed the baby slowly, holding him or her almost upright. Burp your baby periodically. Prop your baby up for 15 minutes after feeding.

- If your baby is bottle-fed, use nipples with holes large enough to drip cold formula at least one drop per second. Babies will swallow more air from around the nipple if the hole is too small.

- Heat formula to body temperature. Don't overheat.

- Babies need to suck up to two hours a day to be satisfied. If feedings aren't enough, use a pacifier.

- Keep a regular routine for meals, naps, and playtime. Mealtime should be quiet and undisturbed by bright lights and loud noise.

- Make sure your baby's diaper is clean, that your baby isn't too hot or cold, and isn't bored.

- Try rocking or walking your baby. Putting him or her stomach-down over your knee or forearm may be helpful.

- Calm your baby with a car ride or a walk outside. Placing your baby near the hum of a clothes dryer, dishwasher, or bubbling aquarium may help soothe him or her.

- Don't worry about spoiling a baby during the first three months; comforting a baby makes both of you feel better.

- Ask a friend or neighbor to baby-sit some evening while you go to dinner and a movie!

- If nothing seems to work, don't feel guilty about shutting the bedroom door and turning up the stereo once in a while; if it will help you relax, it will help your baby. However, don't let your baby cry alone for more than 5 to 10 minutes. After 10 minutes, try the above suggestions again.

When to Call Kaiser Permanente

Colic generally does not require professional treatment unless it is accompanied by vomiting, diarrhea, or other signs of more serious illness. If the baby looks healthy and acts normally between crying episodes, and if your emotions can stand the noise for the first three months, you have little cause for worry.

However, if colic lasts more than four hours a day, or if you feel like you need help, contact your doctor for advice.

In rare cases, colic may be so severe that you and your doctor may consider a medication. Ask about side effects.

Cradle Cap

Cradle cap is an oily yellow scaling or crusting on an infant's scalp. It is caused by a build-up of normal oils on the skin. Cradle cap is common in babies and is easily treated.

Home Treatment

- Wash your baby's head with baby shampoo once a day. Gently scrub the scalp with a soft-bristled brush (a soft toothbrush works well) for a few minutes to remove the scales. Don't worry about hurting your baby's skull; it is sturdier than you think. Rinse well.

- You can also rub mineral oil on the scalp one hour before shampooing to loosen the scales.

- If scrubbing with baby shampoo doesn't work, try using a dandruff shampoo, such as Selsun Blue, Head & Shoulders, or Sebulex. Use these carefully because they can irritate your baby's eyes.

- If the rash is irritated and red, a mild hydrocortisone cream (Cortaid) will probably help.

Croup

Croup is a respiratory problem most common in children ages two to four years. It may accompany a viral infection, such as a cold. The main symptom is a harsh cough that sounds like a seal's bark. A fever of 100° to 101° is common. The child may become very frightened. Croup usually gets worse at night and may last one to seven days, with each night usually better than the last.

Home Treatment

- Stay calm. The child is already frightened and needs reassurance.

- Get moisture into the air to make it easier for the child to breathe. Take the child into the bathroom, turn on all hot-water faucets, then sit on the floor in the steamy room and read a story together.

- Bundle up and take the child outside for a walk in the cool fresh air. Cool, moist air is best.

- Set up a vaporizer or croup tent in the child's bedroom. Put a vaporizer under the crib and drape a blanket over the head of the crib to trap the moisture near the child's head. If the child is older and no longer in a crib, drape the blanket over an umbrella or card table. Stay with your child to provide comfort and to be sure the blanket doesn't fall. With a cold-mist vaporizer, the air will be quite cold. Dress the child in warm pajamas, and place a sheet over the blankets to catch moisture. Don't worry about your child getting chilled. The cool, moist air is the important part.

- If the child starts crying, this may be a positive sign that he or she is breathing more normally.

When to Call Kaiser Permanente

- Call 911 or seek emergency services if the child stops breathing or begins to turn blue. Give rescue breathing (see page 56) until help arrives.

- If these signs of respiratory distress appear and persist despite home treatment:

  ° Squeaky or raspy sound as child inhales (stridor)

  ° Sucking in or retraction between ribs as child inhales

  ° Flaring nostrils

- If the child is so short of breath that he or she can't walk or talk.

- If the child drools or is breathing with the chin jutting out and the mouth open.

- If 20 minutes of steam inhalation or cold outdoor air do not relax the child enough to allow sleep.

- If the child has a fever of 102° or higher.

- If you or your child gets hysterical and cannot calm down.

- If it is the first case of croup in your family and you need reassurance.

- If croup lasts longer than three nights.

Diaper Rash

Diaper rash is a skin reaction, usually to the moisture and bacteria in babies' urine and stools, or to the soap used to wash diapers. While it is uncomfortable, diaper rash is usually not dangerous.

Symptoms of the rash are a red bottom and thighs. It will be easier for you to recognize after you have seen it the first time.

Prevention

- Change diapers as soon as possible after they have been soiled or wet.

- Leave the skin open to the air for 5 to 10 minutes after each diaper change as often as possible.

- Wash diapers with mild detergent and rinse twice. Do not use bleach.

- If your baby has frequent problems, avoid using plastic pants for a while. They trap moisture against the baby's skin.

- Protect the diaper area with zinc oxide or another ointment when your baby has diarrhea. If the problem is due to frequent diarrhea, see Diarrhea on page 210.

Home Treatment

- Change diapers frequently. Rinse and dry the skin in the diaper area at every diaper change. Use a washcloth with water and allow the diaper area to air dry if possible. Wash with a mild soap once a day.

- Try protecting the skin with Desitin, Diaparene, A & D Ointment, or zinc oxide. Apply cream only to dry skin. Discontinue creams if a rash develops or they appear to slow healing.

- Try another brand or type of diaper. Some babies tolerate one kind better than another.

- Avoid bulky or multilayered diapers.

- Stop using plastic pants when the rash appears.

- Try changing detergents if the rash does not clear.

When to Call Kaiser Permanente

- If the diaper rash becomes very red, raw, or sore-looking, or if it has blisters, pus, peeling areas, or crusty patches.

- If the rash is mainly in the skin creases, because this may indicate a yeast infection.

- If a significant rash lasts longer than five days.

 For more information, see the inside front cover.

Diarrhea and Vomiting

 Diarrhea and vomiting may be caused by viral stomach flu or by eating unusual kinds or amounts of food. An infant's developing digestive system sometimes will not tolerate large amounts of juice, fruit, or even milk. Breast-fed babies are less likely to develop diarrhea.

Stomach flu often starts with vomiting that is followed in a few hours (sometimes 8 to 12 hours or longer) by diarrhea. Sometimes there is no diarrhea.

Infants and children under age four, and especially under six months, need special attention when they have diarrhea or are vomiting, because they can quickly become dehydrated. Careful observation of the child's appearance and fluid intake can help prevent problems. For children age four and older, see Diarrhea on page 73 and Vomiting on page 80.

Home Treatment

Infants age 3 months to 2 years:

• If the baby is breast-fed, continue breast-feeding. If the diarrhea gets worse (larger, more frequent stools), or if the child is vomiting, supplement feedings with a children's oral rehydration drink (Pedialyte, Ricelyte, or store brand).

• If the baby is formula-fed, switch to an oral rehydration drink. Gradually add back formula feedings within 24 hours. Return to the usual amount of formula within another day.

• Give four to eight ounces of fluid (breast milk or rehydration drink) for each large, loose stool.

• For children over age six months, you can improve the taste of the rehydration drink by adding a pinch of NutraSweet or sugar-free Kool-Aid or Jell-O powder.

• Do not use sports drinks, fruit juice, or soda. These drinks contain too much sugar and not enough of the minerals (electrolytes) that are being lost.

• Do not use rehydration drinks as the sole source of fluid for more than 12 hours.

• After 12 to 24 hours, offer the child solid foods, if he or she was eating solids before. Allow the child to eat what he or she prefers; the particular food is not important. Avoid high-fiber foods (such as beans) and foods with a lot of sugar, such as juice and ice cream.

• Protect the diaper area with zinc oxide or another cream. Diaper rash is common after diarrhea.

Children age 2 years and older:

• Give one-half to one cup of a children's oral rehydration drink each hour. Give small, frequent sips even if the child is vomiting. Add Nutra-Sweet flavorings if needed.

• Diluted Gatorade or sports drinks may be used temporarily if the diarrhea is mild to moderate, but oral rehydration drinks are better. Do not give fruit juice or soda.

- Offer easily digestible foods (cooked cereal, toast, crackers) in addition to the rehydration drink. Resume a regular diet within a day or so. Do not use a rehydration drink as the sole source of fluids and nutrients for more than 12 hours.

As the child gets better, the stools will become smaller and less frequent. Some types of diarrhea may cause four to six days of watery stools. Watch for signs of dehydration (see below). You can treat the illness at home as long as the child is taking in enough fluids and nutrients, is urinating normal amounts, and seems to be improving.

When to Call Kaiser Permanente

- If vomiting occurs with severe headache, sleepiness, lethargy (child cannot be wakened easily), or a stiff neck (child may cry out when the neck is moved). See page 141.

- If the diarrhea is bloody, tarry, or dark red.

- If the urine becomes bloody or cola-colored.

- If there is blood in the vomit.

- If signs of severe dehydration appear (also see page 73):

  ° Sunken eyes, no tears, dry mouth and tongue

  ° Sunken soft spot on an infant's head

° Little or no urine for eight hours

° Skin that is doughy or doesn't bounce back when pinched

° Rapid breathing and heartbeat

° Sleepy, difficult to wake up, listless, and extremely irritable

- If a child with diarrhea or vomiting refuses to drink or cannot take in enough liquid to replace lost fluids.

- If severe vomiting (vomiting most or all clear liquids and feedings) occurs in an infant under age three months. In older children, call if severe vomiting continues:

  ° Longer than four hours in an infant age 3 to 12 months

  ° Eight hours in a child age one to three years

- If occasional vomiting occurs without other symptoms and the child is able to keep fluids down between vomiting episodes, call if it continues longer than:

  ° One to two days in an infant under three months

  ° Two to four days in an infant age three to six months

  ° One to two weeks in a child age six months to three years

- If severe diarrhea (large loose stools every one to two hours) continues for longer than:

  ° Four hours in an infant under three months

  ° Eight hours in an infant age three to six months

For more information, see the inside front cover.

° One to two days in a child age six months to four years

• If mild to moderate diarrhea continues without obvious cause or other symptoms for longer than:

° 24 hours in an infant under three months

° One to two days in an infant age three to six months

° Four to seven days in a child age six months to four years

• If the child has a fever of 103° or higher, or a lower fever with diarrhea for more than two days.

• If the child has severe stomach pain.

• If stomach pain is persistent and there is frequent vomiting for more than 12 hours with little or no diarrhea.

• If stomach pain starts several hours before the vomiting and seems like more than stomach cramps.

• If stomach pain is not located near the bellybutton, especially if it seems to be in the lower right abdomen. This can be difficult to determine in small children.

Fever

 Fever is usually defined as a temperature above 100.4°. Body temperature can also rise above normal when an infant is overdressed or in a room that is too warm.

For information on taking accurate temperatures in infants and children, see page 23. All temperatures in this section are rectal.

In most, but not all, cases, fever indicates that an illness is present. By itself, a fever is not harmful; in fact, it may help the body fight infections more effectively.

In children, viral infections, such as colds, flu, and chickenpox, can cause high fevers. Flu (see page 140) can cause a high fever for five days or longer, along with body aches, headache, and cold-like symptoms. Bacterial infections, such as strep throat and ear infections, also cause fevers. Teething may cause a low-grade fever up to 100°.

Children tend to run higher fevers than adults. Although high fevers are uncomfortable, they do not often cause medical problems. Convulsions from fever (febrile convulsions) occur only occasionally. See page 214.

There is no medical evidence that prolonged high fevers from infection can cause brain damage. The body limits a temperature from going above 106°. However, when heat from external sources (like a car parked in the sun) raises the body temperature above 107°, brain damage can occur rapidly.

Home Treatment

It can be hard to know when to call your doctor when your child has a fever, especially during the cold and flu season.

The degree of the fever is not always related to the severity of the infection. How your child looks and acts is a better guide than the thermometer.

Most children will be less active when they have a fever. However, if there are periods during the day when your child is more active, cheerful and playing, and is taking fluids well, it is a good sign.

Generally, if a child over three is comfortable, eating well, and playing as usual, leave the fever alone. It will do more good than harm.

• Dress the child lightly, and do not wrap him or her in blankets.

• Encourage the child to drink extra liquids or suck on ice chips or popsicles.

If the fever is over 102° and the child is uncomfortable:

• Give acetaminophen or ibuprofen. See page 317 for dose information. Do not give aspirin to children or teens under age 20.

• If the fever is 104° or higher, sponge the child with lukewarm water for 20 minutes. Do not use cold water, ice, or rubbing alcohol. Check the temperature frequently. It may take up to an hour to reduce the fever.

• Keep encouraging the child to drink extra fluids.

When to Call Kaiser Permanente

• If fever occurs with vomiting, severe headache, sleepiness, lethargy (child cannot be wakened easily), or a stiff neck (child may cry out when the neck is moved). See page 141.

• If fever is accompanied by these symptoms:

° Rapid, difficult breathing

° Drooling or inability to swallow

° Purple rash that does not lighten when you press on it

° Vomiting, diarrhea, and stomach pain (see page 210)

° Signs of dehydration (see page 72)

° Unexplained skin rash (see page 205 for common childhood illnesses that cause rash)

° Ear pain (babies often pull at painful ears)

° Painful urination (crying during urination, not caused by painful diaper rash)

° Joint pain

° Any unusual or significant pain

• If an infant under three months has a fever of 101° or higher.

• If a child has a fever of 104° or higher that does not come down after four to six hours of home treatment.

• If a child age three months to three years has a fever of 103° or higher for 24 hours.

- If a fever of 100° to 103° has lasted more than three days.

- If a child with a fever seems sicker than you would expect from a viral illness such as a cold or flu.

- If fever occurs with pain that isn't relieved by home treatment.

- If a child becomes delirious or has hallucinations.

Fever Convulsions

Fever (febrile) convulsions or "fits" are involuntary muscle spasms that sometimes occur in children who have had a rapid increase in temperature (often before you have realized that your child has a fever). Once a high fever has developed, the risk of a convulsion is probably gone.

A child having a convulsion stiffens up and clenches his or her arms, legs, and teeth. The child's eyes may roll back, and he or she may also stop breathing for a few seconds, vomit, urinate, or pass stools. Convulsions usually last one to five minutes.

Although frightening, fever convulsions in children age six months to five years are seldom serious and do not cause any harm. Two to four percent of children at this age are prone to fever convulsions. About 30 percent of children who have a fever convulsion will have another one, usually within two years.

Home Treatment

During a convulsion:

- Protect the child from injury. Ease the child to the floor, or hold a very small child face down on your lap. Do not restrain the child.

- Turn the head to the side. This will help clear the mouth of any vomit or saliva so the child can breathe.

- Do not put anything in the child's mouth to prevent tongue biting. This may injure the child.

- Try to stay calm, because that will help calm the child.

- Time the length of the convulsion, if possible.

After a convulsion:

- Check for injuries.

- Reduce fever with acetaminophen or ibuprofen and lukewarm sponge baths. See page 213.

- Put the child in a cool room to sleep. Drowsiness is common following a convulsion.

When to Call Kaiser Permanente

- Call 911 or seek emergency services:

  ° If the child stops breathing for longer than 30 to 60 seconds. Begin rescue breathing (see page 56).

  ° If a convulsion lasts longer than five minutes, or a second convulsion occurs.

- If the child is under six months old, is five years or older, or the convulsion only affects one side of the body.

- If a high fever occurs with severe headache, vomiting, stiff neck, or a bulging soft spot on an infant's head, see page 141.

- If a convulsion occurs without fever.

- If it is the child's first convulsion, or if you haven't discussed with your doctor what to do if there is another one.

- If you are unable to reduce fever to 102° after a convulsion.

Impetigo

Impetigo is a bacterial infection that is much more common in children than in adults. It often starts when a small cut or scratch becomes infected. Symptoms are oozing, honey-colored, crusty sores that often appear on the face between the upper lip and nose, especially after a cold. Scratching the sores may spread impetigo to other parts of the body.

Prevention

- Wash all scratches and sores with soap and water.

- If your child has a runny nose, keep the area between the upper lip and nose clean to prevent infection.

- Keep fingernails short and clean.

Home Treatment

Small areas of impetigo may respond well to prompt home treatment.

- Remove crusts by soaking the area in warm water (use a warm washcloth for the face) for 15 to 20 minutes, then scrub gently with a washcloth and antibacterial soap such as Betadine or Hibiclens. Pat dry gently; do not rub. Repeat several times a day.

- Apply an antibiotic ointment (see page 311). Cover the area with gauze taped well away from the sores. This will help keep the infection from spreading and prevent scratching.

- To prevent spreading the infection, do not share towels, washcloths, or bath water. Men should shave around the sores, not over them, and use a clean blade daily. Do not use a shaving brush.

When to Call Kaiser Permanente

- If impetigo covers a total area larger than two inches in diameter.

- If impetigo is not improving after three to four days of home treatment, or any new infected areas appear. Your doctor may prescribe an antibiotic.

- If the area around the nostrils, lips, or face swells and becomes tender.

- If other signs of infection develop:

  ○ Pain, swelling, or tenderness

  ○ Redness or red streaks extending from the area

° Discharge of pus

° Fever of 100° or higher with no other cause

Pinworms

Pinworms are tiny, thread-like worms that infect the digestive tracts of young children. Pinworms are most common in four- to six-year-olds, although anyone may be infected. The worms live in the upper end of the large intestine, near the appendix, and travel to the outside of the anus to lay their eggs.

The egg-laying almost always occurs at night and usually causes the child to scratch the anal area.

When the child later sucks a thumb or licks a finger, the eggs are ingested and the cycle begins again. The eggs are very sticky and can survive on clothing and bedding for days, where they can be picked up by other family members.

Rectal itching, especially at night, is the most common symptom of pinworm infection. If the infection is severe, there may also be abdominal pain and loss of appetite.

Pinworms are common and affect many families. If you suspect pinworms, it's easy to find out for sure in your own home and at no cost. Go into your child's darkened bedroom several hours after bedtime and shine a flashlight on the child's anus. The light will make the worms move back into the anus. If you don't see the worms after checking for two or three nights, it is unlikely that the child is infected.

Prevention

Teach children to wash their hands after using the toilet and before meals.

Home Treatment

• Ask your pharmacist for an over-the-counter medication (Pin-X) for pinworms.

• Treat every child in the house between the ages of 2 and 10. If infection recurs, consider treating everyone in the family over age two.

• On the first day of treatment, wash all underwear, nightclothes, bedding, and towels in hot water to get rid of any eggs and prevent reinfection. Sanitize toilet and sleeping areas with a strong disinfectant.

• Trim and keep all fingernails short.

• Require frequent hand washing, morning showers, and daily changes of pajamas and underwear.

When to Call Kaiser Permanente

• If the medication causes side effects such as vomiting or pain.

• If you suspect pinworms but the nighttime checks reveal nothing.

• If you continue to see worms at night after three days of home treatment. Stronger prescription drugs are available.

Prickly Heat (Sweat Rash)

Prickly heat, also called heat rash, sweat rash, or miliaria, is a rash of red or pink dots that appears over an infant's head, neck, and shoulders. The dots look like tiny pimples.

Prickly heat is often caused by well-meaning parents who dress their baby too warmly, but it can happen to any baby in really hot weather. An infant should be dressed just as lightly as an adult and will be comfortable at the same temperature. It is normal for a baby's hands and feet to feel cold to your touch.

Prevention

Do not overdress your baby. Place your hand between the baby's shoulder blades. If the skin is hot or moist, the baby is too warm.

Home Treatment

• Dress the baby in as few clothes as possible during hot weather.

• Keep the skin cool and dry.

• Keep the baby's sleeping area cool.

• Hydrocortisone cream (0.5 percent) can help heal the rash.

Measles, Mumps, and Rubella

Measles (rubeola), mumps, and rubella (German measles) were once common childhood illnesses. Today, they are quite rare, thanks to the measles, mumps, and rubella (MMR) vaccine. Two shots, one given between ages 12 and 15 months and a second at ages 4 to 6 or 11 to 12 years, provide lifelong protection. Adults who have not been immunized, who have only had one shot, or who have not had the illnesses may also need one or both shots.

Local outbreaks of measles, mumps, or rubella can occur where immunization rates are low.

Measles symptoms:

• Fever, runny nose, hacking cough

• Reddened eyes

• Spotty red rash on entire body

Mumps symptoms:

• Swelling along the jawline

• Fever and vomiting

Rubella symptom:

• Fine pink rash starting on face and covering entire body

Call your health professional for information about the MMR vaccine, or if you suspect your child has measles, mumps, or rubella.

For more information, see the inside front cover.

When to Call Kaiser Permanente

- If the rash looks infected or persists over three to four days.

- If the infant looks sick.

- If sweat rash is accompanied by a fever of 100.4° in a baby under three months of age and the fever doesn't come down after you remove the baby's extra clothing.

Roseola

Roseola (roseola infantum) is a mild viral illness that often starts with a sudden high fever (103° to 105°) and irritability. The fever lasts two to three days. As the fever drops, a rosy pink rash appears on the torso, neck, and arms. It may last one to two days. Since the fever is quite high and may come on quickly, fever convulsions may occur (see page 214). Roseola is most common in children six months to two years of age. It is rare after age four.

Home Treatment

- If the child is uncomfortable, reduce the fever. See page 213.

- Give lots of liquids.

- If a convulsion occurs, see page 214.

When to Call Kaiser Permanente

See When to Call Kaiser Permanente under Fever on page 213.

Fifth Disease

Another common childhood illness that causes a rash is erythema infectiosum, or "fifth disease." The main symptom is a red rash on the face that looks like slapped cheeks, and a lacy pink rash on the backs of the arms and legs, torso, and buttocks. There may be a low fever. The rash may come and go for several weeks in response to changes in temperature and sunlight.

This illness is most contagious the week before the rash appears. Once the rash has developed, the child is no longer contagious.

Home treatment for fifth disease is simply to keep the child comfortable and watch for signs that a more serious illness is present (fever over 102°; child seems very sick).

Fifth disease is harmless in otherwise normal children, but it poses a slight risk to developing fetuses. Pregnant women should avoid exposure if possible. If you are pregnant and are exposed to a child with fifth disease, or if you develop a fifth disease-like rash, contact your obstetrician.

I live with the expectation that life is not fragile;
that if I push, it will not break.
Andrew Sullivan

13

Chronic Conditions

Most of the conditions described in this book get better after a short while. These are called acute diseases. Chronic diseases, on the other hand, last long periods of time or come and go, often for the rest of your life. Having a chronic disease does not mean you can no longer enjoy the good things of life; while these diseases may not be curable, they are often controllable.

Some conditions that can be chronic are covered in other places in this book.

- Allergies, see page 123.
- Arthritis, see page 103.
- Asthma, see page 127.
- Back Problems, see page 87.
- Depression, see page 296.
- Headaches, see page 165.
- Irritable Bowel Syndrome, see page 78.
- Neck Problems, see page 98.
- Osteoporosis, see page 114.

Diabetes

 During digestion the starches and sugars in the food you eat are converted to glucose, a sugar that your body uses for fuel. Insulin is a hormone produced by the pancreas to control the amount of glucose in the blood. Without insulin, the body cannot use or store glucose, so too much sugar stays in the blood.

Type 1 occurs when the pancreas fails to make insulin. It usually occurs in childhood or adolescence but can develop at any age. People with type 1 diabetes must inject insulin every day.

Type 2 occurs when body cells become resistant to insulin. This reduces the amount of glucose that can be used by the cells at any one time. Type 2 diabetes is more common among adults, especially those who are overweight and over age 40.

Many people with type 2 diabetes are able to control their blood sugar through weight control, regular exercise, and healthy eating. Some may need insulin injections or oral medications to lower blood sugar.

Risk factors for type 2 diabetes include:

- Age 40 or over
- Overweight (20 percent more than ideal weight)
- Family history of diabetes
- African American, Hispanic, Native American, or Pacific Islander
- Delivery of a baby over 9 pounds or previous diabetes during pregnancy

The symptoms of diabetes are vague, and by themselves, seldom lead to a doctor visit. They include:

- Increased thirst
- Frequent urination (especially at night).
- Increased appetite
- Unexplained weight loss
- Fatigue
- Skin infections
- Slow-healing wounds
- Recurrent vaginal infections
- Difficulty with erections
- Blurred vision
- Tingling or numbness in hands or feet

A blood test is needed to accurately diagnose diabetes. Blood glucose tests are inexpensive and very low-risk. Ask your doctor if you should eat or fast before the test.

Prevention

At this time, there is no known way to prevent type 1 diabetes.

In most cases, the risk of type 2 diabetes can be reduced by regular exercise (see Chapter 17) and by maintaining a healthy body weight.

Home Treatment

- Believe that you can control diabetes. Diabetes requires making significant, long-term lifestyle changes and can be overwhelming at first. Focus on making one change at a time, and soon you will have good control over your life and your diabetes.

- Eat a healthy diet to help keep your blood sugar in control and maintain a healthy weight. Pay special attention to eating low-fat foods, portion size, and the other eating recommendations in Chapter 18.

- Get regular aerobic exercise to help regulate your blood sugar, reduce your risk of heart disease, and control your weight. Work closely with your doctor to determine how your activity level affects your blood glucose levels and medication needs.

- Depending on how strictly you are controlling your blood sugar levels and how difficult they are to control, you may wish to track the following daily:

  ° The time and content of each meal

  ° The kind and amount of exercise you get

  ° How tired or energetic you feel

  ° If you have a home glucose monitor, check your blood sugar level as directed by your doctor. This record will help you understand how your body reacts to different foods and exercise, so you can correct glucose imbalances before they get out of control.

- If drugs are prescribed to control your blood sugar, take them as directed. Too little medication will make your blood sugar higher than normal; too much will make it lower than normal. As you improve your diet and exercise, you may need less medicine. Check with your doctor.

- Take good care of your feet. Diabetes impairs nerve function and blood flow to the feet, increasing your risk of infection. Take care to avoid cuts and sores, and promptly treat any injuries to your feet.

- Get regular eye exams to check the retina at the back of your eyes. Eye changes caused by diabetes often have no symptoms until they are quite advanced. Early treatment may slow their progress and save your sight.

- Monitor your blood pressure.

- Have a flu shot every year.

- Check your cholesterol and blood lipids regularly.

- If you smoke, stop (see page 150). Avoid secondhand smoke.

The National Diabetes Information Clearinghouse (1 Information Way, Bethesda, MD 20892) is a good resource for more information on diabetes.

When to Call Kaiser Permanente

- Call 911 or seek emergency services if a person with diabetes loses consciousness and remains unconscious.

- If signs of high blood sugar develop in a person who has diabetes:

  ° Frequent urination

  ° Strong thirst

  ° Dim vision

  ° Rapid breathing

  ° Fruity-smelling breath

- If signs of low blood sugar persist longer than 15 minutes after a person who has diabetes has eaten something containing sugar:

  ° Fatigue, weakness, nausea

  ° Hunger

  ° Double or blurred vision

° Pounding heart

° Confusion, irritability, appearance of intoxication

• If your blood sugar levels on home monitoring fall outside the range your doctor has recommended.

• For a blood glucose test, if you suspect diabetes but have not been diagnosed.

High Blood Cholesterol

 Cholesterol is a waxy substance that is produced by the human body and is also found in animal products. Cells need cholesterol to function. Unfortunately, any excess cholesterol in the blood builds up inside the arteries. Cholesterol deposits (arteriosclerosis) are major causes of heart attacks and strokes.

A high cholesterol level in your blood is a risk factor for heart disease and stroke. The higher your cholesterol level, the higher the risk. However, not all cholesterol is bad.

Good and Bad Cholesterol

Fat travels through your bloodstream attached to protein, in a combination called a lipoprotein. Two lipoproteins are the main carriers of cholesterol: low-density lipoprotein (LDL, sometimes called bad cholesterol) and high-density lipoprotein (HDL, sometimes called good cholesterol).

LDL acts like a fat delivery truck. It picks up cholesterol from the liver and delivers it to the cells. When more cholesterol is ready for delivery than the cells can take, LDL deposits the extra cholesterol on the artery walls. A lot of LDL cholesterol in your blood increases your risk of heart disease and stroke.

What Do the Numbers Mean?

Doctors don't agree on which cholesterol numbers are most useful in determining your risk of heart disease. The most commonly used values are listed here. The importance of these numbers will vary depending on your risk factors.

Desirable: All of the following:

• Total cholesterol below 200

• HDL cholesterol above 35

• LDL cholesterol below 130

Borderline high-risk: One or more of the following:

• Total cholesterol 200–239

• LDL cholesterol 130–159

High-risk: One or more of the following:

• Total cholesterol 240 or higher

• HDL cholesterol below 35

• LDL cholesterol above 160

HDL works like a garbage truck. It removes excess cholesterol from the bloodstream and takes it to the liver. A lot of HDL cholesterol in your blood decreases your risk of heart disease and stroke.

Cholesterol Screening

Check the recommended schedule for cholesterol screening in the preventive care guidelines for Kaiser Permanente in your area. If you have any of the following risk factors, discuss with your health care professional when to begin screening tests and how frequently to have them.

- Family history of early heart attack (before age 55 in father or brother; before age 65 in mother or sister)

- Current cigarette smoking

- High blood pressure (over 140/90) or taking high blood pressure medication

- Diabetes

- Personal history of heart disease

- Postmenopausal women

High cholesterol is one of many factors that increase your risk for heart disease. Smoking, high blood pressure, diabetes, family history, and lack of exercise also increase your heart disease risk.

If your total cholesterol is over 200, consider tests to measure your HDL and LDL levels, which can help further clarify your actual risk. For example, if your HDL and LDL

levels are in the desirable range, a total cholesterol level over 200 may be of less concern. See left for an explanation of HDL, LDL, and total cholesterol levels.

For most people, a low-fat diet (see page 280) and exercise are all they need to lower cholesterol. People who have very high cholesterol or heart disease (or who are at very high risk) may need medication as well as exercise and a low-fat diet to lower their cholesterol.

Reversing Heart Disease

A low-fat diet and lifestyle changes may actually reverse the process of heart disease and help reopen arteries that are clogged by arteriosclerosis.

Participants in the Lifestyle Heart Trial followed a vegetarian diet containing less than 10 percent of calories from fat and no caffeine. They also stopped smoking, got 30 minutes of exercise at least six days a week, and practiced a relaxation technique (deep breathing, stretching, progressive muscle relaxation, etc.) for one hour each day. After a year, over 80 percent of the participants had lost weight, reduced their cholesterol, and most importantly, reduced the amount of blockage in their coronary arteries.

For more information, see page 280 and Resource 40 on page 327.

How to Reduce Your Cholesterol

- Eat less total fat. Because a high-fat diet increases cholesterol, just cutting back on cholesterol is not enough. You must cut back on total fats as well. See page 280.

- Buy a cooking oil that is liquid at room temperature (such as canola, corn, soybean, sunflower, or cottonseed oil) and use less of it.

- Eat two to three servings (three to four ounces) of baked or broiled fish per week. Most fish contain omega-3 fatty acids that help lower blood cholesterol and triglycerides. In general, fish with darker flesh, such as mackerel, lake trout, herring, salmon, and halibut, have more omega-3 oils. The safety and value of fish-oil supplements is not yet known.

- Exercise more. Exercise increases your protective HDL cholesterol level.

- Quit smoking to increase your HDL levels and reduce your risk of heart disease.

- Lose weight. Losing even 5 to 10 pounds can increase HDL levels and lower your total cholesterol.

- Eat more soluble fiber, which lowers overall cholesterol. See page 278.

- Attend a low-fat diet workshop, consult a registered dietitian, or read Resource 61 on page 328 to learn ways to lower your fat intake to 30 percent or less of total calories, based on your goal. For tips on choosing a low-fat diet, see page 280.

High Blood Pressure

 High blood pressure (hypertension) occurs when the pressure of your blood against the artery walls is higher than normal. For information on taking your blood pressure, see page 25.

Doctors rate blood pressure for adults over 18 in the following categories:

- Normal: below 130/85

- High-normal: 130–139/85–89

- High: over 140/90

High blood pressure usually has no symptoms. High blood pressure itself is not a disease, but it can increase your risk of stroke, heart attack, and kidney disease. Risks of these diseases are lowest for people whose blood pressure is below 120/80.

Risk factors for high blood pressure include:

- African-American race

- Overweight

- Family history of high blood pressure

- Inactive lifestyle

- Excess alcohol intake

- Excess sodium (salt) intake

- Use of certain medications, including birth control pills, steroids, decongestants, and anti-inflammatories

In some cases, high blood pressure can be prevented. Many people with high blood pressure can control it by changing their lifestyle and may not require medication.

Taking the following steps is especially important if you are in one of the high-risk groups listed above.

Prevention

- Lose weight. This is especially important if you tend to gain weight around the waist rather than in the hips and thighs. A weight loss of only 10 pounds can lower blood pressure.

- Limit your alcohol intake to two drinks or less per day. Too much alcohol increases blood pressure.

- Exercise regularly. Thirty to 45 minutes of brisk walking three to five times a week will help lower your blood pressure (and will also help you lose weight).

- Reduce your salt intake. This is a good idea for nearly everyone. But for as many as half of those with high blood pressure, reducing salt intake helps control the condition. See page 284.

- Improve your diet. Limit fats, especially saturated fats (fatty meat, fried foods, whole milk, cheese, palm and coconut oil). Eat plenty of fruits, vegetables, whole grains, and low- or nonfat dairy products.

- Eating a healthy diet may help you lose weight, lower your blood pressure, and reduce your risk for heart disease.

- Reduce the saturated fat in your diet. Saturated fat is found in animal products (milk, cheese, and meat). Limiting these foods will help you lose weight and also lower your risk of heart disease. See page 280.

- Stop smoking and avoid tobacco products in any form. Smoking and tobacco use increase your risk of heart disease and stroke. See page 150 for tips on quitting.

Home Treatment

- Follow the prevention tips above even more closely if you have high blood pressure.

- Take any prescribed blood pressure medications exactly as directed.

- Learn how to take your blood pressure at home. See page 25.

- If you have high blood pressure, see your health care professional at least once a year.

When to Call Kaiser Permanente

- If you check your own blood pressure and it is very high, such as 200/120, or if you are having a severe headache or blurred vision, call your doctor immediately.

- If you have had two or more blood pressure readings of 140 or higher systolic or 90 or higher diastolic. Call if either one or both numbers remain high after several readings on separate days.

- If blood pressure remains high even after you have been on blood pressure medication.

Behind every successful woman is herself.
New American Proverb

14

Women's Health

From puberty to menopause, women cope with unique health problems. This chapter covers some health problems that are of special interest to women. Important health issues that affect both men and women are covered in other chapters.

Healthy Lifestyles

Good health habits are the best way to reduce your risk of the five most common causes of death for women of all ages. For older women, heart disease and cancer are the leading causes of death.

1. Cancer

• Quit smoking to reduce your risk of lung cancer (page 150).

• Have regular mammograms and Pap tests (pages 230 and 231).

2. Accidents (especially motor vehicle accidents)

• Buckle up. Seat belts save lives and prevent serious injury.

• Don't drink and drive.

3. Heart Disease

• Quit smoking. Quitting will reduce your risk of heart disease and stroke.

• Limit dietary fat and cholesterol, especially if your cholesterol is high (page 222).

• Maintain a healthy weight and get regular exercise.

• Have your blood pressure checked regularly (see pages 25 and 224) and take prescribed high blood pressure medications as directed.

4. Suicide

• Learn the warning signs of depression and seek help if you have them (page 296).

5. Homicide

• If you are in an abusive personal relationship, take steps to protect yourself (page 303).

Breast Health

Breast cancer is the leading cause of cancer deaths in women ages 40 to 55. Breast cancer is most treatable and curable if detected early. There are three methods of early detection: breast self-exam, clinical breast exam, and mammogram.

One of the most important risk factors for breast cancer is age. The risk goes up significantly after age 40. Women younger than 40 are at relatively low risk of breast cancer (about 1 in 1,200). However, if your mother or a sister had breast cancer before menopause, talk with your doctor about starting breast self-exams and other screenings before age 40.

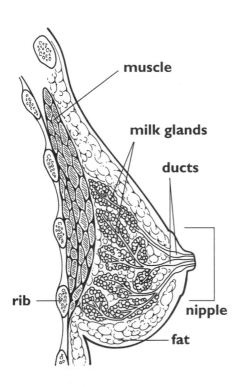

The milk glands swell in a woman who is pregnant or breast-feeding. Most of the rest of the breast is fat.

Breast Self-Exam

Most women's breast tissue has some lumps or thickening. When in doubt about a particular lump, check the other breast. If you find a similar lump in the same area on the other breast, both breasts are probably normal. Be on the lookout for a lump that feels much harder than the rest of the breast. Have any areas of concern checked by your health professional.

The breast self-exam is a simple technique to help you learn what is normal for you and how to recognize any changes.

Establish a regular time to examine your breasts. A few days after your period when your breasts are not swollen or tender is a good time. Women who do not menstruate (after menopause and hysterectomies) can examine their breasts anytime.

The breast self-exam takes place in two stages.

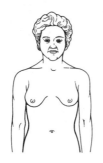

Look at your breasts in a mirror.

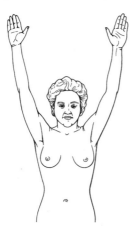

Put your hands on your hips.

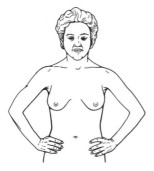

Lift your arms up.

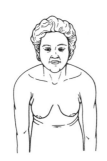

Bend forward, still looking in the mirror.

Stage 1: In front of the mirror

Examine your breasts visually in a mirror. Few women have breasts that match exactly. It is normal for one breast to be slightly larger than the other. Learn what is normal for you.

Stand and look at your breasts in four positions:

- With your arms at your sides
- With your hands on your hips
- With your arms raised overhead
- While bending forward

In each position, look for changes in the contour and shape of your breasts, the color and texture of the skin and nipples, and any discharge from the nipples.

Stage 2: Lying down

To examine your right breast, place a pillow or folded towel under your right shoulder. If your breasts are large, lie on your left side and turn your right shoulder back flat to spread the breast tissue more evenly over your chest wall.

Use the pads of the three middle fingers of your left hand to examine your right breast. Move your fingers in small, dime-sized circles. Use light to medium pressure in each spot to feel the full thickness of the breast tissue. Don't lift your fingers away from the skin. You are feeling for lumps, thickening, or changes of any kind.

Examine your entire breast using a vertical strip pattern (see illustration below). Examine all tissue from the collarbone to the armpit and from the bra line to the breastbone. Start in the armpit and work down to the bottom of the bra line. Move one finger-width toward the middle and work up to the collarbone. Repeat until you have covered all the breast tissue.

If you discover any unusual lumps, thickening, or changes of any kind, or if there is a discharge from the nipple when you are not squeezing it, report them to your doctor immediately. Most lumps are not malignant, but your doctor needs to make a diagnosis.

If you examine your breasts monthly, you will learn what is normal for you and quickly recognize if something changes. The breast self-exam takes some practice. Ask your doctor or health care professional for help in learning the technique.

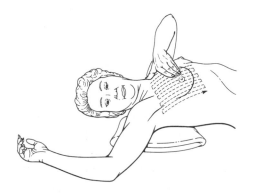

Vertical strip pattern: move your fingers up and down across the breast.

Clinical Breast Exam

The second component for early detection of breast problems is your health professional's physical exam. This exam is very similar to the self-exam. See Kaiser Permanente's recommended schedule for clinical breast exams, or discuss with your doctor.

Mammogram

A mammogram is a special X-ray of the breast that can reveal breast tumors too small to be detected by breast self-exam.

Studies have shown that mammograms save lives in women over 50, reducing breast cancer death rates by up to one-third. Studies in younger women are less clear. Be sure to follow the preventive care guidelines for Kaiser Permanente in your area. Talk to your doctor if you have special concerns, or if your mother or sister had breast cancer before menopause.

Scheduling an Exam

- Schedule your mammogram one to two weeks after your period.

- Do not wear deodorant, perfume, powder, or lotion, because they can affect the quality of the X-ray.

- Wear clothing that allows you to remove only your top.

Breast Health Tips

- Have a clinical breast exam according to the recommended schedule.

- Have a mammogram according to the recommended schedule for your age and risk factors.

- Do a breast self-exam regularly.

- Limit alcohol to one drink per day. Moderate to heavy drinking increases the risk of breast cancer.

Gynecological Health

Regular pelvic exams and Pap smears are a vital component of women's health. These exams can give you early indications of any abnormalities in your reproductive organs. It is better to catch any disease in its early stages, when it is much easier to treat.

Self-Exam

Self-exams will help you better understand your own body and what is normal for you. A female's genitals include two sets of lips: the inner (labia minor) and the outer (labia major). These lips form around the urinary opening, the vaginal opening, and the clitoris.

Periodically examine your entire genital area for any sores, warts, red swollen areas, or unusual discharge. A normal vaginal discharge may be white to yellowish white and smell slightly like vinegar. It can be either thick or thin and present in large or small amounts; every woman is different. During ovulation (the midpoint between periods) there is often a large amount of clear, slippery mucus. If your discharge seems unusual in amount, smell, or texture, see Vaginitis on page 245.

There should be no pain or straining on urination, and the urine should come out in a fairly steady stream. The urine should be pale yellow, and it should not have a strong ammonia smell. If you experience pain or burning on urination, see Urinary Tract Infections on page 243 or Vaginitis on page 245.

The Pelvic Exam and Pap Test

A pelvic exam given by a health professional will generally consist of an external genital exam, a Pap test, and a manual exam.

The Pap test is the screening exam for cancer of the cervix. Pap smears detect 90 to 95 percent of cervical cancers, making it a reliable and important test. The health care professional will insert a speculum into your vagina and gather some cells from your cervix and vagina. You may feel some discomfort. Tell the health care professional if you feel any pain. The speculum can be adjusted to ease the discomfort.

The cells are put on a slide and sent to a lab for classification. If abnormal cells are found, your doctor will ask you to return for more testing. In any case, your doctor should let you know the results of your Pap test. Ask for an explanation of your results.

For a manual exam, the health care professional inserts two gloved and lubricated fingers into your vagina and presses on your lower abdomen with the other hand to feel the ovaries and uterus.

Scheduling an Exam

The first Pap test is recommended when a female becomes sexually active. Therefore, a 16-year-old female who is sexually active should have an exam.

See the Kaiser Permanente preventive care guidelines for how often you should have a Pap smear. Women with a single sexual partner and several consecutive normal Pap smears may not need an annual Pap smear.

Women with multiple sexual partners, other risk factors, or a history of abnormal Paps may need yearly exams. Discuss this with your doctor or health care professional.

Schedule the exam one to two weeks after your period. Do not douche, have intercourse, or use feminine hygiene products for 24 hours before the exam, because they can alter the results.

Women who have had a hysterectomy that included removal of the cervix don't need a Pap smear unless they have a history of cancer or precancerous conditions.

For more information on women's health, see Resources 75 to 77 on page 329.

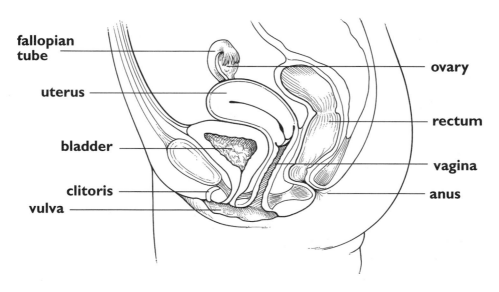

Female pelvic organs

Pregnancy: How to Make a Healthy Baby

You can increase the chances that your baby will be healthy. The following guidelines will help. For more information, refer to the prenatal education materials from Kaiser Permanente in your area.

Before Conception

Your health, both before conception and during the first weeks after, is particularly important for your baby's health. Start helping your baby even before you become pregnant.

- If you have diabetes, high blood pressure, seizure disorders, or any inherited diseases, talk with your doctor before getting pregnant. Your doctor may want to modify your treatment and may be able to prescribe medicine that is safer for the developing baby.

- Before you start trying to get pregnant, have a blood test to check your rubella immunity. If you test negative, you will want to receive an immunization. To avoid harming the baby, do not become pregnant for at least three months following the immunization.

- If you have symptoms of sexually transmitted diseases or are unsure of your partner's sexual history, read pages 260 to 264 and arrange for an examination and testing with your doctor.

- Eat well. Make sure your diet includes plenty of green leafy vegetables and legumes, and take a folic acid supplement containing 0.4 mg of folate. Folic acid helps prevent certain birth defects, such as spina bifida. Other good sources of folic acid include fortified cereal, whole-wheat bread, oranges, and nuts.

- Stop smoking (see page 150) and stop drinking alcohol.

- Stop all illegal drug use and eliminate any medications that are not absolutely essential.

- If you are anxious or depressed, get help. See pages 294 to 299.

- Buy a good book on pregnancy and begin reading. See Resources 64 to 66 on page 328.

Home Pregnancy Tests

If you become pregnant, it is important that you know right away. The quickest way is with a home pregnancy test. Home pregnancy tests are inexpensive and very reliable when done correctly. Select a test that has simple instructions and follow the instructions exactly. Mistakes can lead to false results.

If the test is positive, call your doctor's office or the advice nurse to schedule a repeat test at the laboratory to confirm it. Even if the test is negative, treat yourself as if you are pregnant until you are sure.

Early Pregnancy
(First Trimester)

- Continue to avoid smoking, alcohol, and drugs.

- Make the first visit to your doctor or health care professional in the first 6 to 12 weeks of your pregnancy.

- Get regular prenatal care from your doctor or health care professional.

- Continue to improve your nutrition. Call your local WIC (Women, Infants, and Children) agency to learn if you are eligible for this program. WIC provides vouchers for nutritious food, nutrition education, and breast-feeding support to pregnant women, women with new babies, and children under age 5.

- Continue taking 0.4 mg folic acid daily. As long as you are eating a well-balanced diet, most obstetricians no longer recommend vitamin supplements. In fact, there is some evidence that vitamin supplements may cause more morning sickness early in the pregnancy.

- Avoid touching cat feces and litter boxes. Also, cook all meats well before eating. Cat feces and undercooked or raw meat can carry toxoplasmosis, an infection that can cause miscarriage or brain damage in the fetus.

- Avoid all chemical vapors, paint fumes, and poisons.

Morning Sickness

For many women, the first few months of pregnancy bring morning sickness, which can happen at any time of the day. This is a normal result of the body's adjustment to pregnancy. The following home treatment can help:

- Eat five or six small meals a day to avoid an empty stomach. Include some protein in each of these meals.

- Eat crackers or dry toast before getting up in the morning.

- Increase your intake of vitamin B_6 by eating more whole grains and cereals, wheat germ, nuts, seeds, and legumes. Talk with your caregiver before taking vitamin supplements during early pregnancy. They may cause nausea.

- Keep a positive attitude. Morning sickness usually passes in three to four months.

- If you drink coffee or soda with caffeine, cut back to two cups per day.

Middle Pregnancy
(Second Trimester)

- Continue with the safeguards described above.

- Reduce the risk of injury and falls:

  ° Always wear your seat belt.

° Wear sensible shoes.

° Continue moderate levels of your regular exercises but do not become exhausted or significantly short of breath.

° Avoid sports with a high risk of falls or impact.

• Increase your calcium intake by drinking more milk (a quart of skim or low-fat milk a day) or through other sources of calcium. See page 283.

• Control your weight as advised by your doctor or health care professional.

Late Pregnancy (Third Trimester)

• Maintain all of the other guidelines listed above.

• Get plenty of rest.

• Take childbirth classes with your partner or designated coach.

• Educate yourself about early signs of labor.

• If appropriate, have your other children take a class to help them adjust to the new baby.

• Practice the relaxation exercises on page 272. They will be helpful during labor.

• Develop a written birth plan with your doctor or health care professional that outlines your wishes and expectations throughout the labor and delivery.

• Maintain a good sense of humor.

Cesarean Deliveries

Most babies are delivered vaginally. However, when the health of the baby or mother is at risk, doctors can deliver the baby through an incision in the abdomen. This is called a cesarean delivery or a C-section.

There are three main concerns with cesarean deliveries:

• More risk. Some mothers who have C-sections develop infections or bleeding that requires additional medications or treatment. Although the maternal death rate for C-sections is four times higher than the rate for vaginal deliveries, the rate for both types of delivery is very low.

• Longer recovery. You can usually go home within one to two days after a vaginal delivery. Hospital stays after cesarean deliveries may be three or more days. After a cesarean, you must limit your activity over the next four to six weeks to allow the incision to heal.

• Less involvement. The mother and other family members can be more involved with a vaginal delivery. Cesarean delivery is a surgery, which limits family involvement.

C-sections are a good idea when either the baby or the mother is in danger. A cesarean should not be done just because it is easier to schedule or because you have previously had a C-section delivery. Ask your doctor or health care professional what you can do to help avoid the need for a cesarean delivery.

Breast-Feeding

Breast milk is the ideal food for your new baby. Consider taking a breast-feeding class before your baby is born. See page 200.

Bleeding Between Periods

Many women experience bleeding or spotting between periods. It does not necessarily mean a serious condition is present. Use of an intrauterine device (IUD) may increase your chances of spotting. Some minor bleeding is common during ovulation and during the first three months of using birth control pills. It is also common to spot or bleed while breast-feeding.

If the bleeding is not heavy and occurs only occasionally, it is probably not a cause for concern.

Use tampons or pads, and avoid aspirin, which may prolong the bleeding.

When to Call Kaiser Permanente

- If bleeding is accompanied by unusual pain, cramping, or fever.

- If the bleeding is heavy (changing a maxi pad or super tampon every hour for more than six hours).

- If bleeding between periods lasts more than 10 days in a row or occurs three months in a row.

- If bleeding occurs after intercourse.

- If you are over age 35 and have any bleeding between periods or prolonged bleeding with periods.

Menopause

For most women, menopause occurs between the ages of 45 and 55, when the production of female hormones (estrogen and progesterone) begins to decline. These hormonal changes will cause irregular menstrual periods before periods stop altogether. You may also experience hot flashes, vaginal dryness, and mood changes. Osteoporosis is also directly linked to the decrease in estrogen that comes with menopause. See page 114.

Irregular periods may mean lighter or heavier menstrual flows, either shorter or longer intervals between flows, or spotting. Some women have irregular periods for years during menopause. Others have regular periods until periods suddenly stop. Every woman is unique and will experience menopause differently.

Hot flashes are sudden periods of intense heat, sweating, and flushing. A hot flash usually begins in the chest and spreads out to the neck, face, and arms. Seventy-five to 80 percent of women going through menopause will have hot flashes. Hot flashes may occur as frequently as once an hour and last as long as three to four minutes. If they occur at night, they may disrupt your sleep. Hot flashes usually stop within one or two years but may persist for several years.

Vaginal dryness, the loss of lubrication and moisture in the vagina, may lead to soreness during and after intercourse. These vaginal changes may also increase the risk of infections. See Vaginitis on page 245.

Mood changes are caused by the hormonal and physical changes of menopause. Symptoms such as nervousness, lethargy, insomnia, moodiness, or depression are common.

With menopause, many women fear emotional upheaval and the loss of sexuality. On the other hand, many women look forward to the freedom that menopause brings, particularly freedom from menstrual cycle discomfort and freedom from contraception.

Understanding what is happening to you and using home care techniques to relieve any discomfort will help you through menopause.

Home Treatment

Irregular periods:

- Keep a written record of your periods in case you need to discuss them with a health professional.

Hot flashes:

- Keep your home and work place cool.

Birth Control During Menopause

Some women may continue to ovulate during menopause, which means there is a slight chance that they could become pregnant, even though they are no longer menstruating regularly.

Women who have their last period before age 50 and who do not want to become pregnant should continue using contraceptives (other than birth control pills) for two years. Birth control pills may be used with medical supervision.

Women who have their last period after age 50 generally need to use contraceptives only for one year.

- Wear layers of loose clothing that can be easily removed.

- Drink lots of water and juices. Avoid caffeine and alcohol if they bring on hot flashes.

- Exercise regularly. This will help to stabilize hormones and prevent insomnia.

Vaginal dryness:

- Use a water-soluble vaginal lubricant such as Astroglide, Surgilube, or Today Personal Lubricant to relieve painful intercourse. Do not use a petroleum-based product such as Vaseline.

 For more information, see the inside front cover.

Mood changes:

- The best thing you can do for yourself is to realize you are not alone. Discuss your symptoms with other women. Give yourself, and ask others for, abundant amounts of love, caring, and understanding.

When to Call Kaiser Permanente

- If you have prolonged irregular bleeding, particularly if you are overweight.

- If you are considering hormone replacement therapy.

- If mood changes are causing problems, and home treatment isn't helping.

- If you bleed after not having a period for 6 months.

Hormone Therapy

Hormone therapy helps relieve the short-term symptoms of menopause and reduces some long-term risks associated with lower estrogen levels. There are two types of hormone therapy. **Estrogen replacement therapy** (ERT) is estrogen alone. **Hormone replacement therapy** (HRT) combines estrogen with progestin, another hormone.

ERT is usually prescribed only for women who have had a hysterectomy, because it increases the risk of endometrial cancer. HRT is usually prescribed only for women who have a uterus. Women with a uterus who take ERT need regular check-ups for uterine lining changes.

Hormone therapy reduces some health risks and increases others. Consider the following factors in your decision.

Osteoporosis

Both ERT and HRT reduce the risk of osteoporosis and slow the rate of bone loss that occurs after menopause, which helps reduce the risk of fractures. See page 114 for information on preventing osteoporosis.

Heart Disease

ERT reduces a woman's risk of heart disease by increasing high-density lipoprotein (HDL or "good" cholesterol). Studies of HRT suggest it also has a significant "heart-protective" effect.

Because the risk of heart disease is much greater than other health risks for postmenopausal women, the "heart-protective" effect of ERT may make it a wise choice for many women.

Breast Cancer

It is not clear whether hormone therapy increases the risk of breast cancer. Some studies find that it may increase the risk slightly; others find no increase in risk. However, women who currently have breast cancer should not take ERT or HRT. Some women who have had breast cancer in the past but have been cancer-free for at least two to three years may be able to take HRT. Discuss this with your doctor.

Endometrial Cancer

Estrogen alone (ERT) increases the risk of endometrial (uterine) cancer (although the risk is still very low). Estrogen combined with progestin (HRT) protects against this increased risk.

Gallbladder Disease

Both ERT and HRT increase the risk of gallbladder disease.

Considerations

Hormone therapy reduces the discomfort caused by menopausal symptoms. However, HRT also has side effects that may be unacceptable to some women. They include periodic vaginal bleeding, bloating, cramping, nausea, and breast tenderness. Your doctor may be able to ease these side effects by adjusting the dose.

To gain the long-term benefits of hormone therapy, the medications must be taken for many years. Women on long-term hormone therapy need regular visits to a health professional.

Should You Take Hormones?

Hormone therapy is not usually recommended for women who have had breast cancer, trouble with blood clots, liver disease, or undiagnosed vaginal bleeding.

Discuss the risks and benefits of hormone therapy with your doctor. Few risks appear to be associated with short-term (up to one year) hormone therapy to relieve menopause symptoms. If you are considering longer-term therapy, keep the following in mind:

- If your risk of osteoporosis and heart disease is already low, long-term hormone therapy may not give you enough additional benefits to justify the added risk and inconvenience.

- If your risk of osteoporosis and heart disease is normal to high, the benefits of long-term therapy may outweigh the added risk and inconvenience.

- If taking hormones is inconvenient or is causing side effects, you may want to consider not using them, especially if your risk for osteoporosis and heart disease is low.

Menstrual Cramps

Many women suffer from painful menstrual cramps (dysmenorrhea). Symptoms include mild to severe cramping in the lower abdomen, back, or thighs, headaches, diarrhea, constipation, nausea, dizziness, and fainting.

During the menstrual cycle, the lining of the uterus produces a hormone called prostaglandin. This hormone causes the uterus to contract, often painfully. Women with severe cramps may produce higher than normal amounts of prostaglandin or may be more sensitive to its effects.

 For more information, see the inside front cover.

Home Treatment

- Exercise. Regular workouts decrease the severity of cramps. See Chapter 17.

- Ibuprofen and naproxen (Aleve) generally help ease cramps better than aspirin or acetaminophen. Take either of these the day before your period starts, or at the first sign of pain. Take ibuprofen or naproxen with milk or food; otherwise, these medications can upset your stomach.

- Use heat (hot water bottles, heating pads, or hot baths) to relax tense muscles and relieve cramping.

- Herbal teas, such as chamomile, mint, raspberry, and blackberry, may help soothe tense muscles and anxious moods.

- Try using sanitary napkins instead of tampons.

- If you have symptoms other than cramping, such as weight gain, headache, and tension, see Premenstrual Syndrome on page 241.

When to Call Kaiser Permanente

- If sudden, severe pelvic pain occurs, with or without menstrual bleeding.

- If your period is accompanied by sudden high fever, diarrhea, or skin rash.

- If painful cramping is significantly worse than typical.

- If pelvic pain seems unrelated to your menstrual cycle.

- If menstrual bleeding is very heavy (changing more than one maxi pad or super tampon an hour for more than six hours) or lasts longer than 10 days.

- If periods come closer than 21 days apart.

- If you suspect that your intrauterine device (IUD) is causing cramps.

- If cramps begin five to seven days before your period begins, or if cramps do not cease when menstrual flow stops.

- If cramps fail to respond to home treatment.

Missed or Irregular Periods

Missed or irregular periods have a variety of causes. Pregnancy is usually the first cause to be considered, but other common causes include:

- Stress, weight loss or gain, increased exercise (missed periods are common in endurance athletes), and travel.

- Use of birth control pills, which may cause lighter, less frequent, or skipped periods.

- Menopause or menarche (starting of menstrual periods). For the first few years of menstruation, periods may be irregular.

- Medications, including steroids, tranquilizers, and diet pills.

- Hormone imbalance or problems in the reproductive system.

If you've skipped a period, try to relax. Restoring your life to emotional and physical balance will help. Many women miss periods now and then. Unless you are pregnant, chances are your cycle will return to normal next month. If you could be pregnant, treat yourself as if you are until you know for sure.

Home Treatment

• If you had sex during the previous month, do a home pregnancy test. See page 233.

• Avoid fad diets that greatly restrict calories and food variety, and avoid rapid weight loss. To maintain a healthy weight, focus on eating a variety of low-fat foods. See page 280.

• Increase exercise gradually. If you are an endurance athlete, cut back on training or talk with a doctor about hormone and calcium supplements to protect against bone loss.

• Learn and practice relaxation exercises to reduce and cope with stress. See Chapter 17.

• If you are age 45 or older, you may be starting menopause. See page 236.

When to Call Kaiser Permanente

• If pregnancy is possible, see a doctor to confirm your home pregnancy test and begin pregnancy counseling and/or prenatal care.

• If you have missed two regular periods, are not pregnant, are not approaching menopause, are not dieting or exercising a lot, and are not under psychological stress.

• If you are an endurance athlete who is unable to cut back on training. You may need hormones or calcium supplements.

• If you miss two or three periods while taking birth control pills, and you have not skipped any pills.

Premenstrual Syndrome

Premenstrual syndrome (PMS) occurs 7 to 10 days before the menstrual period begins. It is estimated that 90 percent of women have had some of the symptoms associated with PMS. Only about 10 percent of women have severe problems with PMS. Symptoms generally improve when menstrual bleeding starts.

Over 150 physical and psychological symptoms are associated with PMS. Physical symptoms include headaches, backaches, weight gain, breast tenderness, water retention and bloating, food cravings and increased appetite, diarrhea or constipation, dizziness or fainting, and clumsiness.

Emotional symptoms include irritability and anger, mood swings, anxiety, sudden bouts of crying, sadness, fatigue, poor concentration, diminished sex drive, and aggression.

A self-test to determine if you have PMS:

- Do the same symptoms occur each month?

- Do they occur within 10 days of your period?

- Do symptoms improve or disappear when bleeding begins?

- Do you have at least one symptom-free week per month?

Keep a diary charting your premenstrual symptoms, their timing, and severity. If symptoms appear fairly consistent over several months, chances are you have PMS.

Home Treatment

- Eat smaller meals every three to four hours with plenty of whole grains, fruit, and vegetables. Limit fats and sweets, and reduce salt to help limit bloating.

- Eliminating tobacco, alcohol, and caffeine may help relieve some symptoms.

- Get some exercise. Regular exercise will help minimize PMS symptoms.

- Try an over-the-counter PMS medication, such as Midol or Pamprin. Many products contain a combination of drugs to help relieve symptoms of cramps, bloating, and headache.

- Take a calcium supplement of 600 mg twice a day every day of the month. A recent study has shown a 50 percent reduction in PMS symptoms for most women taking the supplemental calcium.

- Be good to yourself. Reduce your stress level as much as possible. Try relaxation techniques such as yoga and deep breathing. See Chapter 17.

- Talk with others. Your PMS also affects those with whom you live and work. Join a PMS self-help group. You can ask for information and referrals from your doctor or health care professional.

When to Call Kaiser Permanente

- If physical or emotional symptoms are severe and home treatment does not help.

- If symptoms do not stop when menstrual bleeding starts.

Urinary Tract Infections

Urinary tract infections (UTIs), also called bladder infections or cystitis, are a common health problem for women, young girls, and some infant boys. They may also occur in men.

Early symptoms may include burning or pain during urination and itching or pain in the urethra (the tube that carries urine from the bladder). There may be discomfort in the lower abdomen and a frequent urge to urinate without being able to pass much urine. Men with these symptoms may have an infection of the prostate gland. See page 252.

Urinary infections are generally caused by *E. coli* bacteria, which are normally present in the digestive system. Because women have shorter urethras, they are much more susceptible to the infection than men.

Other causes of irritation to the genital area that may be associated with bladder infection include intercourse, diaphragms, wearing tight jeans or pants, bike riding, infrequent urination, perfumed soaps and powders, even spicy food.

Prevention

- Drink more fluids; water is best.

- Urinate frequently.

- Women should wipe from front to back after going to the toilet to reduce the spread of bacteria from the anus to the urethra. Teach young girls this habit during toilet training.

- Avoid frequent douching, and do not use vaginal deodorants or perfumed feminine hygiene products.

- Wash the genital area once a day with plain water or mild soap. Rinse well and dry thoroughly.

- If you are susceptible to urinary infections, drink extra water before intercourse and urinate promptly afterwards.

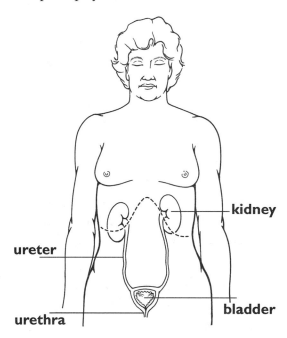

The kidneys filter blood. The waste products from the blood become urine. The ureters carry urine to the bladder. Urine flows out of the body through the urethra (in men, the urethra is inside the penis). Infections can occur in any of the structures of the urinary tract.

- Wear cotton underwear, cotton-lined pantyhose, and loose clothing.

- Drinking cranberry or blueberry juice may protect against infection, especially in postmenopausal women.

Home Treatment

Apply home care at the first sign of irritation or painful urination. A day or so of home treatment may eliminate minor symptoms. However, if your symptoms last longer than a day or worsen despite home care, call your doctor. Because the organs of the urinary tract are connected, untreated bladder infections can spread and can lead to kidney infections and other serious problems.

- Drink as much water as you can (think in terms of gallons) as soon as you notice the symptoms and for the next 24 hours. This will help flush bacteria out of the bladder.

- Avoid alcohol and caffeine.

- A hot bath may help relieve pain and itching. Avoid using bubble bath.

- Check your temperature and examine the genital area twice daily. Fever may indicate a more serious infection is present.

- Avoid intercourse until symptoms improve.

- If vaginal burning and redness occur in a young girl, consider the possibility of an allergy to bubble bath or soap.

When to Call Kaiser Permanente

- If painful urination occurs with any of the following symptoms:

  ° Fever over 101° and chills

  ° Inability to urinate when you feel the urge

  ° Low back pain just below rib cage

  ° Blood or pus in the urine

  ° Unusual vaginal discharge

  ° Nausea or vomiting

- If symptoms do not improve after 24 hours of home treatment.

- If you are pregnant or have diabetes, and have symptoms of a urinary tract infection.

- If you suspect a child has a urinary tract infection.

Blood in the Urine

A blow to the kidneys, excessive running, or an infection can cause blood in the urine. Blood in the urine can be a sign of a serious illness in both women and men and should always be discussed with a health professional.

Eating foods such as beets, blackberries, and foods containing red artificial food colorings can temporarily color the urine pink or red.

Vaginitis

 Vaginitis is any vaginal infection, inflammation, or irritation that causes a change in normal vaginal discharge. General symptoms include a change in the amount, color, odor, or consistency of the discharge; itching; painful urination; and pain during intercourse. Common types of vaginitis include yeast infection (see page 246) and bacterial vaginosis. Some types of sexually transmitted diseases can cause an unusual vaginal discharge. See page 260. If you have burning and pain on urination and feel the need to urinate often, see Urinary Tract Infections on page 243.

Symptoms of bacterial vaginosis often include a thin, grayish white, "fishy-smelling" vaginal discharge. The odor is often worse after intercourse.

Bacterial vaginosis is commonly associated with using tampons, an intrauterine device or diaphragm, and multiple sex partners. In addition, irritation caused by frequent douching, tight clothing, or use of strong soaps or perfumed feminine hygiene products may contribute to vaginal irritation or infection.

Prevention

- Limit the number of your sexual partners and use condoms during intercourse. Multiple sexual partners may increase the risk of bacterial vaginosis by changing the normal environment of the vagina.

- If you think frequent vaginal infections are related to diaphragm or IUD use, discuss other birth control options with your doctor.

- Wipe from front to back after using the toilet to avoid spreading bacteria from the anus to the vagina.

- Wash the genital area once a day with plain water or a mild, non-perfumed soap. Rinse well and dry thoroughly. Avoid douching.

- Avoid using feminine deodorant sprays and other perfumed products. They irritate tender skin.

- Change tampons at least three times a day or alternate tampons with pads. Be sure to remove the last tampon used during your period.

Home Treatment

Bacterial vaginosis may clear up without treatment in three or four days. If symptoms persist, call your doctor.

- Avoid intercourse for two weeks to give irritated vaginal tissues time to heal.

- Avoid scratching. Relieve itching with a cold water compress.

- Make sure that the cause of the vaginitis is not a forgotten tampon or other foreign object.

When to Call Kaiser Permanente

- If you have pelvic or lower abdominal pain, fever, and unusual vaginal discharge.

- If you have an unusual, foul-smelling vaginal discharge that is especially noticeable after intercourse.

- If the discharge and other symptoms are very uncomfortable.

- If you think you've been exposed to a sexually transmitted disease (see page 260). Your partner may need to be treated as well.

- If you have pain with intercourse and it is not eased by use of a vaginal lubricant, such as Astroglide, Surgilube, or Today Personal Lubricant.

- If any unusual discharge lasts more than two weeks.

If you plan to see a health professional, do not douche, use vaginal creams, or have intercourse for 48 hours before your appointment, because they may make diagnosis difficult.

Yeast Infections

A yeast infection is an excess growth of yeast organisms in the vagina due to an imbalance among the normal vaginal microorganisms. Yeast infections are common in women of childbearing age. They can cause severe discomfort but rarely cause serious problems.

Common symptoms of yeast infection include itching (often severe) in the genital area, white, curdy, usually odorless vaginal discharge, painful urination, and pain during intercourse. The skin around the vagina (labia) may be red and irritated. If you have burning and pain on urination and feel the need to urinate often, see Urinary Tract Infections on page 243.

Yeast infections are not sexually transmitted. However, some doctors feel that treating your sexual partner may help prevent chronic, recurrent infections.

Yeast infections (candidiasis) are commonly associated with antibiotic or steroid use, pregnancy, diabetes, and illnesses that impair the immune system. In addition, irritation caused by frequent douching, tight clothing, or use of strong soaps or perfumed feminine hygiene products may contribute to vaginal irritation or infection.

Prevention

- Wear cotton or cotton-lined underwear. Avoid tight-fitting pants and undergarments. They increase body heat, which may allow yeast to grow more easily in your vagina.

- Avoid feminine sprays, talcs, or perfumes in your vaginal area, because they may affect the balance among the microorganisms in your vagina. Do not douche unless told to by your health professional.

- Wipe your vaginal area from front to back after using the toilet and when bathing.

- It is not clear that a high-sugar diet causes yeast infections, but limiting sugar may help prevent them.

Home Treatment

Some women get mild yeast infections toward the end of their menstrual periods. These mild infections sometimes go away without treatment as the menstrual cycle progresses. Be sure your symptoms indicate a yeast infection before trying self-treatment.

- Use an over-the-counter antifungal medication for yeast infections (Gyne-Lotrimin, Monistat 7) as directed.

- Avoid excessive cleaning of the vaginal area. Wash once a day with plain water or a mild, non-perfumed soap.

- Consider using condoms while being treated to avoid (possibly) being reinfected by or infecting your sexual partner. If intercourse is painful, use a water-soluble lubricant (such as Astroglide, Surgilube, or Today Personal Lubricant) to reduce irritation.

When to Call Kaiser Permanente

- If you have pelvic or lower abdominal pain, fever, and unusual vaginal discharge.

- If you think you have a yeast infection for the first time, or if you aren't sure whether your symptoms are due to a yeast infection.

- If home treatment with an over-the-counter product fails to clear up a yeast infection within three or four days, or if you are using antifungal creams repeatedly.

- If you have pain with intercourse and it is not eased by use of a vaginal lubricant.

- If any unusual discharge lasts more than two weeks.

If you plan to see a health professional, do not douche, use vaginal creams, or have intercourse for 48 hours before your appointment, because they may make the diagnosis difficult.

Hysterectomy Guidelines

A hysterectomy is the surgical removal of the uterus. It is sometimes needed to save a woman's life. However, it is often performed unnecessarily. Hysterectomy is often the best solution for:

- Endometrial or cervical cancer

- Severe uterine bleeding of unknown cause

- Ovarian cancer

- Large fibroids with severe bleeding and pain

- Severe prolapse of the uterus

Hysterectomy is generally not the best solution for:

- Non-invasive cervical cancer before menopause

- Fibroids with mild or no symptoms

- Endometriosis without severe symptoms

- Prolapsed uterus that responds to nonsurgical treatments or exercise

- Pelvic inflammatory disease that responds to other treatments

- Abnormal uterine bleeding

The guidelines above may not apply to you. Work with your doctor to decide if a hysterectomy is the best solution for your problem.

The man who says it cannot be done should not interrupt the man doing it.
Old Chinese Proverb

15

Men's Health

This chapter focuses on several health problems that are unique to men. However, it doesn't address basic lifestyle habits, which are the most important health issues for men and also for women.

Healthy Lifestyles

Good health habits are the best way to reduce your risk of the five most common causes of death for men ages 25 to 44. For older men, heart disease and cancer are the leading causes of death.

1. Accidents

• Buckle up, even if your vehicle has airbags. Seat belts save lives and prevent serious injury.

• Don't drink and drive.

2. HIV Infection

• Always use condoms with new sex partners and any partner whose sexual history may not be risk-free (see page 262).

3. Heart Disease

• Limit dietary fat and cholesterol, especially if your cholesterol is high (see page 222).

• Quit smoking, to reduce your risk of heart attack and stroke (see page 150).

• Maintain a healthy weight and get regular exercise.

• Have blood pressure checked regularly (see pages 25 and 224) and take prescribed high blood pressure medications as directed.

4. Cancer

• Quit smoking. Lung cancer is the most common type of cancer among both men and women.

5. Suicide

• Learn the warning signs of depression and seek help if you have them (see page 296).

If your health is already good, these habits will help you stay healthy and active as you get older. If you have some health problems, good habits are even more important. Specific tips for controlling cholesterol, blood pressure, and weight, for getting enough exercise, quitting smoking, and managing stress are included in other chapters. Check the page numbers above and the index for help in getting started.

Genital Health

Daily cleaning of the penis, particularly under the foreskin of an uncircumcised penis, can prevent bacterial infection. Daily washing also reduces the already low risk of penile cancer. Boys should be taught by age three or four to start to gently retract the foreskin. The foreskin

may not be fully retractable until puberty. Wash the penis, and replace the foreskin over the head of the penis after cleaning. Do not forcibly retract a child's foreskin if it is painful or difficult to do so.

Testicular Self-Exam

 Teen males and young men who are at increased risk of testicular cancer (those who have had undescended testicles or a family history of testicular cancer) are encouraged to examine their testes once a month. Testicular cancer is very rare and highly curable.

The best time to do the exam is after a warm bath or shower when the scrotal skin is relaxed.

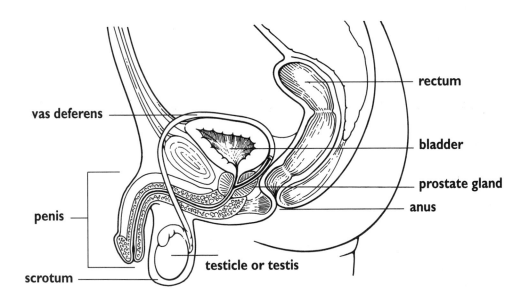

Male pelvic organs

- Stand and place your right leg on an elevated surface. A tub side or toilet seat works fine.

- Examine the surface of the right testicle by gently rolling it between the thumb and fingers of both hands. Feel for any hard lumps or nodules. The testicle should feel round and smooth.

- Notice any enlargement of the testicle or a change in its consistency. It is normal for one testicle to be slightly larger than the other. Report any major size differences to a health professional.

- Repeat, lifting your left leg and examining your left testicle.

When to Call Kaiser Permanente

- Unusual lumps or nodules in the testes

- Unexplained pain or swelling in the testes or scrotum

- If you notice any penile discharge or sores on your penis, see pages 260 and 261 and discuss it with your doctor.

Gently feel each testicle for hard lumps or a change in size.

Erection Problems

Erection problems are common and can often be solved with self-care. By definition, an erection problem is difficulty in raising or maintaining an erection capable of intercourse.

Erection problems are often due to stress at work, tension in relationships, depression, fatigue, lack of privacy, physical injury, or side effects of medications. These causes are generally temporary and will usually resolve with home treatment. Other, less reversible causes include diabetes, a long history of smoking, or vascular disease.

The ease of gaining and sustaining erections generally decreases with age. However, with the right foreplay and environment, there is no age limit to the ability of healthy men to have erections.

Prevention

Most erection problems can be resolved by taking a more relaxed approach to lovemaking and watching for possible side effects from medications or illnesses.

Home Treatment

- Rule out medications first. Many drugs have side effects that can cause erection problems, especially blood pressure medicines, diuretics (water pills), and mood-altering drugs. Ask your doctor or pharmacist to check your medications for possible side effects on sexual function, or look it up yourself. See Resource 2 on page 325.

- Avoid alcohol and smoking, which make erection problems worse.

- Cope with stress (see Chapter 17). Tension in your life can distract you and make erections difficult. Regular exercise and other stress-relieving activities may help ease tension.

- Take time for more foreplay. Let your partner know that you would enjoy some stroking. Slow down, then slow down some more.

- Make sure you're ready. If you have experienced a recent loss or change in a relationship, you may not yet be emotionally ready for erections. Generally, the stress will subside and the erection problem will disappear over time. Do what you can to relax.

- Find out if you can have erections at other times. If you can have an erection during masturbation or on awakening from sleep, the problem is probably stress-related or due to an emotional problem.

When to Call Kaiser Permanente

- If you think that a medication may be causing the problem. Substitutes may be available.

- If you are unable to have an erection at all, or think that your problem may be a physical one.

- If you are still having problems after a few months of self-care.

- After all other options have been tried for several months without success, you may wish to talk with your doctor about erection-producing injections, a vacuum device, or penile implant.

Prostate Problems

The prostate is a doughnut-shaped gland with two lobes located at the bottom of the bladder about halfway between the rectum and the base of the penis. It encircles the urethra, the tube that carries urine from the bladder out through the penis. This walnut-sized gland produces most of the fluid in semen.

The three most common prostate problems are: infection (prostatitis), prostate enlargement (benign prostatic hypertrophy), and prostate cancer. Infection and enlargement do not lead to cancer.

Prostate Infection (Prostatitis)

There are two types of prostate infection, acute and chronic. Acute infections come on suddenly and have some or all of the following symptoms:

- Fever and chills

- Pain and burning during urination and ejaculation

- Strong and frequent urge to urinate while passing only small amounts of urine

- Low back or abdominal pain

- Blood in the urine (occasionally)

Symptoms of chronic prostatitis are usually milder than those of an acute infection, and fever and chills are usually not present. Either infection may occur with a urinary tract infection. See page 243.

Prostate infections usually respond well to home care and antibiotics. If the infection recurs, long-term antibiotic treatment may be needed.

Sometimes men will have painful urinary symptoms without infection. This condition, called prostatodynia, is often related to stress or anxiety.

Prevention

- Increase your fluid intake to as much as 8 to 12 glasses per day, until you are urinating more often than usual. Extra fluids help flush the urinary tract clean.

- Avoid alcohol and caffeine. Caffeine can cause a strong and frequent urge to urinate. Remember that colas as well as coffee and tea contain caffeine.

- Keep stress under control. Stress is closely associated with painful urinary symptoms.

- Drink as much water as you can tolerate.

Home Treatment

- Eliminate all alcohol and caffeine from your diet.

- Hot baths help soothe pain and reduce stress.

- Aspirin or ibuprofen may help ease painful urinary symptoms.

When to Call Kaiser Permanente

- If urinary symptoms occur with fever, chills, vomiting, or pain in the back or abdomen.

- If urine is red or pink with no dietary reason (see page 244). Always call your doctor if you have blood in your urine.

- If symptoms continue for five days despite home care.

- If there is a sudden change or worsening of symptoms.

- If you have pain on urination or ejaculation and a discharge from the penis. See pages 260 and 261.

Prostate Enlargement (Benign Prostatic Hypertrophy)

As men age, the prostate may enlarge. This seems to be a natural process and is not really a disease. However, as the gland gets bigger, it tends to squeeze the urethra and cause urinary problems, such as:

- Difficulty getting urine started and completely stopped (dribbling)

- Urge to urinate frequently, or being wakened by the need to urinate

- Painful urination

- Decreased force of the urine stream

- Incomplete bladder emptying

An enlarged prostate gland is not a serious problem unless urination becomes extremely difficult or backed-up urine causes bladder infections or kidney damage. Some dribbling after urination is very common and not necessarily a sign of prostate problems.

Surgery is usually not necessary for an enlarged prostate. Although surgery used to be a common treatment, recent research shows that most cases of prostate enlargement do not get worse over time as previously thought. Many men find that their symptoms are stable and some even clear up on their own. In these cases, the best treatment may be no treatment at all. Drugs are available that may help improve symptoms in many men. Your doctor can advise you on the various treatment options.

Prevention

Since the prostate produces seminal fluid, there is a long-standing belief that regular ejaculations (two to three times per week) will help prevent an enlarged prostate. There is no scientific proof of this, but it is risk-free.

Home Treatment

- Avoid antihistamines and decongestants, which can make urinary problems worse.

- If you are bothered by a frequent urge to urinate at night, cut down on beverages before bedtime, especially alcohol and caffeine.

- Don't postpone urinating, and take plenty of time. Try sitting on the toilet instead of standing.

- If dribbling after urination is a problem, wash your penis once a day to prevent infection.

- Also see Urinary Incontinence on page 84.

When to Call Kaiser Permanente

- If fever, back or abdominal pain, or chills develop.

- Diuretics, tranquilizers, antihistamines, decongestants, and antidepressants can aggravate urinary problems. If you take these drugs, ask your doctor if there are other medications that do not cause these side effects.

- If the symptoms of an enlarged prostate last longer than two weeks without letting up. Early examination enables you to confirm the diagnosis and consider treatment options.

Prostate Cancer

 Prostate cancer is the most common cancer and the second leading cause of cancer deaths in men. It is usually a small and slow-growing cancer. When detected early, before it has spread to other organs, the cancer may be curable. Risk increases with age, and most cases are in men over 65. Since it is more common in older men, it usually does not shorten life. However, when it is large, advanced, or appears at a younger age, it can be very serious.

There are no specific symptoms of prostate cancer. Most men have no symptoms at all. In a few cases, it can cause urinary symptoms very similar to those of prostate enlargement. In advanced cases, other symptoms, such as pain, may be caused by spread of the cancer to other organs such as bone.

Prostate cancer sometimes runs in families, is more common in African-American men, and tends to be more common in men who eat a high-fat diet.

Prevention

Maintaining a low-fat diet is the only known way to reduce the risk of prostate cancer.

There is a great deal of controversy about the value of using digital rectal exams and the prostate-specific antigen (PSA) blood test to screen men who do not have any symptoms of prostate cancer. Using these tests to detect early prostate cancer has not been shown to improve the quality of life or to prolong life. Therefore, many experts are uncertain whether routine digital rectal exams or PSA tests are appropriate for all men.

Talk with your doctor for more information about screening.

Home Treatment

Prostate cancer treatment is tailored to each individual. Work together with your doctor to be sure that you will receive long-term benefit from treatment.

Learn all you can about the available treatment options, which may include watchful waiting, so that you and your doctor can select the one best suited for you.

Your age, overall health, other medical conditions, and the characteristics of the cancer are all important factors to consider in making treatment decisions.

When to Call Kaiser Permanente

- If you have any of the symptoms listed under When to Call Kaiser Permanente for prostate infection (page 253) or prostate enlargement (page 254).

- If there is severe bone pain.

I wasn't kissing her, I was whispering in her mouth.
Groucho Marx

16

Sexual Health

Sexuality is an important aspect of our health. It influences how we love, how we show affection, how we value ourselves, and how we bond with and befriend each other. Sexuality is based on deep personal values we learn from our parents, our culture, our religion, and who we are.

Sexuality can be confusing; there are myths and misunderstandings about it. Parents have a special obligation to help their children develop sexual values. Talk with your children about their sexuality and give them good information. Help them learn to make responsible and safe choices about sex and sexuality.

This chapter covers specific health issues of concern to people who are sexually active, from birth control to sexually transmitted diseases (STDs), including AIDS.

Birth Control

 Birth control can help prevent unplanned pregnancies. However, no birth control method (except abstinence) is 100 percent effective and without risks. Each method has different risks and effectiveness. The text below and the chart on page 258 briefly describe the most common birth control methods. Review each method with your partner before deciding which one meets your needs. Your health professional can help you better understand the effectiveness and risks of each method.

Use all birth control methods exactly as your doctor or the package instructions recommend. Proper use helps ensure the most effectiveness. If you have sexual intercourse without using a birth control method and are concerned about a possible pregnancy, call your doctor or advice nurse as soon as possible for information about emergency contraception.

Birth Control

Method	Pregnancies*	Comments
Sterilization Tubal ligation (women) Vasectomy (men)	Less than 1	Consider it permanent.
Hormonal Methods Oral contraceptives (the Pill)	3 (less than 1 with proper use)	Increased risk of circulatory disorders and high blood pressure in smokers.
Norplant (implant) Depo-Provera (shot)	Less than 1 Less than 1	Either may cause irregular menstrual bleeding.
Intrauterine Device (IUD)	Less than 1	May cause bleeding and cramping. May be expelled without being noticed. Increased risk of pelvic infection.
Barrier Methods Condom alone	12	Use properly for best protection.
Condom with spermicide	5	Provides the most reliable protection against STDs.
Diaphragm (with spermicide)	18	
Cervical cap	18–36	
Spermicides Jelly, cream, foam, suppositories	21	Use with a condom for best protection.
Used with condom	5	
Periodic Abstinence (natural family planning: basal body temperature, mucus, or rhythm / calendar method)	20	
Withdrawal	19	
No method (chance)	85	

*Typical number of accidental pregnancies per 100 women in one year. When birth control methods are used exactly as directed, pregnancy rates are lower.

Adapted from: R. Hatcher, et al., *Contraceptive Technology, 1994-1996.*

Hormonal methods of birth control for women require a doctor's prescription. Hormones prevent the ovaries from releasing an egg each month (ovulation). They do not protect against STDs.

Oral contraceptives (the Pill) are pills taken daily. Norplant is a set of small cylinders inserted under the skin that release hormones continuously for up to five years. They can be removed whenever you decide you want to get pregnant. Depo-Provera is an injection given once every three months.

The intrauterine device (IUD) is a plastic or metal device that is inserted into the uterus by a doctor. It appears to prevent pregnancy by keeping the egg from being fertilized. The IUD does not provide any protection against STDs.

Barrier methods of birth control keep sperm from reaching the egg.

Condoms are a thin covering of latex or other material that fits tightly over the man's erect penis to catch the ejaculated semen. There are also condoms for women that fit in the vagina and protect against STDs and unplanned pregnancy.

Spermicides are foams, jellies, and suppositories that contain chemicals that kill sperm.

Condoms used with spermicides provide the most reliable, but not total, protection against STDs, including HIV. You can buy both condoms and spermicides without a doctor's prescription.

The diaphragm and cervical cap are small rubber caps that are filled with spermicide and inserted into the vagina to cover the cervix (opening to the uterus). They are left in place for six hours or longer after intercourse. Both require a doctor's prescription.

These barrier methods provide minimal protection against STDs and HIV.

Surgical methods are the most effective forms of birth control.

During a vasectomy, the tubes (vas deferens) that carry a man's sperm from the testes are cut and tied off, thus preventing pregnancy. A tubal ligation (having your "tubes tied") closes or blocks a woman's fallopian tubes to keep eggs from moving from the ovaries into the uterus.

Both procedures should be considered permanent but may be successfully surgically reversed in some cases.

Natural family planning (fertility awareness) methods help a couple estimate when the woman is most likely to become pregnant (during ovulation) so they can avoid intercourse during that time. To estimate when ovulation occurs, a woman records her temperature, examines her vaginal mucus discharge, and tracks her menstrual periods.

Sexually Transmitted Diseases

 Sexually transmitted diseases (STDs) or venereal diseases (VD) are infections passed from person to person through sexual intercourse or genital contact. Chlamydia, genital herpes, genital warts, gonorrhea, hepatitis B, and syphilis are among the most common STDs. AIDS (acquired immune deficiency syndrome), the most virulent and deadly of all STDs, is discussed on page 262.

Chlamydia (kla-mid-ee-uh) is a bacterial infection that affects millions of men and women. It may be difficult to detect chlamydia; about 75 percent of women and 20 percent of men with the disease have no symptoms. If symptoms do show up, they occur two to four weeks after exposure. In women, symptoms may include vaginal discharge or irregular menstrual bleeding, painful urination, genital itching, or lower abdominal pain. In men, there may be a penile discharge and painful urination.

Chlamydia is easily treated with antibiotics. If undetected and untreated, chlamydia can cause pelvic inflammatory disease (infection in the ovaries and fallopian tubes), which may lead to sterility. All sexually active teenage females should be screened for chlamydia, whether they have symptoms or not. Other sexually active women should discuss screening with their doctor.

Genital herpes is caused by the herpes simplex virus, which also causes cold sores (see page 174). Genital herpes is easily spread through sexual and other direct skin contact.

Symptoms occur 2 to 30 days after contact with an infected person. It is also possible to be infected with herpes and have no symptoms.

The first case of genital herpes may be quite severe, with many painful sores or blisters. Fever, swollen glands, and headache or muscle aches may also occur. If the sores develop inside the urethra or vagina, there may be pain on urination or a vaginal discharge. The sores will crust and disappear in one to three weeks' time. Sometimes the first episode is so mild it is unnoticed.

There is no known cure for herpes. Once infected, most people do not have recurrent outbreaks. For those who do, the recurrent outbreaks are usually shorter and less severe than the first one. Itching, burning, or tingling may occur at the place where the sores will later appear. Medication may be helpful if you have very frequent and severe outbreaks.

Genital warts are caused by the human papillomavirus (HPV), which is spread by sexual contact. They generally appear as small fleshy bumps or flat white patches on the labia (the lips around the vagina), inside the vagina, on the penis or scrotum, or around the anus. The warts may be too small to be seen. HPV seems to increase the risk of cervical cancer in women.

The virus can occasionally be detected by a Pap smear. If warts are bothersome or develop on the cervix, they can be removed by a health professional. In some cases, the warts may recur. There does not appear to be an effective cure at this time.

Gonorrhea, also known as clap, drip, or GC, is a bacterial infection spread through sexual contact.

Symptoms include painful urination, vaginal discharge, irregular menstrual bleeding, or a thick discharge from the penis. Many people who have the bacteria have no symptoms. If untreated, gonorrhea in women may lead to pelvic inflammatory disease and sterility. It can sometimes spread to the joints and cause arthritis.

Hepatitis B is a viral infection spread through sexual contact or contact with infected blood. An infected pregnant woman can also transmit the virus to her baby. Symptoms appear two to five months after exposure and include vomiting, abdominal pain, loss of appetite, and yellow tint to the eyes and skin (jaundice). About one-third of infected people have no symptoms. Long-term effects of the disease include life-threatening liver damage. The hepatitis B vaccine is recommended for all infants, adolescents (especially those at risk), and for people in high-risk groups (people with many sexual partners, men who have sex with men, intravenous drug users, infants born to women who have hepatitis B, and health care workers). See page 19.

Syphilis is a bacterial infection spread through sexual contact or by sharing contaminated needles. Symptoms appear in two weeks to one month when passed by sexual contact. The first symptom is a chancre, a small red blister, ulcer, or sore that appears on the genitals, rectal area, or mouth. This sore is painless and may go unnoticed. The lymph nodes in the groin may also swell.

If syphilis is not treated early, it can proceed to a second phase in two to eight weeks. Symptoms of the second phase include skin rash, patchy hair loss, fever, swollen lymph glands, and flu-like symptoms, which are easily confused with other illnesses.

Syphilis can be treated with antibiotics. If untreated, syphilis may cause serious problems and premature death.

Prevention

Preventing a sexually transmitted disease is easier than treating an infection once it occurs. Only monogamy (you and your partner have sex with each other only) between uninfected partners or sexual abstinence completely eliminates the risk.

- Avoid sexual contact while you or your partner is being treated for a sexually transmitted disease.

- If you or your partner has herpes, avoid sexual contact when a blister or any open ulcer or sore is present, and use condoms at all other times.

• The same behaviors that reduce your risk of HIV (such as using condoms) also reduce your risk of getting other STDs. See page 264 for additional prevention guidelines, including condom use.

When to Call Kaiser Permanente

Call if you notice any unusual vaginal or penile discharge, sores, redness, or growths on the genitals, or if you suspect that you have been exposed to an STD.

STDs need to be diagnosed and treated by a health professional. Your doctor or a health department can diagnose and treat STDs. Your sexual partner must also be treated, even if he or she has no symptoms. Otherwise, your partner may reinfect you or develop serious complications.

HIV Infection and AIDS

 AIDS (acquired immune deficiency syndrome) is caused by the human immunodeficiency virus (HIV). HIV destroys the immune system, so that it is impossible for the body to fight off disease or even minor illnesses. AIDS is the last phase in HIV disease, when the body is unable to fight a disease or infection.

A person is said to be HIV-positive if antibodies to the virus are detected in his or her blood. It may take up to six months after infection for the antibodies to appear. Someone who is HIV-positive may appear to be healthy for 10 years or longer before the symptoms of AIDS develop.

HIV is not spread by mosquitoes, toilet seats, being coughed on by an infected person, casual contact with someone who is HIV-positive or who has AIDS, or by donating blood.

Because all blood has been tested for HIV since 1985, the risk of getting the virus from blood or blood products is extremely low.

HIV is spread only when blood, semen, or vaginal fluids from an infected person enter someone else's body. The specific behaviors that spread HIV include:

1. Sharing injection needles, syringes, or drug-use equipment with someone who is HIV-positive.

2. Unprotected (without a condom) rectal entry intercourse (anal sex) with someone who is HIV-positive. Anal sex often tears the rectal blood vessels, allowing the virus to enter the body.

3. Vaginal intercourse without a condom or oral sexual activity with someone who is HIV-positive.

Babies born to or breast-fed by women who are HIV-positive are also at high risk of contracting the virus.

Being touched, hugged, or lightly kissed by someone who is HIV-positive will not transfer the virus to you. As long as you practice the prevention behaviors on page 264, you have virtually no risk of contracting the virus.

If you may been exposed recently to HIV, contact your health care professional or advice nurse to make an appointment for testing.

A simple, confidential blood test, available from your doctor or a health department, can determine if you are HIV-positive. All pregnant women and any individual who is at high risk should have this test. Although new tests may detect HIV as early as three weeks after infection, it may take up to six months for HIV antibodies to develop. The virus can be transmitted even before antibodies have developed. Even after antibodies develop, some people remain free of symptoms for well over 10 years but can still transmit the virus to others.

Researchers believe that most people who are HIV-positive will eventually develop AIDS. Although there is still no cure for HIV infection or AIDS, new treatments have dramatically improved the lives and health of people with HIV. Early diagnosis by testing is the key. If you find out that you have been infected, there are many resources available to help you.

Symptoms of HIV Infection and AIDS

In early infection, people usually have no symptoms. However, some people may experience:

- Rapid, unexplained weight loss
- Persistent unexplained fever and night sweats
- Persistent severe fatigue
- Persistent diarrhea
- Swelling of glands in neck, armpits, or groin

As the immune system deteriorates, a variety of other symptoms may appear, including:

- Unusual sores on the skin or in the mouth; white patches in the mouth
- Increased outbreaks of cold sores or genital herpes
- Unexplained shortness of breath and dry cough
- Severe numbness or pain in the hands and feet
- Personality change or mental deterioration
- Unusual cancers and infections

These symptoms also are caused by many illnesses other than HIV infection or AIDS. However, if any symptom develops or persists without a good explanation, especially if your behavior puts you at risk of HIV infection, call your doctor.

Prevention

Only monogamy (you and your partner have sex with each other only) between uninfected partners or sexual abstinence completely eliminates the risk of HIV and other sexually transmitted diseases. The following actions will reduce your risk:

 For more information, see the inside front cover.

- If you are beginning a sexual relationship, take time before having sex to talk about HIV and other STDs. Find out if your partner has ever been exposed or infected or if your partner's behavior puts him or her at risk of HIV infection. Talk about your own risks and history of infection as well. Remember that it is possible to be infected without knowing it.

- Use condoms every time you have anal or vaginal intercourse until you are certain that neither you nor your partner has any sexually transmitted diseases. Also be sure that neither of you will have unprotected sexual contact with anyone else while your relationship lasts.

- Remember that it can take up to six months before HIV can be detected in the blood. If you plan to use HIV testing to decide whether condoms are needed, wait six months after any unprotected sexual contact or other high-risk behavior. During this time, both you and your partner need to avoid unprotected sexual contact and use condoms every time you have sexual contact.

- Avoid unprotected sexual contact with anyone who has symptoms of or who has been exposed to an STD, or whose behavior puts him or her at risk of HIV infection. Keep in mind that a person may have no symptoms but still be able to transmit the diseases.

- Avoid unprotected vaginal and anal intercourse and oral sex with anyone whose sexual history may not be risk-free. Use latex condoms from the beginning to the end of sexual contact. "Natural" or lambskin condoms do not protect as well against HIV infection.

- People who are allergic to spermicides containing nonoxynol-9 may develop genital sores, which can increase the risk of HIV infection.

- Do not rely on spermicidal jelly, birth control pills, or the diaphragm alone to protect against STDs. Condoms offer the most reliable protection against HIV and other STDs.

In addition to the guidelines above, taking the following precautions will reduce your risk of getting HIV and hepatitis B:

- Avoid activities that spread HIV (see page 262). Safer activities include closed-mouth kissing, hugging, massage, and other pleasurable touching.

- Never share needles, syringes, or other personal items that could be contaminated with blood. Even needles that have been boiled can remain contaminated.

For more information, call the National AIDS Hotline at 1-800-342-AIDS. Also see Resource 6 on page 325.

If exercise could be packed into a pill, it would be the single most widely prescribed, and beneficial, medicine in the nation.
Robert Butler, M.D.

17

Fitness and Relaxation

Staying fit and relaxed is not only good for your health, it is good for you. If you want to enjoy life more, the tips in this chapter can help.

The Benefits of Exercise

No amount of exercise can guarantee a long life. However, even moderate amounts of exercise can improve the likelihood of a healthy life. Along with a positive attitude and a healthy diet, your fitness level plays a major role in how well you feel, what illnesses you avoid, and how much you enjoy life.

Consider the benefits of fitness presented here and find one or more reasons to commit to your own fitness program.

Benefits of Exercise

- Relieves tension and stress
- Provides enjoyment and fun
- Stimulates the mind
- Helps maintain stable weight
- Controls appetite
- Boosts self-image
- Improves muscle tone and strength
- Improves flexibility
- Lowers blood pressure
- Relieves insomnia
- Increases "good" (HDL) cholesterol
- Reduces risk of diabetes
- Increases energy and helps decrease fatigue
- Reduces anxiety and depression
- Improves balance and coordination
- Helps prevent constipation

Your Personal Fitness Plan

No one can prescribe the perfect fitness plan for you. You have to figure it out based on what you enjoy doing and what you will continue to do. The next few pages can be a big help.

Consistency is the most important, the most basic, and the most often neglected part of fitness. Consistency in regular exercise or moderate activity delivers all of the fitness benefits.

A good fitness plan has three parts: aerobic fitness, muscle strengthening, and flexibility. Read the section on each part. Then see "Setting Your Fitness Goals" on page 270.

Aerobic Fitness

Aerobic conditioning strengthens your heart and lungs. Good aerobic exercises include brisk walking, running, stair climbing, biking, swimming, aerobic dance, or anything else that raises your heart rate and keeps it up for a while.

How Hard Should I Exercise?

Nice and easy does it. Exercise does not have to be intense to be of value. In fact, if you exercise too hard, you get less benefit than if you go at a moderate pace.

Above all, listen to your body. If the exercise feels too hard, slow down. You will reduce your risk of injury and enjoy the exercise much more.

Try the "talk-sing test" to determine your ideal exercise pace:

- If you can't talk and exercise at the same time, you are going too fast.

- If you can talk while you exercise, you are doing fine.

- If you can sing while you exercise, it would be safe to exercise a little faster.

Your exercise is most effective when you can talk, but not sing, while doing it.

Target Heart Rate

Another way to see how hard you are exercising is to check your heart rate. You gain the most aerobic benefits when your exercise heart rate is 60 percent to 80 percent of your maximum heart rate. This is your target heart rate. After exercising for about 10 minutes, stop and

Target Heart Rate	
Age	10-second heart rate
20	20–27
25	20–26
30	19–25
35	19–25
40	18–24
45	18–23
50	17–23
55	17–23
60	16–22
65	16–21
70	15–20

Target heart rate is 60 percent to 80 percent of maximum heart rate (maximum heart rate = 220 minus your age).

Are You Ready to Get Started?

- Any activity is better than no activity...and you never have to run a marathon. You can start with a five-minute walk **today,** and presto! You're started!

- Then, you can look for ways to liven up every day with a few minutes of walking, gardening, bicycling, dancing, swimming, taking the stairs, basketball, hiking, skating, playing games, etc.

- Some people like to write down all of their activity on their calendar. Then they can step back and say, "I did it!"

take your pulse for 10 seconds (see page 25). Compare the number to the chart on page 266. Adjust the intensity of your exercise so that your heart rate stays between the two numbers. However, the target heart rate is only a guide. Each individual is different, so pay attention to how you feel.

How Often and How Long Should I Exercise?

Most studies show that exercising for 30 minutes on most days each week is what it takes to improve fitness. However, sometimes it's easier to make exercise a habit if you do it every day.

With aerobic exercise, harder is not better, but longer is. Although you can get good fitness benefits from as little as 10 minutes of aerobic exercise per day, extending your exercise time will increase your rewards. This is true for up to one hour of exercise per day. Beyond that, there may be diminishing health returns and increasing risk of injuries.

Warm Up and Cool Down

For the first five minutes of your exercise routine, start out slowly and easily so your muscles have a chance to warm up.

End your exercise with a little cool-down period. If you've been running or walking quickly, gradually slow your pace, then do a few light stretches to improve flexibility. See page 268.

Drink some extra water before and after exercising.

Muscle Strengthening

Strengthening your muscles improves your work and athletic performance and prevents fatigue. Muscle-strengthening exercises will also improve your posture and help you feel more energetic.

Resistance training, with free weights, weight-training equipment, or inexpensive rubber tubing, can quickly increase your muscle strength.

Other simple, safe, and effective strengthening exercises include bent-knee curl-ups, chin-ups, push-ups, side leg-lifts, and other calisthenics to improve abdominal, neck, arm, shoulder, and leg strength.

triceps stretch   latissimus stretch

calf stretch

hamstring stretch

outer hip stretch

quadriceps stretch

groin stretches

Stretching exercises

Flexibility

Stretching can increase your range of motion and reduce stiffness and pain. Stretching is particularly important during the cool-down phase after exercising when your muscles are warm. See the stretches on page 268 and Resource 36 on page 327.

- Stretch slowly and gradually. Don't bounce. Maintain a continuous tension on the muscle.

- Relax and hold each stretch for a count of 20.

- Exhale as you stretch, to further relax your muscles. If stretching hurts, you have gone too far or you are doing something incorrectly.

Try to stretch a little every day. Take a stretch break instead of a coffee break.

Overcome Barriers to Exercise

There are six barriers to exercise that are all easy to overcome.

1. No time? Try shorter periods of activity spread throughout the day, such as three 10-minute walks.

2. Too tired? It's often lack of exercise that makes you tired. Exercise gives you energy. Try it.

3. Embarrassed? Many people are, especially at first. Be proud that you're taking care of your body.

Exercise Caution

Moderate exercise is safe for most people. To be safe, start slowly and gradually increase the intensity of your exercise. However, if you can answer yes to any of the following questions, talk with your doctor before beginning an exercise program.

- Do you have heart trouble?

- Do you have undiagnosed chest pains?

- Do you have high blood pressure?

- Do you often feel faint or dizzy?

- Do you have arthritis or other bone or joint problems that might be aggravated by improper exercise?

- Do you have diabetes? You may want to talk with your doctor about how increased exercise affects your insulin needs.

Men over age 40 who have been inactive or who have two or more risk factors for heart disease* and who plan to start a vigorous exercise program (running or fast bicycling or swimming) may wish to talk with their doctors about any possible risks.

....

*Cholesterol over 200, blood pressure over 140/90, smoking, diabetes, or family history of heart disease before age 45.

---

4. No partner? Yes, it's more fun to exercise with a friend. If your regular exercise partner quits, find another one. You could also join a fitness club, take a class, or exercise to a video.

5. Bad weather? Too hot, too cold, too wet, too windy—it never seems right for exercise. Lots of people exercise come rain or shine. Try a variety of indoor and outdoor activities.

6. Too costly? You had to let the fitness club membership expire. You can't afford a mountain bike. You panic at the price of running shoes. It all costs money. But can you afford not to exercise? Try a low-cost option, such as walking instead of driving.

Setting Your Fitness Goals

Are you as strong, flexible, and physically fit as you would like to be? If you are, good for you. We hope this chapter has helped you reaffirm the exercises you are already doing. However, if you want to make some improvements, here's one piece of advice: Try to improve a little bit at a time.

The only way to walk a mile is to take one step at a time. The only way to improve your fitness level is to take it one step at a time.

• Pick one aspect of fitness (aerobic, strength, flexibility) you want to improve first.

• Pick an activity that you enjoy. You're more likely to keep doing something you like.

• Set a one-month goal that you think you can reach. For example, plan to walk for 10 minutes at lunch three days a week, or stretch for five minutes each morning.

• Start today. Keep a record of what you do.

• When you reach your first goal, reward yourself! Then set a new one.

Consistency brings success. Each success may be a small one, but small successes can quickly add up to physical fitness that will make a big difference in your life.

Stress and Distress

Stress is the physical, mental, and emotional reactions you experience as the result of changes and demands in your life.

Stress is part and parcel of common life events, both large and small. It comes with all of life's daily hassles, traffic jams, long lines, petty arguments, and other relatively small irritations. Stress also comes with crises and life-changing events, such as illness, marriage problems or divorce, losing a job, getting a new job, or children leaving home.

All these events may force you to adjust, whether you are ready to or not. Unless you can regularly release the tension that comes with stress, it can greatly increase your risks of physical and mental illness.

Because many major life events are beyond your control, take charge of those aspects of your life that you can manage. One major change doesn't mean that all areas of your life must change. Continue to participate in the same activities you did before the event happened.

Not all stress is bad. Positive stress (eustress) is a motivator, challenging you to act in creative and resourceful ways. When changes and demands overwhelm you, negative stress (distress) sets in. This section has specific techniques you can use to cope with stress in your life.

What Stress Does to the Body

At the first sign of alarm, chemicals released by the pituitary and adrenal glands and the nerve endings automatically trigger these physical reactions to stress:

- Heart rate increases to move blood to the muscles and brain.

- Blood pressure goes up.

- Breathing rate increases.

- Digestion slows down.

- Perspiration increases.

- Pupils dilate.

- You feel a rush of strength.

Your body is tense, alert, and ready for action. For primitive people, these reactions were an advantage in the face of sudden danger, preparing them for survival by either "fight or flight." Today, our bodies still react the same way, but it is not as acceptable to either fight or run away (although we often wish we could).

After the natural "alarm" reaction to a real or perceived threat, our bodies stay on alert until we feel the danger has passed. When the stressor is gone, the brain signals an "all clear" sign to the pituitary and adrenal glands. They stop producing the chemicals that caused the physical reaction, and the body gradually returns to normal.

Problems with stress occur when the brain fails to give the "all clear" signal. If the alarm state lasts too long, you begin to suffer from the consequences of constant stress. Unrelieved stress can lead to many health problems.

Recognizing Stress

Sometimes it's difficult to recognize or admit that stress is affecting your health. If you can learn to watch for its effects and take corrective action quickly, you will be able to cope with your stress.

The signs of stress are classic. You may get a headache, stiff neck, nagging backache, rapid breathing, sweaty palms, or an upset stomach. You may become irritable and intolerant of even minor disturbances. You may lose your temper more often and yell at your family for no good reason. Your pulse rate may increase and you may feel jumpy or exhausted all the time. You may find it hard to concentrate.

When these symptoms appear, recognize them as signs of stress and find a way to deal with them. Just knowing why you're crabby may be the first step in coping with the problem. It is your attitude toward stress, not the stress itself, that affects your health the most.

Managing Stress

Some people try to relieve stress by smoking, drinking, overeating, or taking pills. There is a better way. Avoid the dangerous side effects of tobacco, alcohol, and drugs by learning to control your stress level. You can do this by using your body to soothe your mind and using your mind to soothe your body.

Stress and tension affect our emotions and feelings. By expressing those feelings to others, we are able to better understand and cope with them. Talking about a problem with a spouse or a good friend is a valuable way to reduce tension and stress.

Crying can also relieve tension. It's part of our emotional healing process. Expressing yourself through writing, crafts, or art may also be a good tension reliever.

Exercise is a natural response to stress; it is the normal reaction to the fight-or-flight urge. Walking briskly will take advantage of the rapid pulse and tensed muscles caused by stress and release your pent-up energy. After a long walk, your stress level is usually lower and more manageable.

The rest of this chapter is devoted to other skills and techniques that will help you increase your resistance to stress and better cope with those stressors you choose to accept.

Relaxation Skills

Whatever you do to manage stress, you can benefit from the regular use of relaxation skills. Relaxation is the exact opposite to the fight-or-flight response.

When learning relaxation skills, you must remove yourself from all outside distractions. It may take some practice to become comfortable with these techniques. Once you've trained your body and mind to relax (two to three weeks), you'll be able to produce the same relaxed state whenever you want.

The following three methods of relaxation and meditation are among the simplest and most effective. They should be done once or twice a day for about 10 to 20 minutes. Pick a time and place where you won't be disturbed or distracted.

Belly Breathing

The object of belly breathing is to develop full use of your lungs and get in touch with the rhythm of your breathing. It can be practiced in any position, but it is best to learn it lying on your back, with your knees bent.

1. Place your left hand on your abdomen and your right hand on your chest. Notice how your hands move as you breathe in and out.

2. Practice filling your lower lungs by breathing so that your left hand goes up when you inhale and your right hand remains still. Always inhale through your nose and exhale through your mouth.

3. When you have filled and emptied your lower lungs 8 to 10 times, add the second step to your breathing: inhale first into your lower lungs as before, and then continue inhaling into your upper chest. As you do so, your right hand will rise and your left hand will fall a little as your abdomen falls.

4. As you exhale slowly through your mouth, make a quiet, whooshing sound as first your left hand and then your right hand falls. As you exhale, feel the tension leaving your body as you become more and more relaxed.

5. Practice breathing in and out in this manner for three to five minutes. Notice that the movement of your abdomen and chest is like rolling waves rising and falling in a rhythmic motion.

Practice belly breathing daily for several weeks until you can do it almost anywhere, providing you with an instant relaxation tool any time you need one.

CAUTION: Some people get dizzy the first few times they try belly breathing. If you begin to hyperventilate or become lightheaded, slow your breathing. Get up slowly.

Progressive Muscle Relaxation

The body responds to tense thoughts or situations with muscle tension, which can cause pain or discomfort. Deep muscle relaxation reduces the muscle tension as well as general mental anxiety. You can use an audiotape to help you go through all the muscle groups or you can do it by just tensing and relaxing each muscle group. Deep muscle relaxation is effective in combatting stress-related health problems and often helps people get to sleep.

Muscle Groups and Procedure

Pick a place where you can lie down on your back and stretch out comfortably, such as a carpeted floor.

Tense each muscle group for 4 to 10 seconds (hard but not to the point of cramping), then give yourself 10 to 20 seconds to release it and relax. At various points, review the muscle groups and relax each one a little more each time.

How to Tense Muscle Groups

Hands: Clench them.

Wrists and forearms: Extend them and bend the hands back at the wrist.

Biceps and upper arms: Clench your hands into fists, bend your arms at the elbows, and flex your biceps.

Shoulders: Shrug them. (Check the arms and shoulders area for tension.)

Forehead: Wrinkle it into a deep frown.

Around the eyes and bridge of the nose: Close your eyes as tightly as possible. (Remove contact lenses before beginning the exercise.)

Cheeks and jaws: Grin from ear to ear.

Around the mouth: Press your lips together tightly. (Check the face area for tension.)

Back of the neck: Press your head back hard.

Front of the neck: Touch your chin to your chest. (Check the neck and head area for tension.)

Chest: Take a deep breath and hold it; then exhale.

Back: Arch your back up and away from the floor.

Stomach: Suck it into a tight knot. (Check the chest and stomach area for tension.)

Hips and buttocks: Press the buttocks together tightly.

Thighs: Clench them hard.

Lower legs: Point your toes toward your face, as if trying to bring the toes up to touch your head.

Lower legs: Point your toes away and curl them downward at the same time. (Check the area from the waist down for tension.)

When you are finished, return to alertness by counting backwards from five to one.

Relaxation Response

The relaxation response is the exact opposite of a stress response. It slows heart rate and breathing, lowers blood pressure, and helps relieve muscle tension.

Technique (adapted from Herbert Benson, MD):

1. Sit quietly in a comfortable position with your eyes closed.

2. Begin progressive muscle relaxation. See page 273.

3. Become aware of your breathing. Each time you exhale, say the word "one" (or any other word or phrase) silently or aloud. Concentrate on breathing from your abdomen and not your chest.

Instead of focusing on a repeated word, you can fix your gaze on a stationary object. Any mental stimulus will help you to clear your mind.

Continue this for 10 to 20 minutes. As distracting thoughts enter your mind, don't dwell on them, just allow them to drift away.

4. Sit quietly for several minutes, until you are ready to open your eyes.

5. Notice the difference in your breathing and your pulse rate.

Don't worry about becoming deeply relaxed. The key to this exercise is to remain passive, to let distracting thoughts slip away like waves on the beach.

Practice for 10 to 20 minutes once or twice a day, but not within two hours after a meal. When you have set up a routine, you can achieve the relaxation response with little effort.

For a more complete description of the relaxation response, see Resource 70 on page 328.

Never eat more than you can lift.
Miss Piggy

18

Nutrition

This chapter gives some guidelines for good eating and some hints on how to help your children establish healthy eating habits. Children learn best by example, so practice good eating habits along with them. For more information about healthy eating, see Resource 62 on page 328.

Seven Simple Guidelines for Eating Well

(Dietary Guidelines for Americans, USDA, 1995)

1. Eat a variety of foods.

2. Balance the food you eat with physical activity to maintain or improve your weight. See page 285.

3. Choose a diet with plenty of grain products, vegetables, and fruits. See information at right.

4. Choose a diet low in fat, saturated fat, and cholesterol. See pages 280 and 281.

5. Choose a diet moderate in sugars. See page 279.

6. Choose a diet moderate in salt and sodium. See page 284.

7. If you drink alcoholic beverages, do so only in moderation. Alcohol is high in calories and has no nutrients. For men, this means not more than two drinks per day; for women, not more than one. A drink is equal to 12 ounces of beer, 5 ounces of wine, or $1\frac{1}{2}$ ounces of distilled alcohol (vodka, gin, etc.).

Eating Well: A Basic Plan

Eat a variety of foods from the Guide to Eating Well every day. Eat more from the bread and cereal and fruit and vegetable groups than from the other groups. Most people who follow this plan will get all the vitamins, minerals, and other nutrients their bodies need and will have little trouble controlling their weight.

 For more information, see the inside front cover.

Breads, Cereals, and Starches

Starches are carbohydrates, which have less than half the calories per gram than fat. Unprocessed starches (whole grains, vegetables) also contain large amounts of vitamins, minerals, fiber, and water.

Contrary to popular belief, bread, potatoes, rice, and pasta are not fattening! Starchy foods do not contain a lot of calories compared to the fat you add to them. Try nonfat yogurt, nonfat sour cream, or salsa instead of butter and sour cream on baked potatoes. Use fresh vegetable and tomato sauces instead of creamy sauces on pasta. Choose basic breads and cereal grains, and avoid high-fat muffins, croissants, and bakery items.

Fruits and Vegetables

Fresh fruits and vegetables provide vitamins, minerals, and fiber and are naturally low in fat. Many fruits and vegetables contain a lot of vitamins A (beta carotene) and C, especially oranges and other citrus fruits, broccoli, sweet potatoes, winter squash, carrots, spinach, and other leafy greens. A diet that includes lots of fruits and vegetables helps protect you against heart disease, stroke, and cancer.

Fruits and vegetables are most nutritious when eaten fresh and raw or lightly cooked. Steam or microwave vegetables to retain more vitamins.

Fruits and Vegetables Against Cancer

Fruits and vegetables are important for good basic nutrition. They are naturally low in fat and contain a lot of fiber. A diet high in fiber may protect you against colon cancer. Fruits and vegetables also contain other important food components. They are excellent sources of vitamin C, carotenoids, and other plant compounds that are natural antioxidants. The antioxidants in plant food may play an important role in reducing your risk of cancer. Carotenoids are found in carrots, dark green leafy vegetables, sweet potatoes, tomatoes, papaya, cantaloupe, and broccoli. Vitamin C is found in citrus fruits such as oranges, and in cantaloupe, strawberries, peppers, broccoli, and tomatoes.

Scientists are continuing to study the other compounds found in fruits and vegetables to learn about the role those compounds may play in preventing cancer.

Whatever the reason, the evidence is strong that we should all eat five or more servings of fruits and vegetables every day to help us lower the risk of cancer.

Guide to Eating Well

Grains (breads, cereals, rice, pasta) form the foundation of a healthy diet. Serving sizes: 1 slice of bread, 1 oz. of cereal, ½ bagel, ½ cup of cooked pasta or rice.

Eat plenty of fruits and vegetables. Serving sizes: ¾ cup fruit or vegetable juice; ½ cup raw, canned, or cooked fruits or vegetables; medium apple or banana; 1 cup raw leafy vegetables.

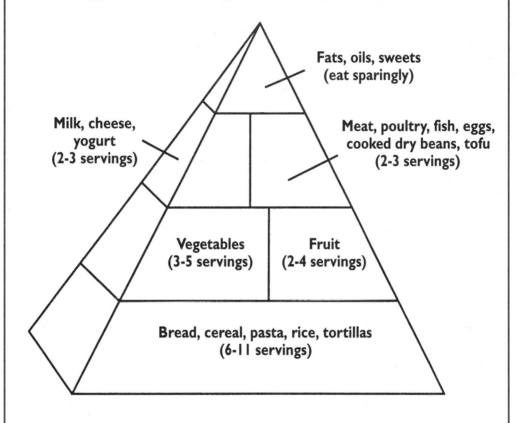

Fats, oils, sweets (eat sparingly)

Milk, cheese, yogurt (2-3 servings)

Meat, poultry, fish, eggs, cooked dry beans, tofu (2-3 servings)

Vegetables (3-5 servings)

Fruit (2-4 servings)

Bread, cereal, pasta, rice, tortillas (6-11 servings)

The Food Guide Pyramid (USDA)

Choose lean meats, fish, or poultry, and cooked dry beans to reduce fat. Serving sizes: 2 – 3 oz. cooked lean meat, poultry, or fish; ½ cup cooked dry beans; 1 egg; 2 tbsp. peanut butter.

Choose nonfat or low-fat dairy products. Serving sizes: 1 cup milk or yogurt, 1½ – 2 oz. low-fat cheese, ½ cup cottage cheese.

Eat foods from the top of the pyramid only in moderation. Examples: cooking oil, butter or margarine, high-fat salty snacks, alcohol, candy.

Fiber

Fiber is not a nutrient because it is not absorbed; yet it is important to the health of your digestive tract. There are two types of fiber.

Insoluble fiber in whole-grain products provides bulk for your diet. Together with fluids, insoluble fiber stimulates the colon to keep waste moving out of the bowels. Without fiber, waste moves too slowly, increasing your risk for constipation, colon and bowel cancer, and diverticulosis.

Soluble fiber found in fruit, beans, peas and other legumes, and oats helps lower cholesterol, reducing your risk of heart disease. The fiber in legumes can also help regulate blood glucose and cholesterol levels.

Small Changes Can Make a Big Difference

You don't have to change your whole diet at once. Pick one easy change and stick with it. Add others once you've had success with the first change.

- Buy only whole-grain bread.

- Buy only skim or 1% milk.

- Use less oil for cooking.

- Eat fish at least twice a week.

- Eat a raw vegetable at lunch.

- Drink an extra glass of water when you wake each morning.

Caffeine

There is no convincing evidence that a moderate amount of caffeine (two to three cups of coffee or cola per day) will do you any harm if you are healthy.

Caffeine is mildly addictive, and cutting back too quickly may cause a headache. Gradual reductions will prevent headaches.

Do you need more fiber? If your bowel movements are soft and easy to pass, you probably get plenty of fiber. If they are hard and difficult to pass, more fiber and water may help. See page 70 for more information on constipation.

To increase fiber in your diet:

- Eat at least five servings of fruits and vegetables a day. Eat fruits with edible skins and seeds: kiwis, figs, blueberries, apples, and raspberries. Eat more of the stems of broccoli and asparagus.

- Switch to whole-grain and whole-wheat breads, pasta, tortillas, and cereals. The first ingredient listed should be whole-wheat flour. If it just says wheat flour, it means white flour, from which much of the fiber has been removed.

- Eat more cooked dry beans, peas, and lentils.

- Popcorn is a good high-fiber snack. However, avoid added oil, butter, and salt.

Artificial Sweeteners

Although artificial sweeteners do help you avoid sugar, losing weight depends more on reducing calories from fat. Avoid using artificially sweetened foods to justify eating more high-fat food.

Aspartame (NutraSweet) and saccharin are considered safe, but the effects of long-term use are not known. Use them in moderation.

Water

One easy way to improve your diet is to drink more water. Active people need two quarts of water a day, and people who exercise regularly need even more. If you drink other fluids, you can get by with less, but plain water is best.

Sugar

What's wrong with sugar? It comes from a vegetable (sugar beets or sugar cane), is relatively cheap, tastes good, is fat-free, and is even a carbohydrate. Can sugar be all that bad?

From a health point of view, the biggest problem with sugar is that it is stripped of all vitamins, minerals, and fiber. What is left are crystals of pure calories.

In moderation (10 percent of calories), sugar does no harm. However, if too many of your calories come from sugar, you will either gain weight or not get enough of the other nutrients you need. Sugar also contributes to cavities.

- All sugars are basically alike. Honey and brown or raw sugar have no advantage over other sugars.

- Be aware of hidden sugars in flavored yogurt and canned and processed foods. Check the label for words that end in "-ose," like dextrose, fructose, sucrose, lactose, and maltose, which are forms of sugar. Corn syrup is another common form of sugar.

- Limit foods that list sugar among the first few ingredients.

- Look for breakfast cereals that have six grams or less of added sugar per serving.

- You can reduce the sugar in homemade baked goods by up to one-half without affecting the texture.

- Eat a sweet piece of fruit instead of a sugary dessert.

Fats

Fat (butter, lard, cream, oil, margarine, mayonnaise, and grease in food) accounts for 34 percent of the calories in the average American diet. Fat has more than twice as many calories per gram as carbohydrates or protein.

How much fat is too much? The USDA Dietary Guidelines recommend that less than 30 percent of total calories come from fat. Reducing dietary fat from 34 percent to 30 percent may slow the development of heart disease, reduce cancer risk, and improve your overall diet. But is it enough?

 For more information, see the inside front cover.

Many scientists think a diet with 30 percent fat is still too high for a healthy heart. A diet of 20 percent fat will reduce the risk of heart disease even more. There is some evidence that a 10-percent fat diet, along with other lifestyle changes, can even reverse narrowing of the arteries (arteriosclerosis). However, a 10-percent fat diet is challenging to maintain.

Based on your heart disease risks, you may wish to set a goal for how much fat to include in your diet. A class or appointment with a registered dietitian can help you develop a menu plan to meet your goal.

15 Simple Ways to Reduce Fat

When eating meat:

1. Choose lean poultry and fish. Use lean cuts of meat, such as tenderloin or top and bottom round.

2. Remove all visible fat before cooking. Poultry skin may be removed either before or after cooking.

3. Broil or bake instead of frying.

4. Reduce serving sizes to two or three ounces and don't take seconds.

5. Replace some meat with cooked dry beans and grains.

When using dairy products:

6. Use skim or 1 percent milk.

7. Choose lower-fat cheeses like Gruyère, farmer's, Jarlsberg Swiss, mozzarella, or ricotta. Look for low-fat or nonfat cheddar and Monterey Jack cheeses.

8. Substitute low-fat or nonfat cottage cheese and yogurt for cream and sour cream, or use fat-free sour cream and cream cheese.

In cooking:

9. Steam vegetables, saute with one teaspoon of oil or less, or cook with wine or defatted broth.

10. Use nonstick pans or add oil to a preheated pan (less oil goes farther this way).

11. Season vegetables with herbs and spices instead of butter and sauces, or try Butter Buds or Molly McButter.

12. Experiment using less oil than is called for in recipes. You may need to increase other liquids. Use applesauce or prune puree to replace some or all of the fat in baked goods.

The 80-20 Rule

If you are generally healthy, you don't need to worry about maintaining a perfect diet. If you make healthy eating choices 80 percent of the time, occasional high-fat or high-calorie foods the other 20 percent of the time won't be a problem.

In general:

13. Avoid crackers, chips, cookies, and margarines made with hydrogenated oil, palm oil, coconut oil, or cocoa butter.

14. Eat plenty of carbohydrates to fill you up (fruits, vegetables, grains, bread, pasta, etc.).

15. Let salads go naked, modestly dressed with lemon juice, or use fat-free mayonnaise or dressings.

Cholesterol

For many people a diet high in saturated fat or cholesterol raises the amount of cholesterol in the blood. To reduce cholesterol in your diet, see page 224.

Protein

Protein is important for maintaining healthy muscles, tendons, bones, skin, hair, blood, and internal organs. Most adult Americans get all the protein they need.

Using Food Nutrition Labels

The Nutrition Facts label on food packages provides information on selected nutrients and can help you make good nutrition choices. It can help you limit your fat, cholesterol, and sodium intake and improve your intake of fiber, vitamins, and minerals.

The Nutrition Facts label lists the total calories in a serving of the food. It also tells you how many calories in a serving come from fat. To convert this to percent fat calories, simply divide the calories from fat by the total calories and multiply by 100. It is recommended that not more than 30 percent of your calories come from fat. However, it is not necessary that every food you eat have less than 30 percent of calories from fat. Instead, look at the average for your entire diet.

Another easy way to do this is to use the "% Daily Value" column on the Nutrition Facts label. If you add up the % Daily Values for a nutrient in your diet (from all the servings of everything you eat in a day) and you get a number close to 100 percent, you are getting enough of that nutrient in your diet. For fat calories, a 100 percent result means you are getting 30 percent or less of your calories from fat.

The % Daily Value is based on a 2,000-calorie diet. If you eat more or less than this, you will need to add to or subtract from the percentages. For example, if you need 3,000 calories, your percentages can total 150 percent. If you need only 1,500 calories, your percentages can total 75 percent.

Protein deficiencies are rare. If you eat animal products (milk, cheese, eggs, fish, meat), your diet will contain plenty of protein. Even if you don't eat animal products (vegans), if your diet includes a wide variety of vegetables, legumes, fruits, breads and cereals, you will get all the protein you need.

Vitamins

Vitamins are exciting! These 13 tiny, unseen elements of food have no calories, yet are essential to good health.

Vitamins A, D, E, and K are fat-soluble and can be stored in the liver or fat tissue for a relatively long time. The other nine vitamins are water-soluble and can be retained by the body for only short periods. They include:

- Thiamine
- Riboflavin
- Niacin
- Pantothenic acid
- Biotin
- Folate (folic acid)
- Vitamin B$_6$
- Vitamin B$_{12}$
- Vitamin C

For most people, a diet that contains a variety of foods from the Food Guide Pyramid (page 277) provides all the vitamins needed for good health.

If you eat less than 1,500 calories per day, consider a low-dose vitamin-mineral supplement (see right).

Vitamin-Mineral Supplement Buyer's Guide

Research shows that vitamins from food may help prevent some diseases, but it remains unproven whether supplements do the same. However, if you choose to take vitamin and mineral supplements, the following guidelines may be helpful:

- Choose a balanced, multiple vitamin-mineral supplement rather than a specific vitamin or mineral, unless it has been prescribed by a doctor. Too much of any one vitamin or mineral might be toxic and can interfere with the body's ability to use other vitamins and minerals.

- Choose a supplement that provides about 100 percent of the RDA (Recommended Dietary Allowances) for vitamins and minerals.

- Avoid taking much more than 100 percent of the RDA for any vitamin or mineral. This is particularly important for the fat-soluble vitamins A, D, E, and K and for minerals. Because they are stored in the body, large doses can build up to toxic levels.

- Don't use a supplement to make up for a poor diet.

- High-priced brand-name vitamins are no better than store or generic brands.

- Check expiration dates.

If you are a woman who could potentially become pregnant (even if using birth control), make sure you get enough folate (folic acid), 0.4 mg/day, in your diet or vitamin supplements. The B vitamin folate helps prevent birth defects, particularly spina bifida (or "open spine"). Foods highest in folate include oranges, nuts, beans, leafy green vegetables, breads, and fortified cereals. An alternative is to take a multivitamin with folate (0.4 mg) daily. Make sure you get enough folate beginning at least one month prior to conception and continue throughout the first trimester of pregnancy.

Minerals

Minerals help regulate the body's water balance, as well as providing structure and functioning as part of hormones, enzymes, and vitamins. The body maintains minerals in a delicate balance to ensure proper functioning of the systems they serve. Eating a variety of foods is the best way to get all the minerals you need.

A total of 60 minerals have been discovered in the body, and 22 are essential to health. We know the most about calcium, sodium, and iron.

Calcium

Calcium is the primary mineral needed for building and maintaining strong bones. Calcium is especially important for growing children and women, especially in the peak bone-building years between the

---

Lactose Intolerance

People whose bodies produce too little of the enzyme lactase have trouble digesting the lactose (milk sugar) in milk. Symptoms of lactose intolerance include gas, bloating, cramps, and diarrhea after drinking milk or eating dairy products.

Tips for dealing with lactose intolerance include:

- Eat small amounts of dairy products at any one time.

- Drink milk only with snacks or meals.

- Try cheese, which usually does not cause symptoms. Most of the lactose is removed during processing.

- Yogurts made with active cultures provide their own enzymes and cause fewer tolerance problems.

- Pretreated milk, enzyme treatments, and enzyme tablets (Lactaid, Dairy Ease) are available in most stores.

- If you cannot tolerate milk in any form, include other calcium-rich foods in your diet. See left.

- Severe lactose intolerance may increase your need for calcium supplements. Ask your doctor.

---

teens and early 30s. Calcium also helps women prevent osteoporosis, which can occur after menopause. See page 115.

Children age 1 to 3 need 500 mg of calcium per day. Children age 3 to 9 need 800 mg. Older children and teens age 10 to 18 need 1,300 mg of calcium daily. From age 19 to 50, adults need 1,000 mg, and after age 50, 1,200 mg of calcium daily. Pregnant or nursing women need 1,300 mg of calcium daily.

A cup of skim milk, nonfat yogurt, or low-fat yogurt has 300 to 400 mg of calcium. Other good sources of calcium include calcium-fortified juices, dark green vegetables, tofu set in calcium, and beans. To get 1,000 mg of calcium, choose three to four servings of foods highest in calcium (milk, yogurt, cheese, or calcium-fortified orange juice). You'll need four or more servings of these foods to get 1,200 to 1,300 mg of calcium.

While dietary calcium is preferred, low-dose calcium supplements can also help keep bones strong. One 500-mg Tums (calcium carbonate) tablet provides about 200 mg of calcium. A few Tums tablets per day can help adults meet their calcium needs but should not replace calcium-rich foods such as low-fat milk and other dairy products, tofu, soy milk, broccoli, greens, or calcium-fortified orange juice.

Creative Salt Substitute

Mix together and put in a shaker:

$\frac{1}{2}$ teaspoon cayenne pepper

$\frac{1}{2}$ teaspoon garlic powder

1 teaspoon each:

Basil	Onion Powder
Black pepper	Parsley
Mace	Sage
Marjoram	Savory
Thyme	

Sodium

Salt is the most familiar source of sodium. About 40 percent of salt is pure sodium. Sodium is also hidden in foods that don't taste salty, such as cheddar cheese and processed foods. Sodium is also a major ingredient of monosodium glutamate (MSG), disodium phosphate, and baking powder.

Most people get far more sodium than they need. Our bodies need only 500 mg of sodium per day. Anything over 2,500 mg of sodium per day is probably too much.

For some people, excess sodium causes high blood pressure. If you are not sodium-sensitive, salt may not be a problem for you. See page 224.

If you want to cut back on the sodium in your diet:

- Limit ready-mixed sauces and seasonings, frozen dinners, canned soups, and salad dressings, which are usually packed with sodium. Products labeled "low sodium" contain less than 140 mg of sodium per serving.

- Eat lots of fresh or frozen fruits and vegetables. These foods have very little sodium.

- Don't put the salt shaker on the table, or get a shaker that lets very little salt come out. Or, use "lite" salt or salt substitute sparingly.

- Always measure the salt in recipes and use half of what is called for.

Iron

The body needs small amounts of iron to make hemoglobin, which carries oxygen in the blood. Adults need about 10 to 15 mg of iron per day. People who have increased blood loss from ulcers or heavy menstrual periods, or who lose blood from taking blood thinners (anticoagulants) or arthritis medications (such as aspirin), may need more iron. An inexpensive blood test can determine if you need additional iron.

To get more iron in your blood:

- Vitamin C helps you absorb more iron from food. Drink a glass of orange or other citrus juice and eat a bowl of iron-enriched cereal. High-iron cereals have at least 25 percent of the Daily Value of iron.

- Increase absorption of plant sources of iron by eating meat, poultry, or fish along with vegetables and grains. The iron in animal tissue improves the absorption of the iron in plants.

Iron Supplements

Women who menstruate and who eat less than 1,500 calories per day may wish to consider a multivitamin-mineral supplement that contains iron. (Men are much less likely to need iron supplements.) A low-dose ferrous-form iron supplement containing no more than 20 mg is safe for most women. However, too much iron can cause a number of serious medical problems or mask the development of others. Do not take more than 20 mg without consulting your doctor. Take the supplement with orange or other citrus juice. Keep iron supplements away from children.

Iron Deficiency Anemia

Chronic blood loss of any kind depletes the body's store of iron. Symptoms of iron deficiency anemia include paleness and fatigue. A blood test is needed to confirm the diagnosis, and further testing may be needed to determine the cause of the blood loss.

A Healthy Weight

People come in all shapes and sizes. Genetics, exercise, and the food you eat all play a role in determining your body's shape and size.

 For more information, see the inside front cover.

Focus on Health, Not Weight

Eating well, enjoying physical activity, and accepting your body size are the keys to good health. Although excess body fat may increase your risk of heart disease, diabetes, and stroke, it is more important to focus on healthy habits rather than trying to achieve a certain body size or shape.

Eating healthy, lower-fat foods and adding regular physical activity to your life can help you lose weight and establish some good health habits that you can maintain for life.

Exercise Makes It Easier

Regular exercise makes you feel stronger, more energetic, and in better overall health. As a bonus, regular exercise makes maintaining a healthy weight a little easier.

Even short periods of exercise, done every day or every other day, can make a big difference. Pick an exercise you enjoy enough to stick with for a long time. Even a five-minute walk every day is a good start. Add more exercise when you can.

Exercise Keeps You Strong

Exercise helps build your lean muscle mass when you are losing weight. One of the biggest problems with diets is that if you don't exercise while you diet, you will lose both fat and lean muscle mass. Dieters often suffer from weakness and low energy. If you are trying to lose weight, include a regular exercise program.

Never Go Hungry

Skipping meals is not a good way to lose weight. Going hungry can make you more likely to overeat later. Take time to savor your food and relax during meals.

Focus on Reducing Fat, Not Calories

Eat a variety of nutritious, low-fat foods. Rather than counting calories, focus on eating more fruits and vegetables and less fat. See the ways to reduce fat on page 280.

Get Help From Your Friends

The food customs and habits of friends and family affect what you eat. Ask friends and family to:

- Encourage you to respect yourself regardless of what you weigh.

- Celebrate events with a variety of nutritious foods and activities that everyone can enjoy.

- Serve low-fat options with meals, and make water and low-fat snacks available.

- Offer small servings, and don't insist on second helpings.

- Join you in a walk, swim, or other enjoyable activity.

Help Yourself to Good Thoughts

Develop a positive attitude about yourself. Think of yourself as healthy, and take pride in making positive nutrition and exercise choices. Focus on living a healthy life regardless of your weight.

Nutrition for Children

 Your whole family can eat from the Food Guide Pyramid (page 277). Offer nutritious foods as well-planned, pleasant meals and snacks. Then sit back and let your child decide how much to eat (or even if he or she wants to eat it at all!). This is a good division of responsibility that allows children to tune in to their own appetite and takes the pressure off the parents.

Child-Sized Environment

Imagine yourself eating at a giant's table. That's how a child can feel eating at an adult-sized table in an adult-sized chair.

- Provide a booster seat and child-sized utensils. However, fingers are fine until a child can hold utensils easily.

- Give children smaller plates and smaller servings (one tablespoon per year of age is a good serving size guide). Let the child ask for seconds.

Healthy Snacks

Young children have small stomachs and high energy needs, so they need frequent snacks to supplement meals. Plan between-meal snacks as part of the day's total food intake. They should provide good nutrition, not just empty calories.

Food Allergies

Less than one percent of adults have true food allergies. Most adverse reactions to foods are due to food intolerances, reactions to food additives, or food poisoning. Most true food allergies are to legumes, nuts, shellfish, eggs, wheat, and milk. An allergic reaction to a food can result in anaphylactic shock. See page 125.

Consider breast-feeding your child for at least the first six months if either parent has a history of any allergy, including hay fever. Children who are breast-fed develop fewer food allergies than those who are not. By gradually introducing simple solid foods into your child's diet, any allergy will be more easily found. Children often outgrow food allergies by age six. If your child was allergic to a food when younger, try reintroducing it as he or she gets older (unless the reaction was severe).

- Fruits and fruit juices are good snacks. Other good choices are raw vegetable sticks with fat-free dressing, cereal, yogurt, cheese, or soup.

- Serve meals and snacks on a regular schedule. Do not serve snacks so close to a meal that they interfere with the child's appetite.

- Choose desserts that are low in fat and high in nutrients. Fig bars or oatmeal raisin cookies are good choices.

- For more information on feeding children, see Resource 25 on page 326.

He who laughs, lasts.
Mary Pettibone Poole

19

Mental Self-Care and Mental Wellness

Mental health problems are similar to other health problems: some can be prevented; others will go away on their own with a little care and home treatment; and some need professional attention.

This chapter is organized in two sections. The first section, Mental Self-Care, covers some common mental and emotional health problems and describes what you can do at home and when you should seek professional help.

The second section, Mental Wellness, describes how you can use your mind and emotions to boost your immune system and improve your health.

Mental Self-Care

Medical science is discovering that mental health problems often have a physical cause. Psychological problems are no longer thought of as character weaknesses or flaws.

We now know that mental health problems can begin when psychological or emotional stress (such as the loss of a loved one) triggers chemical changes in the brain. While some people can withstand more stress than others, nobody is immune to mental illness.

Because mental health problems have both physical and psychological causes, both self-care and professional care are often needed. The goal is to reduce stress and to restore the normal chemical processes in the brain.

Seeking Professional Help

This chapter does not cover all mental health problems. If you have mental or emotional symptoms that are not addressed here, contact your health professional. In general, it is a good idea to seek professional help when:

- A symptom becomes severe or disruptive.

Therapist Selection Tips

Here are some ways to improve the likelihood of finding the therapy that's right for you.

- Ask people you trust for a good referral.

- Ask mental health professionals to help you identify the real problem and develop a self-management plan to resolve it.

- Emphasize the importance of self-care in your treatment plan.

- Ask about group therapy options.

- Cultivate special friends, join support groups, or look for peer counseling opportunities. Understanding and acceptance can help you resolve the problem.

- Check out 12-step programs such as Alcoholics Anonymous, Overeaters Anonymous, and other groups that can help you deal with addiction problems. Such programs are usually free, effective, and available in most communities.

There is a wide range of professional and lay resources to choose from for mental health problems.

Family doctors: Mental health problems may have physical causes. Your doctor can review your medical history and medications for clues, provide some counseling, prescribe medications, or refer you to other resources.

Psychiatrists: Psychiatrists are medical doctors who specialize in mental disorders. They counsel patients, prescribe medications, and order medical treatments.

Psychologists, social workers, and counselors: These professionals receive special training in helping people deal with mental health problems. They help patients identify, understand, and work through disturbing thoughts and emotions.

Pastors: People often turn to their clergy for counseling and advice in times of emotional distress. Many pastors have formal training in counseling, and many do not.

Support groups: Talking with others who are coping with the same problem is often helpful. See Resource 67 on page 328.

- A disruptive symptom becomes a continuous or permanent pattern of behavior and does not respond to self-care efforts.

- Symptoms become numerous and affect all areas of your life and do not respond to self-care or communication efforts.

- You are thinking of suicide.

Alcohol and Drug Problems

 The overuse or abuse of alcohol or other drugs is called substance abuse. It is common, costly, and associated with many medical problems.

Alcohol Problems

A person has an alcohol problem if the use of alcohol interferes with his or her health or daily living. A person develops **alcoholism** if he or she becomes physically or psychologically dependent on alcohol.

Long-term heavy drinking causes liver, nerve, heart, and brain damage, high blood pressure, stomach problems, sexual problems, and cancer. Alcohol abuse can also lead to violence, accidents, social isolation, and difficulties at work and home or with the law.

Symptoms of an alcohol problem include personality changes, blackouts, drinking more and more for the same "high," and denial of the problem. A person with alcoholism may gulp or sneak drinks, drink alone or early in the morning, and suffer from the shakes. He or she may also have family or work problems, or get in trouble with the law due to drinking.

Alcohol abuse patterns vary. Some people get drunk every day. Some drink large amounts of alcohol at specific times, such as weekends. Others may be sober for long periods and then go on a drinking binge that lasts for weeks or months.

Someone with alcoholism may suffer serious withdrawal symptoms (such as trembling, delusions, hallucinations, sweating, and seizures) if he or she stops drinking suddenly ("cold turkey"). Once alcohol dependency develops, it becomes very difficult to abstain without outside help. Medical detoxification may be needed.

Drug Problems

Drug abuse includes the use of marijuana, cocaine, heroin, or other "street drugs," and the abuse of legal prescription drugs. Some people turn to drugs as a way to get a "high" or to deal with stress and emotional problems.

Tranquilizers, sedatives, painkillers, and amphetamines are misused most often, sometimes unintentionally.

Drug dependence or addiction occurs when you develop a physical or psychological "need" for a drug. You may not be aware that you have become dependent on a drug until you try to stop taking it suddenly. Withdrawing from the drug can cause uncomfortable symptoms such as muscle aches, diarrhea, or depression. The usual treatment is to reduce the dose of the drug gradually until it can be stopped completely.

Screening Test

Many people will deny that they have a problem with alcohol or other drugs. The questions in the "Are You a Problem User?" chart on page 293 may help you, or others, recognize a problem.

Answering yes to two or more questions raises the possibility of an alcohol or drug problem and signals the need to seek help.

Prevention

- Look for signs of mental stress. Try to understand and resolve sources of depression, anxiety, or loneliness. Don't use alcohol or drugs to deal with these problems.

- If you drink, consider stopping or drink in moderation: less than two drinks a day for men and one drink a day for women. One drink is 12 ounces of beer, 5 ounces of wine, or $1\frac{1}{2}$ ounces of hard liquor.

- Provide nonalcoholic beverages at parties and meals.

- Ask your pharmacist or doctor if any of your current medications could potentially lead to overuse or dependency. Be especially cautious of painkillers, tranquilizers, sedatives, and sleeping pills. Follow the instructions carefully, and do not exceed the recommended dose.

- Do not regularly use medications to sleep, lose weight, or relax without careful supervision by your doctor. Seek nondrug solutions.

Signs of Drug Use

- Chronic red eyes, sore throat, dry cough, and fatigue (in the absence of allergies).

- Major changes in sleeping or eating habits.

- Moodiness, hostility, or abusive behavior.

- Work or school problems, absenteeism.

- Loss of interest in favorite activities.

- Social withdrawal or changes in friends.

- Stealing, lying, and poor family relationships.

- Do not suddenly stop taking any medication without your doctor's supervision. Serious symptoms can result if some medications are abruptly withdrawn.

- Avoid alcohol when you are taking medications. Alcohol can react with many drugs and cause serious complications.

Home Treatment

- Recognize early signs that alcohol or drug use is becoming a problem. See page 293.

- Attend an Alcoholics Anonymous meeting (a self-help group devoted to helping members get sober and stay sober).

- If you are concerned about another person's alcohol or drug use:

  ° Never ignore the problem. Discuss it as a medical problem.

  ° Build up the person's self-esteem and reaffirm his or her value as a person. Help the person see that he or she can be successful without alcohol or drugs. Let the person know you will support his or her efforts to change.

  ° Ask if the person would accept help. Don't give up after the first no; keep asking. When the person agrees, act that very day to arrange for help. Call a health professional or Alcoholics Anonymous for an immediate appointment.

  ° Attend a few meetings of Al-Anon, a support group for family members and friends of alcoholics. Read some 12-step program information.

Are You a Problem User?

Answer the questions honestly. Answer "yes" if the statement is true for alcohol or drugs (including prescribed, recreational, or illegal substances that can be described as mood-altering).

1. Have you ever tried to stop using alcohol or drugs for a week or so but could stop for only a couple of days?
2. Do you resent the advice of others who try to get you to stop or cut down your use of alcohol or drugs?
3. Have you tried to control your use of alcohol or drugs by changing from one type of drink or drug to another?
4. Do you envy people who can use alcohol or drugs without getting into trouble?
5. Has your use of alcohol or drugs impaired your family relationships, your work, your driving safety, or any other aspect of your life?
6. During the past year, have you missed days of work because of your use of alcohol or drugs?
7. Do you tell yourself you can stop using alcohol or drugs any time you want?
8. Do you sometimes go on binges with alcohol or drugs?
9. Do you ever have blackouts related to your alcohol or drug use?
10. Have you ever felt that your life would be better if you did not use alcohol or drugs?

If you answer "yes" to two or more questions, you may have a problem with alcohol or drugs. If so, talk with a health professional.

When to Call Kaiser Permanente

- If you answer yes to two or more questions on the "Are You a Problem User?" chart.

- If you recognize an alcohol or drug problem and are ready to accept help. A range of useful treatment programs is available.

Anger and Hostility

Anger signals your body to prepare for a fight. When you get angry, adrenalin and other hormones are released into the bloodstream. Blood pressure goes up.

Hostility is being ready for a fight all the time. Continual hostility keeps your blood pressure high and may increase your risk for heart attack and other illnesses. Being hostile also isolates you from other people.

Home Treatment

- Notice when you start getting angry. Don't ignore anger until it erupts.

- Identify the cause of the anger.

- Express anger in a healthy way:

  ° Count to 10. Give your adrenalin level a little time to go down.

  ° Try screaming or yelling in a private place, not at others.

  ° Go for a short walk or jog.

  ° Talk about it with a friend.

  ° Draw or paint to release the anger.

° Write in a daily journal.

- Use "I" statements, not "you" statements, to discuss your anger. Say "I feel angry when my needs are not being met," instead of "You make me mad when you are so inconsiderate."

- Forgive and forget. Forgiving helps lower blood pressure and ease muscle tension so you can feel more relaxed.

- Read books on anger and how to handle it. See Resources 10 to 12 on page 325.

- See page 303 for additional information on anger and violent behavior.

When to Call Kaiser Permanente

- If anger has led or could lead to violence or harm to you or someone else.

- If anger or hostility interferes with your work, family, or friends.

Anxiety

 Feeling worried, anxious, and nervous is a normal part of everyday life. Everyone frets or feels anxious from time to time. However, when anxiety becomes overwhelming and interferes with daily life, it is not normal.

Anxiety can cause both physical and emotional symptoms:

Physical Symptoms

- Trembling, twitching, or shaking
- Muscle tension, aches, or soreness
- Restlessness
- Fatigue
- Insomnia
- Breathlessness or rapid heartbeat
- Sweating or cold, clammy hands

Emotional Symptoms

- Feeling keyed up and on edge
- Excessive worrying
- Fearing that something bad is going to happen
- Poor concentration
- Excessive startle response
- Irritability or agitation
- Constant sadness

Anxiety from a specific situation or fear can cause some or all of these symptoms for a short time. When the situation passes, the symptoms become less intense.

Many people, including children and adolescents, develop anxiety disorders in which many of these symptoms occur when there is no identifiable cause.

Phobias and panic disorder are two common anxiety-related disorders. Phobias are irrational, involuntary fears of common places, objects, or situations. Panic disorder is characterized by distinct periods of intense fear and anxiety that occur when there is no clear cause or danger. Physical symptoms that may occur during a panic attack include hyperventilation, shaking, pounding of the heart, and feeling faint. Self-care, often combined with professional treatment, can be effective in managing these disorders.

Home Treatment

The following home treatment tips can relieve simple anxiety and also help in combination with medical care.

- Recognize and accept your anxiety about specific fears or situations. Then say to yourself, "Okay, I see the problem. Now I'll start to deal with it."

- Be kind to your body:

  ○ Relieve tension with vigorous exercise or massage.

  ○ Practice relaxation techniques. See page 272.

  ○ Get enough rest. If you have trouble sleeping, see Sleep Problems on page 300.

  ○ Avoid alcohol, caffeine, chocolate, and nicotine. They increase your anxiety level.

- Engage your mind:

  ○ Get out and do something you enjoy, such as going to a funny movie or taking a walk or a hike.

  ○ Plan your day. Having too much or too little to do can make you more anxious.

- Keep a record of your symptoms. Discuss your fears with a good friend. Confiding with others sometimes relieves stress.

Sadness or Depression?

If you have experienced four or more of the following symptoms nearly every day for more than two weeks, you may be suffering from depression:

• Feelings of sadness, anxiety, or hopelessness

• Lack of interest or pleasure in usual activities or pastimes

• Increase or decrease in appetite or unexplained gain or loss of weight

• Frequent backaches, headaches, stomach problems, or other aches that don't respond to treatment

• Insomnia or excessive sleepiness

• Low energy, fatigue, tiredness

• Feeling restless or irritable

• Feeling worthless or guilty

• Inability to concentrate, remember, or make decisions

• Frequent thoughts of suicide or death

Home treatment (see page 298) may be all that is needed for mild depression. However, if you are feeling suicidal or if home treatment doesn't help lift your mood within two weeks, contact a health professional. With counseling and medication, and continued home treatment, you can overcome most cases of depression.

• Get involved in social groups or volunteer to help others. Being alone makes things seem worse than they are.

• Learn more about anxiety. See Resources 13 and 14 on page 325.

When to Call Kaiser Permanente

• If anxiety interferes with your daily activities.

• If symptoms are severe and one week of home treatment has not helped.

• If you have sudden, severe attacks of fear or anxiety with intense physical symptoms (shaking, sweating) when there is no apparent reason to be afraid.

• If intense, irrational fears of common places, objects, or situations interfere with your daily life.

• If you suffer from nightmares or flashbacks to traumatic events.

• If you are unable to feel certain about things (e.g., whether you unplugged the iron) no matter how many times you check, or if repetitive, compulsive behaviors interfere with your daily activities.

Depression

Most people experience some form of depression at some point in their lives. Depression can range from a minor problem to a major life-threatening illness. Depression usually is treatable. For many people, treatment can mean a whole new life.

Medical science is getting closer to understanding depression. Ongoing depression affects the body, the mind, and social behavior. Most major depressions involve problems with the chemical messengers (neu-rotransmitters) in the brain. Many things can trigger these problems:

- Loss of a loved one or something that is highly valued

- Chronic stress or a stressful event

- Major illness

- Reaction to medications

- Alcoholism, drug abuse, demen-tia, and other mental health problems

- After childbirth

Some people are genetically suscep-tible to problems with the chemical messengers in the brain. Fortu-nately, effective treatments are available for them and others at high risk for depression.

Everyone gets sad. Gauging how deep and pervasive your sad feel-ings are can help you decide what to do. See "Sadness or Depression?" on page 296 to help determine if you are suffering from depression.

Feeling sad doesn't always mean you are heading for a major depression. Bad news or a disappointment can make you feel sad, perhaps for sev-eral days. This is normal and healthy as long as those sad feelings don't continue indefinitely. Grief can also cause a normal sadness. See page 299.

Seasonal Affective Disorder (Winter Depression)

There is increasing evidence that a lack of sunlight during winter months can cause depression in some people. Symptoms include melancholy moods, changes in sleeping habits, cravings for sweets and starchy foods, and chronic fatigue. If you notice such a pattern developing during the winter, consider the following:

- When the sun does shine, go outside and soak it up. Protect your skin—it is the eye's expo-sure to sunlight that makes the difference.

- Go south for a sunny vacation, if you can.

- Some people may benefit from light therapy: sitting in front of a set of bright, fluorescent lights for 15 minutes to three hours a day, depending on illumination level (2,500 to 10,000 lux). Depression often improves by the end of the first week of daily treatments.

Because light therapy is a new approach to winter depression, the National Institutes of Health recommends that the therapy be supervised by a health professional.

Job Stress

On-the-job stress can bring on feelings of anxiety, anger, and depression which affect our lives and our health. If your work environment or job responsibilities are causing such negative feelings, don't let your emotions rule your actions. Try the following instead:

• Check and recheck the facts before you react.

• Find out what your rights are; don't tolerate abuse.

• Talk to your employer and try to work things out.

• Use appropriate resources: your union, your company's personnel department, Employee Assistance Program, or Equal Employment Opportunity Commission.

When to Call Kaiser Permanente

• If you have thoughts of hurting yourself, the people you work with, or anyone else.

• If you have problems with sleeping, eating, or day-to-day functioning.

• If your preoccupation with work problems begins to interfere with your life outside of work.

Home Treatment

Most people will improve or recover from depression. Self-care may be enough to pull you out of a mild depression. For more serious depression, self-care can add to the benefits of professional treatment.

• At the first sign of depression, ask a friend for some extra attention. You can lose objectivity about yourself when you feel blue.

• Consider what might be causing or adding to your depression:

  ° Are medications causing it? Review your prescription and over-the-counter medications with a pharmacist or doctor.

• Stay active. It is easier to do yourself into feeling better than to feel yourself into doing better.

• Get regular exercise. If nothing else, go for long walks. They help to clear the mind.

• Look for a laugh. Laughter, like exercise, can help restore balance to your system.

• Boost your self-esteem. Read the Mental Wellness section of this chapter.

• Believe that this mood will pass. Then look for signs that it is ending.

• Surround yourself with happy, upbeat people.

• Books can help. See Resource 49 on page 327.

Grief

Grief is a natural healing process that allows you to adjust to a significant change or loss. Grief may be expressed physically or emotionally and may have some of the same symptoms as depression. The following tips may help ease the grieving process.

- Take as much time as you need to grieve. Review mementos, play nostalgic music, and read old letters.

- Let yourself cry. If you can let go and sob, do it.

- Talk about your grief with a friend. If your friend tells you to "snap out of it," find a more sympathetic listener. Your clergy may also help you understand and deal with your loss.

- Friends may feel awkward about mentioning your loss. Let them know it is all right to talk about it.

- See Resources 37 to 39 on page 327.

When to Call Kaiser Permanente

Because many things can contribute to depression, combining self-care and professional treatment is often most effective. The most common form of treatment combines counseling (psychotherapy) with medication. Inpatient treatment is sometimes needed in severe cases. Call for help:

- If you are feeling suicidal.

- If you suspect you are very depressed. See "Sadness or Depression?" on page 296.

- If you suspect you are depressed and two weeks of home treatment has not helped.

- If grieving continues without improvement for more than four weeks.

Eating Disorders

In a society where "thin is in," many of us have tried skipping meals or going on diets to lose weight. Unlike dieting, eating disorders are medical problems that cause disturbances in eating behavior.

Anorexia nervosa is a disorder of severe self-imposed dieting. It affects teenage girls most often. Symptoms include refusing to eat, extreme weight loss, a distorted body image (thinking she's fat when she is actually very thin), a preoccupation with food, low self-esteem, and excessive physical exercise.

Bulimia nervosa is an eating disorder characterized by binge eating and purging (forced vomiting or abuse of laxatives and diuretics). The binges are usually triggered by emotional upset, not hunger. Other symptoms include dry skin and brittle hair, swollen glands under the jaw from vomiting, depression and mood swings, a distorted body image, and secrecy to keep others from discovering the person's abnormal behavior.

People who have anorexia usually look starved, but most people who have bulimia maintain a normal weight and look healthy. Most people with anorexia deny they have a problem; people with bulimia know that they do, but keep it a secret.

Compulsive overeating is characterized by binging on food. An overeater will consume thousands of calories at a time, quickly and without pleasure. Because there is no purging, a compulsive overeater becomes obese.

Eating disorders appear to be caused by emotional and psychological factors. They tend to run in families, so there may be a genetic link.

Eating disorders require professional treatment. If untreated, they can lead to major health problems or even death. Treatment usually involves nutritional counseling, individual psychotherapy, family therapy, and medication. A hospital stay may be required in extreme cases.

Prevention

- Teach and model healthy eating and exercise habits at home and at school.

- Help young people develop confidence and self-esteem. Accept them for who they are.

- Be careful about encouraging a young person to lose weight. Communicate that you love and care for the person, regardless of how much he or she weighs.

- Don't set unrealistic expectations for your child. Striving to live up to them may lead to an eating disorder.

- Be alert to the stress in your child's life. Be available to talk over any problems.

When to Call Kaiser Permanente

If you recognize any of these warning signs of an eating disorder:

- Using body weight as a primary measure of self-worth.

- Having an unrealistic body image and an unrealistic fear of gaining weight.

- Significant unexplained weight loss or gain.

- Constant dieting on highly restricted diets.

- Obsessive exercise routines, especially leading to injury.

- Withdrawal from family and friends.

- If you are purposely causing yourself to vomit or you are using laxatives excessively.

Sleep Problems

 The term insomnia can mean:

- Trouble getting to sleep (taking more than 45 minutes to fall asleep).

- Frequent wakenings with inability to fall back to sleep.

- Early morning awakening.

However, none of these are problems unless they make you feel chronically tired. If you are less sleepy at night or wake up early, but still feel rested and alert, there is little need to worry.

Short-term insomnia, lasting from a few nights to a few weeks, is usually caused by worry over a stressful situation. Long-term insomnia, which can last months or even years, is often caused by general anxiety, medications, chronic pain, depression, or other physical disorders.

Sleep apnea is a sleep disorder usually caused by blockage in the upper airways. When airflow through the nose and mouth is blocked, breathing may stop for 10 seconds or longer. People who have sleep apnea usually snore loudly and are very tired during the day. They are not aware of waking up at night, but do have very restless sleep. Sleep apnea can affect children and adults.

Prevention

- Get regular exercise but avoid strenuous exercise within two hours before bedtime.

- Avoid alcohol and smoking before bedtime. Drink caffeine in moderation and not after noon.

- Drink a glass of warm milk at bedtime.

- Avoid drinking more than a glass of fluid before bedtime.

Home Treatment

- Don't take sleeping pills. They can cause daytime confusion, memory loss, and dizziness. Continued use of sleeping pills actually increases sleeplessness in many people.

- Try the following seven-step formula for two weeks:

  1. Engage in relaxing activities in the evening (e.g., take a warm bath or do some light reading or stretching).

  2. Use your bed for sleeping. Don't eat, watch TV, or even read in it.

  3. Sleep only at bedtime. Don't take naps. (However, naps are fine if you don't have sleep problems.)

  4. Go to bed only when you feel sleepy.

  5. If you lie awake for more than 15 minutes, get up and leave the bedroom.

  6. Repeat steps 4 and 5 until it is time to get up.

  7. Get up at the same time each day, no matter how sleepy you are.

- Review all of your prescription and over-the-counter medications with a pharmacist to rule out drug-related sleep problems.

- Read about anxiety on page 294.

When to Call Kaiser Permanente

- If you suspect medications are causing sleep problems.

- If you or your partner snores loudly and heavily and feels excessively sleepy during the day.

- If someone has many episodes of sleep apnea (stops breathing, gasps, and chokes) during sleep.

- If your child snores, has difficulty breathing while asleep, sleeps restlessly and awakens frequently, or is very sleepy during the day.

- If a month of self-care doesn't solve the problem.

Suicide

If you are very depressed or feel overwhelmed, you may sometimes think of taking your own life. Occasional thoughts of suicide are not a problem. However, if thoughts of suicide continue, or if you have made suicide plans, it becomes a very serious matter.

People who are considering suicide are often undecided about choosing life or death. With compassionate help, they may choose to live.

Prevention

When there are significant life crises, when you are depressed, or when someone you know is depressed, be alert to the warning signs:

- Verbal warning. Up to 80 percent of people who commit suicide mention their intentions to someone.

- Preoccupation with death. A suicidal person may talk, read, draw, and write about death.

- Previous suicide attempt. Failed attempts are often followed by a completed attempt.

- Giving away prized possessions.

- Depression and social isolation. See page 296.

If you or someone you know is troubled by suicidal thoughts, that person should avoid alcohol.

Home Treatment

- Use your common sense and a direct approach to determine if the suicide risk is high. Ask yourself or the person who you feel is at risk:

  ° Do you feel there is no other way?

  ° Do you have a suicide plan?

  ° How and when do you plan to do it?

- Ask someone you trust to stay with you or the suicidal person until the crisis has passed.

- Encourage the person to seek professional help.

- Don't argue with the person ("It's not as bad as that") or challenge the person ("You're not the type") who is thinking of suicide.

- Don't ignore warning signs, thinking that you or another person will "snap out of it."

- Talk about the situation as openly as possible. Show understanding and compassion.

When to Call Kaiser Permanente

- Call 911 or other emergency services for urgent, life-threatening situations.

- Call your doctor or your local Suicide Prevention hotline (look in the Yellow Pages):

  ° If you are considering suicide.

  ° If you suspect someone has made suicide plans.

Violent Behavior

Anger and arguments are normal parts of healthy relationships. However, anger that leads to threats or violence, such as hitting or hurting, is not normal or healthy. Physical, verbal, or sexual abuse is not an acceptable part of any relationship.

Violent behavior often begins with verbal threats or relatively minor incidents, but over time it can become more serious, involving physical harm. Violent behavior seems to be mostly learned, so it is especially important to help your children learn that violence is not a healthy solution to conflict.

Prevention

- Seek nonviolent ways to resolve conflicts. Arguing is fine, even healthy, so long as it does not turn violent. See page 294 for more on controlling anger.

- Avoid using physical discipline; by avoiding it you will teach your children that violence is not a solution. If you need help with discipline, consider taking a course on parenting skills.

To prevent violence with firearms and other weapons:

- Make sure that everyone in the home who has access to firearms or other weapons knows how to use them safely.

- Lock up firearms unloaded. Lock ammunition in a separate place.

- Do not keep firearms or other weapons in a home where there are children or where there is someone who has a drug or alcohol problem, who is prone to violent behavior, or who has threatened suicide.

If a family member or someone else has threatened to harm you or your child:

- Tell someone: a trusted friend, clergy, or health professional.

- Identify local resources that can help in a crisis. Your local YMCA, police department, or hospital has information on shelters and safe homes.

- Be alert to warning signs, such as threats or drunkenness, so that you can avoid a dangerous situation. If you can't predict when violence may occur, have an "exit plan" for use in an emergency.

When to Call Kaiser Permanente

- If you or someone in your family is physically abused or the victim of violence. Physical abuse is a crime, no matter who does it.

- If you are concerned about violent behavior in yourself, a family member, or friend.

Check the Yellow Pages for hotlines and other resources for victims of abuse.

Mental Wellness

Mental wellness means thinking and feeling positively about yourself. You may have heard of psychosomatic illness, when a person "thinks" him- or herself into being sick. Evidence now supports the idea of psychosomatic wellness. For sickness and for health, what you think has some influence on your health and well-being.

The Mind-Body Connection

Medical science is making remarkable discoveries about how expectations, emotions, and thoughts affect our health. This science is called psycho-neuroimmunology, or PNI. It studies how the brain communicates with the rest of the body by sending chemical messengers into the blood.

Researchers have found that one function of the brain is to produce substances that can improve your health. Your brain can create natural painkillers called endorphins, gammaglobulin for fortifying your immune system, and interferon for combatting infections, viruses, and even cancer.

Your brain can combine these and other substances into a vast number of tailor-made prescriptions for what ails you. The substances that your brain produces depend in part on your thoughts and feelings.

In other words, your immune system's ability to heal the body is linked to your state of mind and your state of mental wellness. Your level of optimism and your expectations of what could happen can affect what goes on inside your whole body.

Positive Thinking

People with positive attitudes generally enjoy life more, but are they any healthier? The answer is often yes.

Optimism is a resource for healing. Optimists are more likely to overcome pain and adversity in their efforts to improve their medical treatment outcomes. For example, optimistic coronary bypass patients generally recover more quickly and have fewer postoperative complications than people who are less hopeful.

Conversely, pessimism seems to aggravate ill health. One long-term study showed that people who were pessimistic in college had significantly higher rates of illness through age 60.

We seem to develop a tendency toward either optimism or pessimism at an early age. However, even if your outlook on life tends to be gloomy, you can enjoy psychosomatic wellness by using your brain to support your immune system.

Boosting Your Immune System

Your immune system responds to your thoughts, emotions, and actions. In addition to staying fit, eating right, and managing stress, the following three strategies will help your immune system function better.

1. Create positive expectations for health and healing.

Mental and emotional expectations can influence medical outcomes. The effectiveness of any medical treatment depends in part on how useful you expect it to be.

The "placebo effect" proves that expectations affect health. A placebo is a drug or treatment that provides no medical benefit except for the patient's belief that it will help. On the average, 35 percent of patients who receive placebos report satisfactory relief from their medical problem, even though they received no actual medication.

Changing your expectations from negative to positive may give your immune system a boost. Here's how to make the change:

- Stop all negative self-talk. Make positive statements that promote your recovery.

- Write your illness a letter. Tell it that you don't need it anymore and that your immune system is now ready to finish it off.

- Send yourself a steady stream of affirmations. An affirmation is a phrase or sentence that sends strong, positive statements to you about yourself, such as "I am a capable person," or "My joints are strong and flexible."

- Visualize health and healing. Add mental pictures that support your positive affirmations.

- Become a cheerleader for your immune system. Talk to it and encourage it to be strong and keep fighting.

2. Open yourself to humor, friendship, and love.

Positive emotions strengthen the immune system. Fortunately, almost anything that makes you feel good about yourself helps you stay healthy.

- Laugh. A little humor makes life richer and healthier. Laughter increases creativity, reduces pain, and speeds healing. Keep an emergency laughter kit of funny videotapes, jokes, cartoons, and photographs. Put it with your first aid supplies and keep it well stocked.

- Seek out friends. Friendships are vital to good health. Close social ties help you recover more quickly from illness and reduce your risk of developing diseases ranging from arthritis to depression.

- Volunteer. People who volunteer live longer and enjoy life more than those who do not. By helping others, we help ourselves.

- Plant a plant and pet a pet. Plants and pets can be highly therapeutic. When you stroke an animal, blood pressure goes down and your heart rate slows. Animals and plants help us feel needed.

3. Appeal to the Spirit.

If you believe in a higher power, ask for support in your pursuit of healing and health. Faith, prayer, and spiritual beliefs can play an important role in recovering from an illness.

Your sense of spiritual wellness can help you overcome personal trials and things you cannot change. If it suits you, use spiritual images in visualizations, affirmations, and expectations about your health and your life.

Hardiness

Some people seem to have more protection from disease than others. Their immune systems appear to be more efficient. Researchers studying these hardy people have identified three personality factors that stand out:

1. Hardy people have a strong commitment to self, work, family, and other values.

2. Hardy people have a sense of control over their lives.

3. Hardy people generally see change in their lives as a challenge rather than a threat.

Developing a Hardy Personality

Can you develop more commitment, control, and acceptance of life's challenges? Apparently so, particularly if you start at an early age. You can help your children become hardy by encouraging them in the following ways:

- Commitment: Be a role model for your children by your commitment to them, to your work, and to the community. The more accepted a child feels, the more he or she will be able to commit to others.

- Control: Provide a variety of tasks that are neither too difficult nor too simple. Experience with both success and failure followed by success helps children build a sense of control.

- The challenge of change: Encourage children to see changes as opportunities to try new things. Accentuate the positive and teach them that life is continually changing.

Adults can also develop hardiness. Training to develop more commitment, control, and acceptance of challenges has proven to be effective.

Avoiding Guilt

There is no value in feeling guilty about health problems. While there is a lot we can do to reduce our risk of health problems and improve our chances of recovery, some illnesses develop and persist no matter what we do. Try to avoid feeling guilty, especially in applying the mental self-care suggestions in this chapter. If what you do helps, terrific. However, if your illness persists despite your best efforts, don't blame yourself. Some things just are. Do the best you can.

Be prepared.
Boy Scout Motto

20

Your Home Health Center

More health care takes place in your home than anywhere else. Having the right tools, medicines, supplies, and information on hand will improve its quality.

Store all your self-care resources in one central location, such as a large drawer in the bedroom or family room. Use the charts on tools and supplies and the list of resources in this chapter as checklists for keeping your home health center well stocked.

Note: If small children are around, keep your supplies out of reach or protected by childproof safety latches.

Be familiar with the disaster preparation and response plan for your area. Keep the appropriate supplies on hand.

Self-Care Tools

Self-care tools are the basic equipment of your home health center.

Cold Pack

A cold pack is a plastic envelope filled with gel that remains flexible at very cold temperatures. Buy two cold packs and keep them in the freezer. Use them for bumps, bruises, back sprains, turned ankles, sore joints, or any other health problem that calls for ice. A cold pack is more convenient than ice and may become the self-care tool you use the most.

You can make your own cold pack:

• Put one pint of rubbing alcohol and three pints of water in a one-gallon heavy-duty plastic freezer bag.

• Seal the bag and then seal it in a second bag. Mark it "Cold pack: Do not eat," and place it in the freezer.

A bag of frozen vegetables will also work as a cold pack.

Humidifier and Vaporizer

Humidifiers and vaporizers add moisture to the air, making it less drying to your mouth, throat, and nose. A humidifier produces a cool mist, and a vaporizer puts out hot steam.

A humidifier makes tiny particles of water that get into your respiratory system better, and the cool mist is more comfortable than hot steam.

However, humidifiers are noisy, produce particles that may be irritating to some people, and need to be cleaned and disinfected regularly. This is especially important for people who have mold allergies.

A vaporizer's hot steam does not contain any irritating particles, and you can add medications such as Vicks VapoRub to ease breathing. Steam may feel good when you have a cold, but the hot water can burn anyone who overturns it or gets too close.

Humidity in the air can help soothe a scratchy throat, ease a dry, hacking cough, and make it easier for someone with a stuffy nose to breathe. Added humidity will make your home more comfortable, especially in the winter when dry air is a problem.

Self-Care Tools

For every household:

• Blood pressure cuff*

• Cold pack*

• Dental mirror

• Eyedropper

• Heating pad

• Humidifier or vaporizer*

• Medicine spoon*

• Nail clippers

• Penlight*

• Scissors

• Stethoscope*

• Thermometer*

• Tweezers

For children under six, add:

• Bulb aspirator/syringe

• Rectal thermometer*

• Otoscope*

*Described in text

Medicine Spoon

Medicine spoons are transparent tubes with marks for typical dosage amounts. A medicine spoon makes it easy to give the right dose of liquid medicine. While the spoons are convenient for anyone, they are

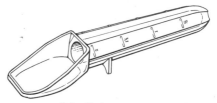

Medicine spoon

particularly helpful for young children. The tube shape and large lip get most of the medication into a child's mouth without spilling. Buy one at your local pharmacy.

Otoscope

An otoscope is a flashlight with a special attachment for looking into the ear. With training, using an otoscope can help you decide if an ear infection is present. Inexpensive consumer model otoscopes are available but do not illuminate the ear canal and eardrum as well as the one your doctor uses. They can also be used as high-intensity penlights. One product is the Earscope, which can be ordered for around $26.95 from Notoco, P.O. Box 300, Ferndale, CA 95536, (707) 786-4400.

Penlight

A penlight has a small, intense light that can be easily directed. It is useful for giving a physical exam and is easier to handle than a flashlight.

Stethoscope and Blood Pressure Cuff

If you have high blood pressure, it's a good idea to have both a stethoscope and a blood pressure cuff (sphygmomanometer) to monitor your blood pressure regularly.

Purchase a flat diaphragm model stethoscope rather than a bell-shaped one. The flat surface makes it easier for you to hear.

Blood pressure cuffs come in many models. If you have difficulty reading the gauge on a regular cuff, look for one attached to an upright mercury column, or an electronic digital model. Ask your pharmacist to recommend a blood pressure kit and show you how to use it.

Thermometer

Buy a thermometer with easy-to-read markings. Digital electronic thermometers are accurate and easy to read. Temperature strips are very convenient and safe but are not as accurate as mercury or electronic thermometers and should only be used to measure axillary (armpit) temperature. Thermometers that measure the temperature in the ear are fast, easy to use, and can be quite accurate, but they are expensive.

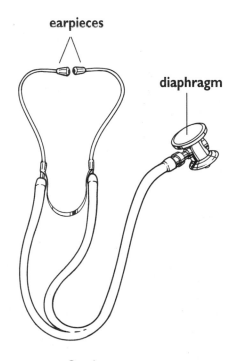

Stethoscope

Rectal thermometers with enlarged bulbs are helpful for children under six or anyone who cannot hold an oral thermometer in his or her mouth. See page 23 for instructions on taking a temperature.

Self-Care Supplies

See the Self-Care Supplies chart (at right) for a list of supplies that are useful to keep on hand in your home health center. These products are inexpensive, easy to use, and generally available at any drugstore or pharmacy.

Over-the-Counter (OTC) Medications and Products

An over-the-counter (OTC) medication is any drug that you can buy without a doctor's prescription. However, don't assume that all OTC drugs are safe for you. These drugs can interact with other medications and can sometimes create serious health problems.

Some medications should only be used by adults or older children. Be sure to read the package instructions carefully, or ask the pharmacist about the use of any product with infants or young children.

Carefully read the label of any over-the-counter drug you use, especially if you also take prescription medications for other health problems. Ask your pharmacist for help in finding the one best suited to your needs.

Self-Care Supplies

Keep these on hand:

- Adhesive strips (band-aids) in assorted sizes
- Adhesive tape, one inch wide
- Butterfly bandages
- Sterile gauze pads, two inches square
- Elastic ("Ace") bandage, three inches wide
- Roll of gauze bandage, two inches wide
- Cotton balls
- Safety pins
- Tweezers
- Dental disclosing tablets and dental floss

Some common OTCs include:

- Antacids and acid blockers
- Antidiarrheals
- Cold and allergy remedies
- Bulking agents and laxatives
- Pain relievers

These drugs can be very helpful when used properly but can also create serious problems if used incorrectly. The following tips will help you use these common OTC drugs wisely and safely. In some cases, you may find that you don't need to take them at all. The chart on page 311 lists common health problems and suggestions for OTC products to treat them.

OTC Products for Home Use

Problem	OTC Product (example)	Comments
Allergies	Antihistamine (Chlor-Trimeton, Benadryl)	Useful for allergies and itching. See page 315.
Colds	Decongestant	See page 313 for precautions.
Constipation	Laxative or bulking agent (Metamucil)	Avoid long-term or regular use of laxatives. (Bulking agents may be used regularly.) See page 316.
Cough, non-productive	Suppressant (Vicks Dry Hacking Cough)	Eases a dry, hacking cough. See pages 137 and 314.
Cough, productive	Expectorant (Vicks 44E)	Thins and helps clear the mucus. See page 315 for precautions.
Diaper rash	Protectant (A & D Ointment, Desitin)	Protects skin from urine and stool. See page 209.
Diarrhea	Antidiarrheal (Pepto Diarrhea Control)	Avoid long-term use. See page 313.
Dry skin	Lubricating cream (Vaseline Intensive Care)	Also see page 187.
Heartburn	Antacid (Tums, Maalox) or acid blocker (Pepcid AC, Tagamet HB)	Avoid long-term use. See page 312.
Itching	Hydrocortisone cream (Cortaid)	Antihistamines are also helpful. See page 188.
Pain, fever, inflammation	Aspirin, ibuprofen, or naproxen	Helps relieve swelling and pain. May cause stomach upset. See pages 316 and 317.
Pain, fever	Acetaminophen (Tylenol)	Less stomach irritation. Safe for children. See page 317.
Poisoning	Syrup of ipecac	To start vomiting if poisoning occurs. See page 318.
Scrapes, skin infections	Antibiotic ointment (Bacitracin, Polysporin)	May cause local allergic reaction. Keep creams cool and dry. Discard if out of date.

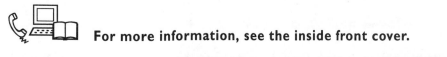

Antacids and Acid Blockers

Antacids are taken to relieve heartburn or indigestion caused by excess stomach acid. While they are safe if used occasionally, antacids may cause problems if taken regularly. There are several kinds of antacids. Learn what ingredients are in each type so that you can avoid any adverse effects.

Acid blockers reduce the amount of acid produced by the stomach. There are several types of OTC acid blockers on the market. Each has slightly different cautions for use. Read and carefully follow the instructions included with the package. If you have a problem with the function of your kidneys or liver, you should be careful in using acid blockers. The drug is broken down and removed from the body by the combined action of the liver and kidneys. If the liver or kidneys are not working correctly, it is possible to build up too high a dose of the drug in the body.

- Sodium bicarbonate antacids (Alka-Seltzer, Bromo-Seltzer) contain baking soda. If you have high blood pressure, or if you are on a salt-restricted diet, avoid these antacids because of their high sodium content. If used too frequently, they may interfere with kidney or heart function.

- Calcium carbonate antacids (Tums, Alka-Mints) are sometimes used as calcium supplements (see page 284). However, these products may cause constipation.

- Aluminum-based antacids (Amphojel) are less potent and work slower than other products. They may also cause constipation. Some may cause calcium depletion and should not be taken by post-menopausal women. Check with your doctor before using aluminum antacids if you have kidney problems.

- Magnesium compounds (Phillips' Milk of Magnesia) may cause diarrhea.

- Aluminum-magnesium antacids (Maalox, Di-Gel, Mylanta, Riopan) are less likely to cause constipation or diarrhea than aluminum-only or magnesium-only antacids.

Antacid Precautions

- Try to eliminate the cause of frequent heartburn instead of taking antacids regularly. See Heartburn on page 74.

- Consult your doctor or pharmacist before taking an antacid if you take other medications. Antacids may interfere with the absorption and action of some drugs, such as antibiotics, digitalis, and anticoagulants. Also consult your doctor if you have ulcers or kidney problems.

Antidiarrheals

There are two types of antidiarrheal drugs: those that thicken the stool and those that slow intestinal spasms.

The **thickening** mixtures (Kaopectate) contain clay or fruit pectin and absorb the bacteria and toxins in the intestine. They are safe because they do not go into the blood, but these products also absorb the bacteria needed for digestion. Long-term use is not advised.

Antispasmodic antidiarrheal products slow the spasms of the intestine. Loperamide (Imodium A-D, Pepto Diarrhea Control) is an example of this type of preparation. Donnagel and Parepectolin contain both thickening and antispasmodic ingredients.

Antidiarrheal Precautions

- Diarrhea helps rid your body of an infection, so try to avoid using antidiarrheal medications for the first six hours. After that, use them only if there are no other signs of illness, such as fever, and if cramping and pain continues.

- Be sure to take a large enough dose. Take antidiarrheal preparations until the stool thickens; then stop immediately to avoid constipation.

- Replace depleted body fluids. Dehydration can develop when someone has diarrhea, especially an infant, child, or older adult. See page 72 for a rehydration drink you can make at home to prevent dehydration.

Cold and Allergy Remedies

In general, whether you take drugs or not for your cold, you'll be getting better in about a week. Rest and liquids are probably the best treatment for a cold (see page 135).

Antibiotics will not help. However, medications help relieve some cold symptoms, such as nasal congestion and cough.

Allergy symptoms, especially runny nose, often respond to antihistamines. Antihistamines are also found in many cold medications, often together with a decongestant. However, the value of antihistamines in treating cold symptoms is under debate.

Decongestants

Decongestants make breathing easier by shrinking swollen mucous membranes in the nose, allowing air to pass through. They also help relieve runny nose and postnasal drip, which can cause a sore throat.

Decongestants can be taken orally or used as nose drops or sprays. Oral decongestants (pills) are probably more effective and provide longer relief but cause more side effects. Sudafed (pseudoephedrine) is an oral decongestant.

Sprays and drops provide rapid but temporary relief. Neo-Synephrine (phenylephrine) is an effective nasal spray. Sprays and drops are less likely to interact with other drugs than oral decongestants are.

Decongestant Precautions

- Do not give cold medicines or oral decongestants to infants under age six months. Over-the-counter cold medicines have not been proven effective for preschool children.

Saline Nose Drops

Over-the-counter saline sprays (NaSal, Ocean) are convenient, inexpensive, and sterile. They will keep nasal tissues moist so they can filter the air and will not cause a rebound effect.

Saline nasal drops can also be easily made at home. Mix $\frac{1}{4}$ teaspoon salt in 1 cup of body temperature water (too much salt will dry nasal membranes).

Place the solution in a clean bottle with a dropper (available at drugstores). Use as necessary. Make a fresh solution every three days.

To insert drops, lie on your back with your head hanging over the side of the bed. This helps the drops get farther back. Try to prevent the dropper from touching your nose.

- Do not use medicated nasal sprays or drops more than three times a day or for more than three days. Continued use will cause a "rebound effect": the mucous membranes swell up more than before using the spray.

- Drink extra fluids when taking cold medications.

- Decongestants can cause problems for people with certain health problems, such as heart disease, high blood pressure, glaucoma, diabetes, and overactive thyroid. They may also interact with some drugs, such as certain antidepressants and high blood pressure medications. Read the package carefully and ask your pharmacist or doctor to help you choose one.

Cough Preparations

Coughing is your body's way of getting foreign substances and mucus out of your respiratory tract. Coughs are often useful, and you shouldn't try to eliminate them. Sometimes, though, coughs are severe enough to impair breathing or prevent rest.

Water and other liquids, such as fruit juices, are probably the best cough syrups. They help soothe the throat and also moisten and thin mucus so that it can be coughed up more easily.

You can make a simple and soothing cough syrup at home by mixing one part lemon juice with two parts honey. Use as often as needed. This can be given to children over one year old. Also see page 137.

There are two kinds of cough medicines. Expectorants help thin the mucus, making it easier to "bring up" when you have a productive cough. Look for expectorants containing guaifenesin, such as Robitussin and Vicks 44E.

Suppressants control or suppress the cough reflex and work best for a dry, hacking cough that keeps you awake. Look for suppressant medications containing dextromethorphan, such as Robitussin-DM or Vicks Dry Hacking Cough.

Don't suppress a productive cough too much (unless it is keeping you from getting enough rest).

Cough Preparation Precautions

• Cough preparations can cause problems for people with certain health problems, such as asthma, heart disease, high blood pressure, and enlarged prostate. They may also interact with some drugs, such as sedatives and certain antidepressants. Read the package carefully and ask your pharmacist or doctor to help you choose one.

• Cough suppressants can stifle breathing. Use them with caution if you have chronic respiratory problems and when giving them to someone who is very old or frail.

• Read the label so you know what the ingredients are. Some cough preparations contain a large percentage of alcohol; others contain codeine. There are many choices. Ask your pharmacist to advise you.

Antihistamines

Antihistamines dry up nasal secretions and are commonly used to treat allergy symptoms and itching.

If your runny nose is due to allergies, an antihistamine will help. For cold symptoms, home treatment and perhaps a decongestant (see page 313) will probably be more helpful. It is usually best to take only single-ingredient allergy or cold preparations, instead of those containing many active ingredients.

Chlor-Trimeton (chlorpheniramine) and Benadryl (diphenhydramine) are single-ingredient antihistamine products.

Dristan, Coricidin, and Triaminic contain both a decongestant and an antihistamine.

Antihistamine Precautions

• Do not give antihistamines to infants under age four months. For children between four months and one year, ask your doctor first.

• Use of antihistamines to treat the stuffiness of a cold will often thicken the mucus, making it harder to get rid of.

• Drink extra fluids when taking allergy medications.

• Antihistamines can cause problems for some people with health problems such as asthma, glaucoma, epilepsy, and enlarged prostate. They may also interact with some drugs, such as certain antidepressants, sedatives, and tranquilizers. Read the package carefully and ask your pharmacist or doctor to help you choose one that will not cause problems.

• The drowsiness that antihistamines often cause usually diminishes with continued use. If it continues, or if the medication isn't helping your allergies after one week, call your doctor for advice.

• Nonsedating antihistamines are available by prescription. These drugs carry some additional risk.

For more information, see the inside front cover.

Bulking Agents and Laxatives

There are two types of products to prevent or treat constipation.

Bulking agents such as bran or psyllium (Metamucil) are not laxatives but ease constipation by increasing the volume of stool and making it easier to pass. Regular use of bulking agents is safe and helps make them more effective.

Laxatives (Correctol, Ex-Lax, Senokot, Dulcolax) speed up the passage of stool by irritating the lining of the intestines. Regular laxative use is not recommended.

There are many other ways to treat constipation, such as drinking more water. See page 70.

Laxative Precautions

• Take any laxative or bulking agent with plenty of water or other liquids.

• Do not take laxatives regularly. Overuse of laxatives decreases tone and sensation in the large intestine, causing laxative dependence. If you need help keeping regular, use a bulking agent (see above).

• Regular use of some laxatives (Correctol, Ex-Lax, Feen-a-Mint) may interfere with your body's absorption of vitamin D and calcium; this can weaken your bones.

Pain Relievers

There are dozens of pain reliever products. Most contain either aspirin, ibuprofen, or acetaminophen. These three and ketoprofen (Orudis) and naproxen (Aleve) all relieve pain and reduce fever. Aspirin, ibuprofen, ketoprofen, and naproxen also relieve inflammation. Generic products are chemically equivalent to more expensive brand-name products, are often less expensive, and will generally work equally well.

Aspirin is widely used for relieving pain and reducing fever in adults. It also relieves minor itching and reduces swelling and inflammation. Most tablets contain 325 mg. Although it seems familiar and safe, aspirin is a very powerful drug.

Aspirin Precautions

• Aspirin causes more childhood poisonings than any other drug. Keep all aspirin, especially baby aspirin, out of children's reach.

• Aspirin can irritate the stomach lining, causing bleeding or ulcers. If aspirin upsets your stomach, try a coated brand, such as Ecotrin. Talk with your doctor or pharmacist to determine what will work best for you.

• Aspirin increases the risk of Reye's syndrome in children. Do not give aspirin to children and teens under age 20 years unless recommended by a doctor.

- Some people are allergic to aspirin. (They may also be allergic to ibuprofen.)

- Throw aspirin away if it begins to smell like vinegar.

- Do not take aspirin if you have gout or if you take blood thinners (anticoagulants).

- Do not take aspirin for a hangover. Aspirin used with alcohol increases the risk of stomach irritation.

- High doses may result in aspirin poisoning (salicylism). Stop taking aspirin and call a health professional if any of these symptoms occur:

  ○ Ringing in the ears

  ○ Visual disturbances

  ○ Nausea

  ○ Dizziness

  ○ Rapid, deep breathing

Other Uses of Aspirin

In addition to relieving pain and inflammation, aspirin is effective against many other ailments. Because of the danger of side effects and the interactions aspirin may have with other treatment, **do not try these uses of aspirin without a doctor's supervision.**

- **Heart Attacks and Strokes:** Aspirin in low but regular doses helps prevent heart attacks and strokes in certain people at high risk. Doses as low as 30 mg per day have helped. Aspirin may also help as a first aid measure for heart attacks. Chewing half a tablet may be enough to help.

- **Stomach and Colon Cancer:** Some studies have shown that one aspirin per day can reduce the risk of cancers in the digestive system.

- **Migraines:** Regular, low-dose aspirin use may reduce the frequency of migraines.

Other Pain Relievers

Ibuprofen (Advil, Nuprin), **ketoprofen** (Orudis), and **naproxen** (Aleve) are other nonsteroidal anti-inflammatory drugs (NSAIDs). Like aspirin, they relieve pain and reduce fever and inflammation. Also like aspirin, they can cause nausea, stomach irritation, and heartburn. These drugs should be used with caution by people who take blood thinners (anticoagulants).

For liquid forms of ibuprofen, follow the dosage instructions on the label. For adults and children over age 12 years, take one to two 200-mg ibuprofen tablets three times a day. Follow the package instructions for ketoprofen and naproxen dosage.

Acetaminophen (Tylenol) reduces fever and relieves pain. It does not have the anti-inflammatory effect of NSAIDS, such as aspirin and ibuprofen, but also does not cause stomach upset and other side effects. For liquid forms, follow the dosage instructions on the label. Take every four hours, as needed:

- 12 pounds or less: consult your doctor.

- 13–23 pounds: 60–80 mg

- 24–35 pounds: 160 mg

- 36–47 pounds: 240 mg

- 48–59 pounds: 320 mg

- 60–71 pounds: 400 mg

- 72–95 pounds: 480 mg

- Adults: 500–1,000 mg (maximum of 4,000 mg per day)

The package label will tell you how many milligrams (mg) are in each pill. Do not exceed dosage limits. People who drink more than three alcoholic beverages a day should discuss use with their doctors. Excess use of acetaminophen can contribute to alcohol-induced liver damage.

Syrup of Ipecac

Syrup of ipecac (ip-uh-kack) is a drug used to induce vomiting when a poison has been swallowed.

In most cases of poisoning, the best treatment is to get the substance out of the victim's stomach as quickly as possible. Syrup of ipecac is excellent for this.

Sometimes, making someone vomit can be harmful. Do not use ipecac if someone has swallowed any of the following:

- Alkalis, such as dishwasher detergents or cleaning solutions.

Poisons

Do not induce vomiting:

- Dishwasher detergent
- Gasoline, kerosene
- Drano
- Oven cleaner
- Oil-based paints
- Furniture polish
- Cleaning solutions
- Antifreeze

Induce vomiting:

- Dishwashing liquid
- Plant food
- Aspirin and other medications
- Ink
- Fingernail polish remover
- Rat poison

- Petroleum distillates, such as furniture polish, kerosene, gasoline, oil-based paints, etc. Give water to dilute the poison without inducing vomiting.

With all poisonings, call your doctor, emergency department, or poison control center immediately!

Dosage for Ipecac

Do not give ipecac to children less than one year old. For children over one year, give one tablespoon. Follow with at least 12 ounces of water, which is essential to ensure vomiting. Try to keep the person walking around.

Repeat in 20 minutes if the person has not yet vomited. Repeat only once. When the person vomits, have him lie on his side with his mouth lower than his chest so vomited material will not enter the airway. If he leans over a toilet, be sure his chest is lower than his stomach.

The vomiting caused by ipecac is very violent. Ipecac should not be used in the following situations:

- If a woman is over five months pregnant.

- If the victim has a history of heart disease.

- If the child is under 12 months old.

- If the victim might choke on the vomited material or inhale it into the lungs:

  ° Persons over age 65

  ° Persons who have taken Valium or any other drug that may cause unconsciousness

  ° Person is drunk

  ° Person is drowsy or lethargic

Keep ipecac on hand and replace it every five years if you haven't used it. It will remain effective for one year after opening.

Prescription Medications

 There are thousands of different prescription medications, used to treat hundreds of different medical conditions. Your doctor and your pharmacist are your best sources of information about your prescription medications. Good books are available that contain information on many different prescription drugs. See Resource 2 on page 325.

Guidelines for taking every kind of prescription medication could fill several books. Common types covered here include antibiotics, minor tranquilizers, and sleeping pills.

Antibiotics

Antibiotics are prescription drugs that kill bacteria. They are effective against bacteria only and have no effect on viruses. Antibiotics will not cure the common cold, flu, or any other viral illness. Unless you have a bacterial infection, it's best to avoid the possible adverse effects of antibiotics, which may include:

- **Side effects**, including **allergic reactions**. Common side effects of antibiotics include nausea, diarrhea, and increased sensitivity to sunlight. Most side effects are mild, but some, especially allergic reactions, can be severe. An allergic reaction can be life-threatening. If you have any unexpected reaction to an antibiotic, tell your health professional before another antibiotic is prescribed.

Medication Guidelines

Basic guidelines for taking prescription and over-the-counter medications include:

- Use medications only if nondrug approaches are not working.

- Know the benefits and side effects of a medication before taking it.

- Take the minimum effective dose.

- Never take a drug prescribed for someone else.

- Follow the prescription instructions exactly or let your doctor know why you didn't.

- Keep medications in their original containers with the caps on tightly and stored according to directions.

- Do not take medications in front of small children. Children are great mimics. Don't oversell the "candy" taste of children's medicines or leave children's vitamins accessible to small children.

- Add a consumer's guide to medications to your home health library. See Resource 2 on page 325.

- **Secondary infections**. Antibiotics kill most of the bacteria in your body that are sensitive to them, including those that help your body. They may destroy the bacterial balance in your body, leading to stomach upset, diarrhea, vaginal infections, or other problems.

- **Bacterial resistance**. Bacteria build resistance to antibiotics that are used frequently; and when only part of a prescription is taken, the stronger bacteria survive. Many common bacteria have developed antibiotic-resistant strains, which are very difficult to treat.

When you and your health professional have decided that an antibiotic is necessary, follow the instructions with the prescription carefully.

- Take the whole dose for as many days as prescribed, unless you have unexpected side effects (in which case, call your health professional). Antibiotics kill off many bacteria quite quickly, so you may feel better in a few days. However, if you stop taking the antibiotic too soon, the weaker bacteria will have been eliminated, but the stronger ones may survive and flourish.

- Be sure you understand any special instructions about taking the medication. They should be printed on the label, but double-check with your doctor and pharmacist.

- Store antibiotics in a dry, cool place. Check carefully to see if they need refrigeration.

- Never give an antibiotic prescribed for one person to someone else.

- Do not save "leftover" antibiotics or take an antibiotic prescribed for another illness without a health professional's approval.

Minor Tranquilizers and Sleeping Pills

Minor tranquilizers like Valium, Librium, Xanax, and Tranxene, and sleeping pills like Dalmane, Restoril, and Ambien are widely prescribed. However, these drugs can cause problems, including memory loss, addiction, and injuries from falls due to drug-induced unsteadiness.

Minor tranquilizers can be effective for short periods of time. However, long-term use is often of limited value and introduces the risk of addiction and mental impairment.

Sleeping pills may help for a few days or a few weeks, but using them for more than a month generally causes more sleep problems than it solves. For other approaches, see page 300.

If you have been taking minor tranquilizers or sleeping pills for a while, talk with your doctor about reevaluating your need for the medication or reducing your dosage. If you have experienced any unsteadiness, dizziness, or memory loss, tell your doctor.

Adverse Drug Reactions

Side effects, drug-drug and food-drug interactions, over-medication, and addiction may cause:

- Nausea, indigestion, vomiting

- Constipation, diarrhea, inability to control urine, or difficulty urinating

- Dry mouth

- Headache, dizziness, ringing in the ears, or blurred vision

- Confusion, forgetfulness, disorientation, drowsiness, or depression

- Difficulty sleeping, irritability, or nervousness

- Difficulty breathing

- Rashes, bruising, and bleeding problems

Don't assume any symptom is a normal side effect that you have to suffer with. Call your doctor or pharmacist any time you suspect your medicines are making you sick.

Medication Problems

Several kinds of adverse medication reactions can occur:

Side effects: Predictable but unpleasant reactions to a drug. They are usually mild but can be inconvenient. In some cases, they are more serious.

Allergies: Some people have severe, sometimes life-threatening reactions (called anaphylaxis) to certain medications. See page 125 for signs of an allergic reaction.

Drug-drug interactions: Occur when two or more prescription or over-the-counter drugs mix in the body and cause an adverse reaction. The symptoms can be severe and may be misdiagnosed as a new illness.

Drug-food interactions: Occur when medications react with food. Some drugs work best when taken with food, but others should be taken on an empty stomach. Some drug-food reactions can cause serious symptoms.

Over-medication: Sometimes the full adult dose of a medication is too much for small people and those over age 60. Too much of a drug is very dangerous.

Medicine Chest

When you open your medicine chest, do you see a history of family illnesses for the past five years or more? If so, it's time to clean house. Most medications lose their potency after a few years, and you should never give an antibiotic prescribed for one person to anyone else. Throw out any medications:

• Prescribed for past illnesses.

• That are past their expiration date (check the label).

• That have no labels.

Addiction: Long-term use of some medications can lead to dependency and cause severe reactions if they are withdrawn suddenly. Narcotics, tranquilizers, and barbiturates must be taken very carefully to prevent addiction. See page 291.

Save Money on Medications

Over-the-counter and prescription medications can be very expensive. Here are some ways to cut your medication costs:

• Buy generic over-the-counter products. They are chemically equivalent to name-brand drugs but are usually cheaper. Ask your doctor if generic forms of your prescription medications are available and appropriate for you.

• Shop around and compare prices between several pharmacies. Prices can vary widely. It may be worth paying a little more if you know and trust the pharmacist.

• Ask your doctor for samples of newly prescribed medications, or ask your pharmacist to fill only the first week's worth of pills. If the medication has to be changed later, you can save the price of the full prescription.

• Consider buying expensive drugs you use regularly from mail-order pharmacies, which charge less. The only disadvantage is that you will not have a partnership with a local pharmacist.

Home Medical Tests

Many common medical tests are now available in home kits. Combined with regular visits to your health professional, home tests can help you monitor your health and, in some cases, detect problems early.

Home medical tests must be very accurate (over 95 percent) to be approved by the Food and Drug Administration. However, they must be used correctly to give such accurate results. Follow the package directions exactly. If you have questions, ask your pharmacist or check the label for the company's toll-free phone number to call.

Home medical tests are especially helpful if you have a chronic condition that requires frequent monitoring, such as diabetes, asthma, or high blood pressure. Ask your doctor which home medical tests would be appropriate for you. Some common tests are described below.

Blood Glucose Monitoring

If you have diabetes, you may already monitor your blood sugar levels (glucose) using a finger prick and a test strip or an electronic monitor.

This test should always be used under a doctor's supervision. Never adjust your insulin dose based on a single abnormal test, unless your doctor has specifically instructed you to do so.

Check with your doctor if you have symptoms of abnormal blood sugar levels, even if the test is normal. See page 220.

Blood Pressure Monitoring

If you have high blood pressure, it is important to monitor your blood pressure frequently. With a little instruction, you can easily monitor your blood pressure at home.

By checking your blood pressure at home, when you are relaxed, you will be able to track changes resulting from your home treatment and medications.

• Do not make any changes to your medications based on your home blood pressure readings without consulting your doctor.

• Check your blood pressure at different times of day to see how rest and activities affect it. For regular readings, check it at the same time of day. Blood pressure is usually lowest in the morning and rises during the day.

• For the most accurate reading, sit still for five minutes before taking your blood pressure.

• Calibrate (adjust) the blood pressure device yearly by checking it against the one in the doctor's office.

Tests for Blood in Stool

The fecal occult blood test can detect hidden blood in the stool, which may indicate colon cancer or other problems. However, this test has a very high rate of false positive and false negative results. Your doctor may recommend a more accurate screening test for colon cancer called a flexible sigmoid-oscopy. See page 22.

Home Pregnancy Tests

Home pregnancy tests are reliable and require only a few steps. Follow the package instructions and report all positive results to your doctor. See page 233.

Home Medical Records

Your home health center is a good place to keep your family's medical records, too. A three-ring binder or wire-bound notebook with dividers for each member of the family is helpful. Each person should have a cover sheet listing:

- Diagnosed chronic conditions: arthritis, asthma, diabetes, high blood pressure, etc.

- Any known allergies to drugs, foods, or insects.

- Information that would be vital in an emergency, such as a pacemaker, a hearing aid, diabetes, epilepsy, or if someone is deaf or blind.

- Name and phone number of primary doctor.

Other important information that should be included:

- An up-to-date list of medications. Include name of drug, purpose, dose, instructions, doctor, and date prescribed.

- Immunization records: childhood immunizations, tetanus, influenza, pneumonia.

- Health screening results: blood pressure, cholesterol, vision, hearing.

- Records of major illnesses and injuries, such as pneumonia, bronchitis, broken bones, or major infections.

- Records of any major surgical procedures and hospitalizations.

- Records listing major diseases in members of your family: heart disease, stroke, cancer, diabetes.

Home Health Library: Self-Care Resources

Good information is the most important self-care resource for the home. Many of the resources listed below are available at your local bookstore or public library. If not, ask the bookstore to order the ones you want.

Other sources of health information may be available in your community. Check the phone book for your local chapter of the American Cancer Society, American Heart Association, Arthritis Foundation, American Diabetes Association, American Lung Association, and other organizations.

If you subscribe to an on-line service such as Prodigy, America Online, or CompuServe, check for health databases, electronic bulletin boards and discussion groups, and other services. You may be able to access medical journal articles, textbooks, and other publications online.

Three Books Every Home Should Have

1. D. Sobel, R. Ornstein, *The Healthy Mind, Healthy Body Handbook*, DRX, 1996. Available from Box 381062, Cambridge, MA 02238-1062, 1-800-222-4745.

2. J. J. Rybacki, J. W. Long, *The Essential Guide to Prescription Drugs: Everying You Need to Know for Safe Drug Use*, Harper-Collins, 1997.

3. *Everything You Need to Know About Medical Tests*, Springhouse, 1997.

General Purpose Resources

4. D. Vickery, J. Fries, *Take Care of Yourself* (6th ed.), Addison-Wesley, 1996.

5. D. E. Larson, ed. *Mayo Clinic Family Health Book* (2nd ed.), William Morrow, 1996.

Special Concerns Resources

AIDS

6. L. Pinsky, P. H. Douglas, *The Essential AIDS Fact Book*, Simon & Schuster, 1996.

Alcohol Problems

7. *Alcoholics Anonymous: The Story of How Thousands of Men and Women Have Recovered From Alcoholism* (3rd ed.), Alcoholics Anonymous World Services, Inc., 1976.

8. A. Mooney et al., *The Recovery Book*, Workman, 1992.

Alzheimer's Disease/Dementia

9. N. L. Mace, P. V. Rabins, *The 36-Hour Day: A Family Guide to Caring for Persons With Alzheimer's Disease, Related Dementing Illnesses, and Memory Loss in Late Life*, The Johns Hopkins University Press, 1991. Also available from the Alzheimer's Association, 1-800-272-3900.

Anger

10. R. Williams, V. Williams, *Anger Kills: 17 Strategies for Controlling the Hostility That Can Harm Your Health*, Random House, 1993.

11. A. Ellis, *Anger: How to Live With and Without It*, Carol Publishing Group, 1985.

12. H. G. Lerner, *The Dance of Anger: A Woman's Guide to the Patterns of Intimate Relationships*, Harper & Row, 1989.

Anxiety

13. E. Bourne, *The Anxiety and Phobia Workbook*, New Harbinger, 1995.

14. R. Z. Peurifoy, *Anxiety, Phobias, and Panic: A Step-by-Step Program for Regaining Control*, Warner Books, 1995.

15. A. Seagrave, F. Covington, *Free From Fears,* Pocket Books, 1989.

Arthritis

16. K. Lorig, J. Fries, *The Arthritis Helpbook* (4th ed.), Addison-Wesley, 1995.

Also see Resource 29.

Asthma

17. A. Weinstein, *Asthma: The Complete Guide to Self-Management of Asthma for Patients and Their Families,* Fawcett, 1987.

Also see Resource 29.

Back Problems

18. R. McKenzie, *Treat Your Own Back,* Spinal Publications, 1993.

19. R. Cailliet, *Low Back Pain Syndrome,* Davis Co., 1995.

Cancer

20. M. Dollinger, E. H. Rosenbaum, G. Cable, *Everyone's Guide to Cancer Therapy* (2nd ed.), Somerville House Books, 1994.

Child Health

21. S. P. Shelov, ed., *Caring for Your Baby and Young Child*, Bantam, 1993.

22. B. Schmitt, *Your Child's Health*, Bantam, 1991.

23. A. Eisenberg et al., *What to Expect the First Year*, Workman, 1989.

24. R. Pantell et al., *Taking Care of Your Child* (4th ed.), Addison-Wesley, 1993.

25. E. Satter, *How to Get Your Kid to Eat…But Not Too Much*, Bull Publishing, 1991.

26. R. Ferber, *Solve Your Child's Sleep Problem*, Simon & Schuster, 1985.

27. D. E. Greydanus, ed., *Caring for Your Adolescent*, Bantam, 1991.

28. D. Dinkmeyer, Sr., G. D. McKay, J. S. Dinkmeyer, *Parenting Young Children*, American Guidance Service, 1989.

Chronic Illnesses

29. K. Lorig, H. Holman, D. Sobel et al., *Living a Healthy Life With Chronic Conditions: Self-Management of Heart Disease, Arthritis, Stroke, Diabetes, Asthma, Bronchitis, Emphysema, and Others*, Bull Publishing, 1994.

Depression

30. M. Seligman, *Learned Optimism*, Random House, 1991.

Also see entries under Mental Self-Care.

Diabetes

31. L. Jovanovic-Peterson, *A Touch of Diabetes*, Chronimed, 1995.

Also see Resource 29.

Elder Care

32. M. Mettler, D. W. Kemper, *Healthwise for Life: Medical Self-Care for People Age 50 and Better* (3rd ed.), Healthwise, 1998.

33. D. W. Kemper et al., *Growing Wiser: The Older Person's Guide to Mental Wellness*, Healthwise, 1986.

Both available from Healthwise, P.O. Box 1989, Boise, ID 83701, 1-800-706-9646.

First Aid

34. *American Red Cross First Aid and Safety Handbook*, Little, Brown & Co., 1992.

Fitness

35. P. Lyons, D. Burgard, *Great Shape: The First Fitness Guide for Large Women*, Bull Publishing, 1990.

36. B. Anderson, *Stretching*, Shelter Publications, 1980.

Grief

37. M. Colgrove, H. Bloomfield, P. McWilliams, *How to Survive the Loss of a Love*, Bantam, 1991.

38. E. Neeld, *Seven Choices: Taking the Steps to New Life After Losing Someone You Love* (3rd ed.), Crown, 1997.

39. H. S. Schiff, *Living Through Mourning: Finding Comfort and Hope When a Loved One Has Died*, Penguin Books, 1987.

Heart Disease

40. D. Ornish, *Dr. Dean Ornish's Program for Reversing Heart Disease*, Ballantine, 1990.

Also see Resource 29.

Incontinence

41. K. L. Burgio, K. L. Pearce, A. J. Lucco, *Staying Dry: A Practical Guide to Bladder Control*, The Johns Hopkins University Press, 1989.

Insomnia

42. P. Hauri, S. Linde, *No More Sleepless Nights*, John Wiley & Sons, 1996.

Irritable Bowel Syndrome

43. E. F. Shimberg, *Relief From Irritable Bowel Syndrome*, Ballantine, 1991.

Medical Consumerism

44. D. W. Kemper et al., *It's About Time: Better Health Care in a Minute (or two)*, Healthwise, 1993. Available from Healthwise, P.O. Box 1989, Boise, ID 83701, 1-800-706-9646.

45. C. Inlander, E. Weiner, *Take This Book to the Hospital With You*, Pantheon, 1991.

46. D. R. Stutz, B. Feder, *The Savvy Patient: How to Be an Active Participant in Your Medical Care*, Consumers Union, 1990.

47. R. Arnot, *The Best Medicine*, Addison-Wesley, 1992.

48. C. B. Inlander, *Good Operations, Bad Operations: The People's Medical Society's Guide to Surgery*, Penguin Books, 1993.

Mental Self-Care

49. D. Burns, *The Feeling Good Handbook*, New American Library/Dutton, 1990.

50. D. Sobel, R. Ornstein, *The Healthy Mind, Healthy Body Handbook*, DRX, 1996. Available from Box 381062, Cambridge, MA 02238-1062, 1-800-222-4745.

51. S. Locke, *The Healer Within*, New American Library, 1997.

52. D. Goleman, J. Gurin, eds., *Mind/Body Medicine: How to Use Your Mind for Better Health*, Consumer Reports Books, 1993.

53. G. Emery, J. Campbell, *Rapid Relief From Emotional Distress*, Fawcett, 1987.

54. B. Moyers, *Healing and the Mind*, Doubleday, 1993.

Men's Health

55. *Staying Strong for Men Over 50: A Common Sense Health Guide.* Available from AARP, Stock No. D15296, 601 E Street NW, Washington, DC 20049.

Neck Problems

56. R. McKenzie, *Treat Your Own Neck* (2nd ed.), Spinal Publications, 1993.

Newsletters

57. *Personal Best*, 420 5th Avenue South, Suite D, Edmonds, WA 98020-3464, 1-800-888-7853.

58. *University of California at Berkeley Wellness Letter.* Available from Health Letter Associates, P.O. Box 420148, Palm Coast, FL 32142, (904) 445-6414.

59. *Columbia University Health and Nutrition Newsletter.* Available from P.O. Box 5000, Ridgefield, NJ 07657.

60. *Mind/Body Health Newsletter*, The Center for Health Sciences, P.O. Box 381062, Cambridge, MA 02238-1062, 1-800- 222-4745.

Nutrition

61. *Health Counts.* John Wiley & Sons, Inc., 1991.

62. E. R. Blonz, *The Really Simple, No-Nonsense Nutrition Guide*, Conari Press, 1993.

Pain

63. M. Caudill, *Managing Pain Before It Manages You*, Guilford, 1994.

Pregnancy

64. A. Eisenberg, *What to Expect When You're Expecting*, Workman Publishing, 1991.

65. P. Simkin et al., *Pregnancy, Childbirth, and the Newborn*, Meadowbrook, 1991.

66. C. Marshall, *From Here to Maternity: Your Guide for the Nine-Month Journey Toward Motherhood*, Marshall Educational Health Solutions, Inc., 1995, 1-800-428-8321.

Self-Help Groups

67. B. White, E. Madara, *The Self-Help Sourcebook: Finding and Forming Mutual Aid Self-Help Groups*, Saint Clares-Riverside Medical Center, 1992, (201) 625-7101.

Smoking

68. T. Ferguson, *The No-Nag, No-Guilt, Do-It-Your-Own-Way Guide to Quitting Smoking*, Putnam, 1988.

Shyness

69. P. Zimbardo, *Shyness*, Addison-Wesley, 1990.

Stress

70. H. Benson, *Beyond the Relaxation Response*, Berkley Books, 1984.

71. M. Davis et al., *The Relaxation and Stress Reduction Workbook*, New Harbinger, 1995.

Wellness

72. H. Benson, E. M. Stuart, *The Wellness Book*, Carol Publishing Group, 1992.

73. D. W. Kemper et al., *Pathways: A Success Guide for a Healthy Life*, Healthwise, 1985. Available from Healthwise, P.O. Box 1989, Boise, ID 83701, 1-800-706-9646.

74. R. Ornstein, D. Sobel, *Healthy Pleasures*, Addison-Wesley, 1989.

Women's Health

75. The Boston Women's Health Book Collective, *The New Our Bodies, Ourselves: A Book By and For Women*, Simon & Schuster, 1992.

76. K. Johnson, *Trusting Ourselves: The Complete Guide to Emotional Well-Being for Women*, Grove-Atlantic, 1991.

77. B. D. Shephard, C. A. Shephard, *The Complete Guide to Women's Health*, Penguin Books, 1997.

78. La Leche League International, *The Womanly Art of Breast-Feeding*, New American Library, 1991.

79. K. Huggins, *The Nursing Mother's Companion* (3rd ed.), Harvard Common Press, 1995.

Also see entries under Pregnancy.

Index